T0155471

Transitions and Trees

An Introduction to Structural Operational Semantics

Structural operational semantics is a simple, yet powerful mathematical theory for describing the behaviour of programs in an implementation-independent manner. This book provides a self-contained introduction to structural operational semantics, featuring semantic definitions using big-step and small-step semantics of many standard programming language constructs, including control structures, structured declarations and objects, parameter mechanisms and procedural abstraction, concurrency, non-determinism and the features of functional programming languages. Along the way, the text introduces and applies the relevant proof techniques, including forms of induction and notions of semantic equivalence (including bisimilarity).

Thoroughly class-tested, this book has evolved from lecture notes used by the author over a 10-year period at Aalborg University to teach undergraduate and graduate students. The result is a thorough introduction that makes the subject clear to students and computing professionals without sacrificing its rigour. No experience with any specific programming language is required.

HANS HÜTTEL is Associate Professor in the Department of Computer Science at Aalborg University, Denmark.

Transitions and Trees

An Introduction to Structural Operational Semantics

HANS HÜTTEL

Aalborg University, Denmark

CAMBRIDGE UNIVERSITY PRESS

CAMBRIDGE
UNIVERSITY PRESS

University Printing House, Cambridge CB2 8BS, United Kingdom

One Liberty Plaza, 20th Floor, New York, NY 10006, USA

477 Williamstown Road, Port Melbourne, VIC 3207, Australia

4843/24, 2nd Floor, Ansari Road, Daryaganj, Delhi - 110002, India

79 Anson Road, #06-04/06, Singapore 079906

Cambridge University Press is part of the University of Cambridge.

It furthers the University's mission by disseminating knowledge in the pursuit of education, learning and research at the highest international levels of excellence.

www.cambridge.org
Information on this title: www.cambridge.org/9780521147095

© H. Hüttel 2010

First published 2010

A catalogue record for this publication is available from the British Library

ISBN 978-0-521-19746-5 Hardback
ISBN 978-0-521-14709-5 Paperback

Additional resources for this publication at www.operationalsemantics.net

Contents

Preface	*page*	ix
About the illustrations		xiii
List of illustrations		xiv
List of tables		xv

	PART I BACKGROUND		1
1	**A question of semantics**		3
	1.1	Semantics is the study of meaning	3
	1.2	Examples from the history of programming languages	4
	1.3	Different approaches to program semantics	6
	1.4	Applications of program semantics	10
2	**Mathematical preliminaries**		16
	2.1	Mathematical induction	16
	2.2	Logical notation	17
	2.3	Sets	19
	2.4	Operations on sets	20
	2.5	Relations	21
	2.6	Functions	22
	PART II FIRST EXAMPLES		25
3	**The basic principles**		27
	3.1	Abstract syntax	27
	3.2	Transition systems	30
	3.3	Big-step vs. small-step semantics	31
	3.4	Operational semantics of arithmetic expressions	31

	3.5	Proving properties	38
	3.6	A semantics of Boolean expressions	39
	3.7	The elements of an operational semantics	40
4	**Basic imperative statements**		**43**
	4.1	Program states	43
	4.2	A big-step semantics of statements	45
	4.3	A small-step semantics of statements in **Bims**	53
	4.4	Equivalence of the two semantics	55
	4.5	Two important proof techniques	60

PART III   LANGUAGE CONSTRUCTS   **63**

5	**Control structures**		**65**
	5.1	Some general assumptions	65
	5.2	Loop constructs	66
	5.3	Semantic equivalence	70
	5.4	Abnormal termination	72
	5.5	Nondeterminism	73
	5.6	Concurrency	76
6	**Blocks and procedures (1)**		**79**
	6.1	Abstract syntax of **Bip**	79
	6.2	The environment–store model	80
	6.3	Arithmetic and Boolean expressions	83
	6.4	Declarations	84
	6.5	Statements	85
	6.6	Scope rules	86
7	**Parameters**		**94**
	7.1	The language **Bump**	94
	7.2	Call-by-reference	96
	7.3	On recursive and non-recursive procedure calls	97
	7.4	Call-by-value	99
	7.5	Call-by-name	100
	7.6	A comparison of parameter mechanisms	110
8	**Concurrent communicating processes**		**113**
	8.1	Channel-based communication – **Cab**	113
	8.2	Global and local behaviour	114
	8.3	Synchronous communication in **Cab**	115
	8.4	Other communication models	119

8.5	Bisimulation equivalence	122
8.6	Channels as data – the π-calculus	123
9	**Structured declarations**	**134**
9.1	Records	134
9.2	The language **Bur**	135
9.3	The class-based language **Coat**	142
10	**Blocks and procedures (2)**	**154**
10.1	Run-time stacks	154
10.2	Declarations	155
10.3	Statements	155
11	**Concurrent object-oriented languages**	**161**
11.1	The language **Cola**	161
11.2	A small-step semantics of concurrent behaviour	163
11.3	Transition systems	163
12	**Functional programming languages**	**171**
12.1	What is a functional programming language?	171
12.2	Historical background	173
12.3	The λ-calculus	174
12.4	**Flan** – a simple functional language	177
12.5	Further reading	181
	PART IV RELATED TOPICS	**183**
13	**Typed programming languages**	**185**
13.1	Type systems	185
13.2	Typed **Bump**	187
13.3	Typed **Flan**	198
13.4	Type polymorphism and type inference	209
14	**An introduction to denotational semantics**	**211**
14.1	Background	211
14.2	λ-Notation	212
14.3	Basic ideas	214
14.4	Denotational semantics of statements	216
14.5	Further reading	220
15	**Recursive definitions**	**222**
15.1	A first example	222
15.2	A recursive definition specifies a fixed-point	224
15.3	The fixed-point theorem	225

15.4   How to apply the fixed-point theorem   231
15.5   Examples of cpos   232
15.6   Examples of continuous functions   236
15.7   Examples of computations of fixed-points   240
15.8   An equivalence result   241
15.9   Other applications   246
15.10 Further reading   248

Appendix A   **A big-step semantics of Bip**   249
Appendix B   **Implementing semantic definitions in SML** 257
       References   264
       Index   269

Preface

About this book

This is a book about structural operational semantics; more precisely it is a book that describes how this approach to semantics can be used to describe common programming language constructs and to reason about the behaviour of programs.

The text grew out of the lecture notes that I have used over a period of more than 10 years in the course *Syntax and semantics* which is taught to all students following the various degree programmes in computer science at Aalborg University. What began as a 10-page set of notes in Danish is now a textbook in English.

The book also includes chapters on related material, namely short introductions to type systems, denotational semantics and the mathematics necessary to understand recursive definitions.

Related work

This work was inspired by lecture notes by Plotkin (1981) (also written in Denmark), where this approach to programming language semantics was first presented.

The topic of structural operational semantics also appears in later books, three of which I will mention here.

Reynolds' book (Reynolds, 1999) is an excellent text that covers some of the same topics as this book but uses denotational and axiomatic semantics as well as structural operational semantics.

The book by Winskel (1993) is another very good textbook that covers many of the same topics as Reynolds' book.

Finally, I should mention Nielson and Nielson (2007), which introduces and relates denotational, axiomatic and structural operational semantics and then gives an introduction to how these can be used in connection with static program analysis.

The book that you are now reading differs from the ones just mentioned in three important ways. First, the main topic is exclusively that of structural operational semantics. Second, both Reynolds and Winskel introduce domain theory early on; this book aims at developing the theory of structural operational semantics and making use of it with mathematical prerequisites of a more modest nature. Third, unlike the book by the Nielsons, the focus here is not that of program analysis. Instead, it is on how operational semantics can be used to describe common features of programming languages.

What you need to know in advance

This text is *not* intended as an introduction to programming; if you are a reader expecting this to be the case, you will probably be disappointed! The ideal reader should already have some experience with programming in a high-level imperative programming language such as C, Java or Pascal.

Programming language semantics is a mathematical theory. Therefore, the reader should also have some mathematical maturity. In particular, you should be familiar with basic notions of discrete mathematics – sets, functions and graphs and the proof techniques of proof by induction and proof by contradiction. Chapter 2 gives a short overview of some of this material. There are several good textbooks that you can consult as a supplement; one that I would recommend in particular is Velleman's book (Velleman, 2006).

Ways through the book

The book falls into four parts. The first two parts must be covered in any course for which this book is the main text, since the contents of these first four chapters are necessary to understand the material in the rest of the book. After that, there are the following dependences:

- Chapter 7 and Chapter 9 are independent of each other but both extend the language introduced in Chapter 6,
- Chapter 8 assumes knowledge of the parallel operator introduced in Chapter 5,
- Chapter 10 on small-step semantics for procedures and blocks also assumes knowledge of Chapter 6,
- Chapter 11 assumes knowledge of Chapters 8 and 10 and finally

- Chapter 15 assumes knowledge of the contents of Chapter 14.

Problems and thoughts

To learn a mathematical subject, one should of course read the text carefully but also learn to apply the content. For this reason, there are quite a few problems scattered throughout the text. As a rule of thumb, a problem will appear at the point in the text where it becomes relevant. I have chosen this approach since I would like you, the reader, to focus on the connection between the problem and the context in which it appears. You can read most of the text without solving the problems but I encourage you to solve as many of them as possible. In some places, I have put problems that are important for understanding the text and they are then marked as such.

I have also introduced mini-problems which I call **A moment's thought**. Here, the idea is to make you think carefully about what you have just read. Do *not* read the text without finding the answers to these mini-problems.

Related resources

The book has its own website, `http://www.operationalsemantics.net`, which has more information, including hints to the mini-problems. The website also holds information about the Danish-language version of the book, *Pilen ved træets rod*, including how to obtain a copy of it.

Acknowledgements

This book grew out of the years I have spent teaching, so, first, I would like to thank the students who have lived with the various incarnations of this text over the years and have made many useful comments that have helped improve and shape its content and form.

Second, I want to thank the people who have inspired me to reflect on the task of teaching mathematical subjects and teaching in general over the years: Jens Friis Jørgensen, Steffen Lauritzen, Finn Verner Jensen, Anette Kolmos, Helle Alrø and Ole Skovsmose.

Third, I would like thank all those who helped me make this book a reality. My thanks go to the people and organizations who have kindly allowed me to use the pictures in Chapter 1 and to David Tranah from Cambridge University Press for his encouragement.

A number of colleagues read parts of the manuscript and provided me with lots of important feedback. Special thanks are due to Denis Bertelsen,

Morten Dahl, Ulrich Fahrenberg, Morten Kühnrich, Michael Pedersen, Willard Rafnsson and last, but by no means least, Gordon Plotkin.

On an entirely personal level, there are others who also deserve thanks. Over the years, I have come to know many inspiring people through my extracurricular activities in human rights activism and music and, most recently, through the extended family of sisters and brothers that I now have. I am very grateful for knowing you all.

Finally, and most importantly, I want to thank my wife Maria and our daughter Nadia for being in my life. This book is dedicated to you.

About the illustrations

- The picture of Alfred Tarski on p. 4 is by George M. Bergman and used courtesy of Wikimedia Commons under the GNU Free Documentation License.
- The picture of Dana Scott on p. 7 is used courtesy of Dana Scott.
- The picture of Christopher Strachey on p. 7 is used courtesy of Martin Campbell-Kelly.
- The picture of Gordon Plotkin on p. 8 is used courtesy of Gordon Plotkin.
- The picture of Robin Milner on p. 9 is used courtesy of Robin Milner.
- The picture of Tony Hoare on p. 9 is used courtesy of Tony Hoare.
- The picture of Joseph Goguen on p. 10 is used courtesy of Healfdene Goguen.
- The pictures of Ariane 5 on p. 12 are used courtesy of the ESA/CNES and are ©AFP/Patrick Hertzog, 1996.
- The picture of the Mars Climate Orbiter on p. 14 is used courtesy of NASA.

Illustrations

1.1	Alfred Tarski	4
1.2	An ALGOL 60 procedure. What is its intended behaviour?	5
1.3	Dana Scott (left) and Christopher Strachey (right)	7
1.4	Gordon Plotkin	8
1.5	Robin Milner	9
1.6	Tony Hoare	9
1.7	Joseph Goguen	10
1.8	The start and end of the maiden voyage of the Ariane 5	12
1.9	The Mars Climate Orbiter	14
3.1	A very small transition system	31
3.2	Derivation tree for a big-step transition for $(\underline{2}+\underline{3})*(\underline{4}+\underline{9}) \rightarrow 65$	35
3.3	Comparison between the derivation trees for the individual steps of a small-step transition sequence and that of a big-step transition	41
6.1	Example of a variable environment and a store	82
6.2	An example **Bip** statement whose behaviour is dependent on the choice of scope rules	88
7.1	A **Bump** statement with recursive calls	98
7.2	Exploiting call-by-name for computing the sum $\sum_{i=1}^{10} i^2$	104
7.3	A **Bump** statement showing where name clashes could occur as a result of an incorrectly defined substitution	108
9.1	A program with nested record declarations	135
9.2	A **Coat** program example	144
13.1	A type system is an overapproximation of safety	198
15.1	Part of the Hasse diagram for $(\mathbb{N}, \leq)$	226
15.2	A Hasse diagram for $(\mathcal{P}(\{1, 2, 3\}), \subseteq)$	233

Tables

3.1	Abstract syntax of **Bims**	29
3.2	Big-step transition rules for **Aexp**	33
3.3	Small-step transition rules for **Aexp**	37
3.4	Big-step transition rules for **Bexp**	40
4.1	Big-step transition rules for **Aexp**	45
4.2	Big-step transition rules for **Bexp**	46
4.3	Big-step transition rules for **Stm**	47
4.4	Small-step transition rules for **Stm**	53
5.1	Big-step transition rules for repeat-loops	67
5.2	Big-step transition rules for for-loops	72
5.3	Big-step transition rules for the **or**-statement	74
5.4	Small-step transition rules for the **or**-statement	75
5.5	Small-step semantics of the **par**-statement	77
5.6	An attempt at big-step transition rules for the **par**-statement	77
6.1	Big-step operational semantics of **Aexp** using the environment–store model	83
6.2	Big-step semantics of variable declarations	84
6.3	Big-step transition rules for **Bip** statements (except procedure calls)	87
6.4	Transition rules for procedure declarations (assuming fully dynamic scope rules)	89
6.5	Transition rule for procedure calls (assuming fully dynamic scope rules)	89
6.6	Transition rules for procedure declarations assuming mixed scope rules (dynamic for variables, static for procedures)	90
6.7	Transition rules for procedure calls assuming mixed scope rules (dynamic for variables, static for procedures)	91
6.8	Transition rules for procedure declarations assuming fully static scope rules	92

6.9   Transition rules for procedure calls assuming fully static scope
      rules   93
7.1   Rules for declaring procedures with a single parameter assuming
      static scope rules   96
7.2   Transition rule for calling a call-by-reference procedure   97
7.3   Revised transition rule for procedure calls that allow recursive
      calls   99
7.4   Transition rules for procedure calls using call-by-value   101
7.5   Transition rules for declaration of call-by-name procedures as-
      suming fully static scope rules   105
7.6   Transition rules for procedure calls using call-by-name   105
7.7   Substitution in statements   111
8.1   Transition rules defining local transitions   116
8.2   Rules defining the capability semantics   117
8.3   Synchronous communication: transition rules for the global level 118
8.4   Asynchronous communication: communication capabilities   120
8.5   Asynchronous communication: the global level   121
8.6   The structural congruence rules   128
8.7   Rules of the reduction semantics of the π-calculus   130
8.8   Rules of the labelled semantics of the π-calculus   132
9.1   Transition rules for generalized variables   137
9.2   Transition rules for arithmetic expressions   138
9.3   Transition rules for variable declarations   139
9.4   Transition rules for procedure declarations   139
9.5   Transition rules for generalized procedure names   140
9.6   Transition rules for record declarations   140
9.7   Transition rules for statements in **Bur**   141
9.8   The semantics of class declarations   146
9.9   The semantics of variable declarations   147
9.10 The semantics of method declarations   147
9.11 The semantics of object declarations   148
9.12 The semantics of object sequences   149
9.13 The semantics of object expressions   150
9.14 Evaluating extended variables (in the semantics of arithmetic
      expressions)   150
9.15 Important transition rules for statements   151
9.16 Transition rule for programs   152
10.1 Transition rules for statements other than procedure calls   157
10.2 Transition rules for procedure calls assuming static scope rules 159
10.3 Transition rule for procedure calls assuming dynamic scope rules 160
11.1 Transition rules for the local transition system   165
11.2 Transition rules of the labelled transition systems   166
11.3 Transition rules for the global level (1) – initialization   167

11.4 Transition rules for the global level (2) – the connection between global and local behaviour 168

11.5 Transition rules for the global level (3) – rendezvous 169

12.1 Big-step semantics for **Flan** 179

12.2 Some of the small-step semantics of **Flan** 180

13.1 Big-step operational semantics of **Exp** (arithmetic part) 188

13.2 Big-step transition rules for Bump statements (except procedure calls) 189

13.3 Type rules for **Bump** expressions 191

13.4 Type rules for variable and procedure declarations in **Bump** 191

13.5 Type rules for **Bump** statements 192

13.6 The error predicate for variable declarations 194

13.7 The error predicate for statements 195

13.8 Type rules for **Flan** 200

13.9 The small-step semantics of **Flan** 201

13.10 The type rule for `letrec` 209

A.1 Big-step operational semantics of **Aexp** 252

A.2 Big-step transition rules for $\to_b$ 253

A.3 Big-step semantics of variable declarations 254

A.4 Transition rules for procedure declarations assuming fully static scope rules 254

A.5 Big-step transition rules for **Bip** statements 256

PART I
BACKGROUND

1

A question of semantics

The goal of this chapter is to give the reader a glimpse of the applications and problem areas that have motivated and to this day continue to inspire research in the important area of computer science known as programming language semantics.

1.1 Semantics is the study of meaning

Programming language semantics is the study of *mathematical models of and methods for describing and reasoning about the behaviour of programs*.

The word *semantics* has Greek roots[1] and was first used in linguistics. Here, one distinguishes among *syntax*, the study of the structure of languages, *semantics*, the study of meaning, and *pragmatics*, the study of the use of language.

In computer science we make a similar distinction between syntax and semantics. The languages that we are interested in are *programming languages* in a very general sense. The 'meaning' of a program is its behaviour, and for this reason programming language semantics is the part of programming language theory devoted to the study of *program behaviour*.

Programming language semantics is concerned only with purely internal aspects of program behaviour, namely what happens within a running program. Program semantics does not claim to be able to address other aspects of program behaviour – e.g. whether or not a program is user-friendly or useful.

In this book, when we speak of semantics, we think of *formal semantics*,

---

[1] The Greek word (transliterated) is *semantikós*, meaning 'significant'. The English word 'semantics' is a singular form, as are 'physics', 'mathematics' and other words that have similar Greek roots.

Figure 1.1 Alfred Tarski

understood as an approach to semantics that relies on precise mathematical definitions.

Formal semantics arose in the early twentieth century in the context of mathematical logic. An early goal of mathematical logic was to provide a precise mathematical description of the language of mathematics, including the notion of truth. An important contributor in this area was the logician Alfred Tarski (Figure 1.1) (Tarski, 1935).

Many of the first insights and a lot of the fundamental terminology used in programming language semantics can be traced back to the work of Tarski. For instance, the important notion of *compositionality* – that the meaning of a composite language term should be defined using the meanings of its immediate constituents – is due to him. So is the insight that we need to use another language, a *metalanguage*, to define the semantics of our target language.

1.2 Examples from the history of programming languages

The area of programming language semantics came into existence in the late 1960s. It was born of the many problems that programming language designers and implementors encountered when trying to describe various constructs in both new and existing programming language.

The general conclusion that emerged was that an informal semantics, however precise it may seem, is not sufficient when it comes to defining the behaviour of programs.

1.2.1 ALGOL 60

The programming language ALGOL 60 was first documented in a paper from 1960 (Backus and Naur, 1960), now often referred to simply as 'the ALGOL 60 report'. ALGOL 60 was in many ways a landmark in the evolution of programming languages.

Firstly, the language was the result of very careful work by a committee of prominent researchers, including John Backus, who was the creator of FORTRAN, John McCarthy, the creator of Lisp, and Peter Naur, who became the first Danish professor of computer science. Later in their careers, Backus, McCarthy and Naur all received the ACM Turing Award for their work on programming languages.

Secondly, ALGOL 60 inspired a great many subsequent languages, among them Pascal and Modula.

Thirdly, ALGOL 60 was the first programming language whose syntax was defined formally. The notation used was a variant of context-free grammars, later known as Backus–Naur Normal Form (BNF).

However, as far as the semantics of ALGOL 60 is concerned, Backus and his colleagues had to rely on very detailed descriptions in English, since there were as yet no general mathematical theories of program behaviour. It turned out to be the case that even a group of outstanding researchers (who for the most part were mathematicians) could not avoid being imprecise, when they did not have access to a formalized mathematical theory of program behaviour. In 1963 the ALGOL 60 committee therefore released a revised version of the ALGOL 60 report (Backus and Naur, 1963) in which they tried to resolve the ambiguities and correct the mistakes that had been found since the publication of the original ALGOL 60 report.

However, this was by no means the end of the story. In 1967, Donald E. Knuth published a paper (Knuth, 1967) in which he pointed out a number of problems that still existed in ALGOL 60.

One such problem had to do with global variables in procedures. Figure 1.2 illustrates the nature of the problem. The procedure awkward is a procedure returning an integer value.

```
integer procedure awkward
begin comment x is a global variable
  x := x+1
  awkward := 3
end  awkward
```

Figure 1.2 An ALGOL 60 procedure. What is its intended behaviour?

The procedure `awkward` manipulates the value of a global variable and therefore has a side effect. However, the ALGOL 60 report does not explain whether or not side effects are allowed in procedures. Because of this, there is also no explanation of how arithmetic expressions should be evaluated if they contain side effects.

Let us consider a global variable x whose value is 5 and assume that we now want to find the value of the expression x+awkward. Should we evaluate x before or after we evaluate `awkward`? If we evaluate x first, the value of the expression will be 8; should we evaluate x after having called `awkward`, we get the value 9!

One consequence of Knuth's paper was that the ALGOL 60 committee went back to the drawing board to remove the ambiguities. The main reason why it took so long to discover these problems was that the language designers had no precise, mathematical criterion for checking whether or not all aspects of the language had been defined.

1.2.2 Pascal

Pascal, a descendant of the Algol family, was created by Niklaus Wirth and first documented in a book written with Kathleen Jensen (Jensen and Wirth, 1975). Ever since then, Pascal has been a common introductory language in computer science degree programmes around the world.

Even though great care was taken in the exposition of the language features, Pascal also suffers from the problems associated with an informal semantics. In particular, there are problems with explaining scoping rules – in fact, the scoping rules are barely explained in the book. There is mention of global variables; however, nowhere in the text is it explained what a global variable is, let alone what its scope should be. Nor are there any rules that specify that a variable must be declared before it is used!

All existing implementations of Pascal assume this (except for pointer variables), but the declaration-before-use convention is not part of the original definition of the language.

1.3 Different approaches to program semantics

The development of a mathematical theory of program semantics has been motivated by examples such as the ones given above. There are several ways of providing such a mathematical theory, and they turn out to be related.

Figure 1.3 Dana Scott (left) and Christopher Strachey (right)

Denotational semantics was the first mathematical account of program behaviour; it arose in the late 1960s (Strachey, 1966, 1967; Scott and Strachey, 1971) and was pioneered by Dana Scott and Christopher Strachey (Figure 1.3), who at the time were both working at Oxford University.

In denotational semantics, the behaviour of a program is described by defining a function that assigns meaning to every construct in the language. The meaning of a language construct is called its *denotation*. Typically, for an imperative program, the denotation will be a *state transformation*, which is a function that describes how the final values of the variables in a program are found from their initial values.

Structural operational semantics – the main topic of this book – came into existence around 1980 and is due to Gordon Plotkin (Figure 1.4), who gave the first account of his ideas in a set of lecture notes written during his sabbatical at Århus University in 1980 (Plotkin, 1981). An important early contribution is that of Robin Milner (Figure 1.5), who used Plotkin's approach to give a labelled semantics to the process calculus CCS (Calculus of Communication Systems) (Milner, 1980). Plotkin (2004) gives a detailed account of the origins and early history of the area.

In structural operational semantics one specifies the behaviour of a program by defining a transition system whose transition relation describes the evaluation steps of a program. One of the underlying motivations for this approach was that it is possible to give a simple account of concurrent programs; previous attempts to give a semantic description of even simple

Figure 1.4 Gordon Plotkin

parallel programming languages had used denotational semantics and had turned out to be quite complicated.

A central insight of this approach, and one to which we shall return repeatedly throughout this book, is that one can describe the evaluation steps of a syntactic entity (such as a program) in a structural fashion, that is, by means of an inductive definition based on the abstract syntax.

Axiomatic semantics is due to Tony Hoare (Hoare, 1969; Apt, 1981) (Figure 1.6) and, like denotational semantics, it is a product of the late 1960s. Here one describes a language construct by means of mathematical logic. More precisely, one defines a set of rules that describe the assertions that must hold before and after the language construct has been executed.

Algebraic semantics is related to denotational semantics and describes the behaviour of a program using universal algebra (Guessarian, 1981; Goguen and Malcolm, 1996). The members of the research collective behind the OBJ specification language, with Joseph Goguen (Figure 1.7) as a prominent contributor, have been important figures in the development of this approach.

These four approaches to programming language semantics are not rivals. Rather, they complement each other. Some approaches are more suitable than others in certain situations. For instance, it is much easier to describe

Figure 1.5 Robin Milner

Figure 1.6 Tony Hoare

parallel and nondeterministic program behaviour using structural operational semantics than by means of denotational semantics.

There are many precise mathematical results relating the four approaches. In this book we give an example of such a result in Chapter 15, where we

Figure 1.7 Joseph Goguen

show that the structural operational semantics and the denotational semantics of the **Bims** language are equivalent in a very precise sense.

1.4 Applications of program semantics

The area of program semantics has turned out to be extremely useful in situations where it is important to give a precise description of the behaviour of a program. Here are some prominent examples.

1.4.1 Standards for implementation

The formal semantics of a programming language is not meant as an alternative to the informal descriptions of programming constructs found in introductory programming textbooks. A formal semantics serves a very different purpose, namely to act as a yardstick that any implementation must conform to.

The examples mentioned in Section 1.2 all helped make computer scientists aware of the fact that *only a precise semantic definition can provide an exhaustive and implementation-independent account of all aspects of a programming language.* Such an account is particularly necessary if one is a 'superuser' of the language whose task is to implement an interpreter or a compiler or, in general, to create a language-dependent programming environment. A prominent example of a formal semantic definition is the operational semantics of Standard ML (Milner *et al.*, 1997), due to Robin Milner, Robert Harper, David MacQueen and Mads Tofte. Later, a lot of effort went into providing a suitable formal semantics of Java and C#; there are now denotational as well as operational semantics of Java (Alves-Foss, 1999) and C# (Börger *et al.*, 2005).

1.4.2 Generating interpreters and compilers

A precise definition of the semantics of a programming language will specify how a program in the language is to be executed. As a consequence, it is a natural step to construct a compiler/interpreter generator which, when given a definition of the semantics of some language *L*, will generate a compiler (or interpreter) for *L*.

Such compiler/interpreter generators have existed for many years. The first such systems were based on denotational semantics (Mosses, 1976; Paulson, 1982); later systems have also used variants of structural operational semantics (Pettersson, 1999; Diehl, 2000; Chalub and Braga, 2007). In general, the idea is not to replace standard compiler implementations as such but to provide a tool for the language developer.

In Appendix B of this book we give a number of small examples that describe how one can create an interpreter directly from a structural operational semantics.

1.4.3 Verification and debugging – lessons learned

Many software systems today are safety-critical in the sense that an execution error may have very unpleasant and wide-ranging consequences. One would of course like to be able to predict such events to prevent them from ever occurring.

In the natural sciences the use of mathematical models allows scientists and engineers to predict many events with great precision. Engineers use the mathematically based theories from physics to design bridges in such a way that these do not collapse and meteorologists use mathematical models of the atmosphere to make weather forecasts.

Similarly, we would like to use mathematically based theories to reason in a precise manner about the behaviour of programs. Programming language semantics makes this possible.

The following examples demonstrate what can happen if safety-critical software is not subjected to analyses of this kind.

Ariane 5

The launch of the Ariane 5 rocket is a notorious example of the consequences of a software bug.

The Ariane 5 is a booster rocket developed by the European Space Agency (ESA). It took the ESA 10 years to develop Ariane 5 and the budget was more than 6 million Euros. The aim was to create a booster rocket capable of placing a payload of up to 6 tonnes in geostationary orbit (ESA, 2001).

On 4 June 1996 the very first Ariane 5 was launched – see Figure 1.8. The ESA had high expectations for the new rocket, so it carried a payload of four expensive satellites.

Figure 1.8 shows the launch but also shows what happened 39 seconds after lift-off: the rocket exploded, and the entire payload was destroyed. There was no insurance covering the loss of the four satellites.

The cause of the explosion was a bug in the onboard control software. The program was meant to keep track of a number of flight data, and among them was the horizontal velocity of the rocket. For this, some parts of the program used 16 bits. This part of the software was legacy software that had been used for the predecessor to the Ariane 5, the Ariane 4. However, the Ariane 5 is a much more powerful rocket capable of reaching a much higher velocity. For this reason, another part of the control software represented the vertical velocity as a 64-bit number (Board, 1996).

The consequences of this design flaw are heartbreakingly obvious: whenever the program tries to store a 64-bit number as a 16-bit number, a run-time error will be the result. If the program were run on a desktop computer,

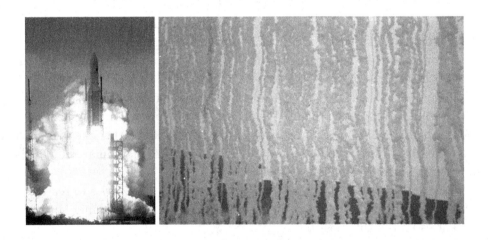

Figure 1.8 The start and end of the maiden voyage of the Ariane 5

the only consequence would be that the run-time environment would report a run-time error, whereupon the program would terminate abnormally. (A type system that could distinguish between the two number representations might have been helpful in preventing this error from ever occurring at run-time.)

However, this was a piece of software intended for an onboard computer on a booster rocket. Not surprisingly, the ESA had taken precautions: if the main computer of the rocket failed, another, identical computer would take over. Unfortunately, this other computer was running exactly the same program!

Even worse, the part of the control software that contained the bug was not even necessary during liftoff. The purpose of this part of the program was simply to ensure that it would be easy to resume the countdown if something unexpected happened.

The Mars Climate Orbiter

Another software bug involving a spacecraft could also have been prevented if the software had been analysed systematically.

The software was used for the Mars Climate Orbiter, an unmanned space probe that was supposed to go into orbit around Mars and take pictures of the weather phenomena on the Red Planet. Figure 1.9 shows what NASA had intended.

The launch itself was a success! The Mars Climate Orbiter reached Mars in September 1999 and the computer on board would now use the onboard engine to place the probe in a stable, low-altitude orbit.

Things turned out differently. NASA lost radio contact with the Orbiter and on 23 September 1999 NASA reported that the probe had gone missing and that they would stop looking for it.

We had planned to approach the planet at an altitude of about 150 kilometers (93 miles). We thought we were doing that, but upon review of the last six to eight hours of data leading up to arrival, we saw indications that the actual approach altitude had been much lower. It appears that the actual altitude was about 60 kilometers (37 miles). We are still trying to figure out why that happened. (Jet Propulsion Laboratories, 1999)

In November 1999 NASA found out what had happened (NASA, 1999), and the explanation was frighteningly simple: some parts of the onboard software used English miles (part of the Imperial system of units, almost only used in the United States nowadays) for representing the altitude of the vessel, while other parts of the software used kilometres (part of the system of SI units, used in almost every other country in the world today,

Figure 1.9 The Mars Climate Orbiter

including the United Kingdom). A type system that could have represented this distinction between units of measurement might very well have been useful here.

Nowadays, NASA devotes a lot of attention to developing ways of finding and preventing software bugs, and these techniques are based on programming language semantics.

Software verification methods and tools

Fortunately, in both of the above cases, no human lives were lost, but the consequences were extremely costly. A common moral of the two stories is that one must perform a systematic and thorough analysis of the behaviour of safety-critical software if one is to prevent the loss of life and/or expensive equipment.

Since the early 1990s a lot of attention has been devoted to creating methods and software tools that can analyse and debug software. These methods and tools are all based on the theory of programming language semantics.

Among the best-known such tools are SPIN (Holzmann, 1990), developed at Bell Labs by members of the team behind Unix, PVS (Owre *et al.*, 1992), developed at the Stanford Research institute, FDR (Roscoe, 1995), developed by the company Inmos together with researchers at Oxford University, and UPPAAL (Bengtsson *et al.*, 1995), developed at the universities in Uppsala and Aalborg.

1.4.4 The principles of programming languages

An important goal of this book is to show how one may give a systematic account of the *principles of programming languages* using structural operational semantics.

All the programming languages considered in the rest of this book are simple toy languages meant to illustrate specific aspects. Actual programming languages contain a plethora of aspects, all of which are important; however, if we were to introduce all these aspects at the same time, the presentation would become overly complicated and would not be helpful to the reader.

The study of the theory of programming languages provides a systematic and, it is hoped, elegant account of the many phenomena found in the realm of programming languages. For instance, it is through the study of programming language semantics that we are able to see how seemingly unrelated phenomena such as pointers, reference parameters and references in object-oriented languages can be described within the same simple framework. This deeper understanding of underlying principles can help language designers create better programming languages and better interpreters and compilers for these.

2
Mathematical preliminaries

This chapter is intended as a short introduction to the mathematical concepts used in the rest of the book. Readers with previous knowledge of set theory and mathematical induction should also have a look at this chapter to familiarize themselves with the notation that will be used in the rest of the book.

2.1 Mathematical induction

In computer science we very often prove theorems by the method of mathematical induction. This simple proof technique is extremely useful when we want to prove theorems of the form

For every natural number $k \geq c$ we have that ...

The underlying idea of mathematical induction is to show that the theorem holds for the case where $k = c$ and is preserved as we count upwards. The strategy is then the following.

1. The *base case* shows that the theorem is true for the least case, i.e. the one where $k = c$.
2. The *induction step* shows that, if we assume that the theorem holds for an arbitrary k where $k \geq c$, then it also holds for $k + 1$.

Here is a small example of how to use this proof technique.

Theorem 2.1 *For every natural number $k \geq 1$, the sum $S(k)$ defined by*

$$S(k) = 1 + \cdots + k = \sum_{i=1}^{k} i$$

satisfies that $S(k) = k(k+1)/2$.

Proof This is a statement of the form 'for every natural number k', so we proceed by induction on k.

Base case – $k = 1$: We have that $\sum_{i=1}^{k} i = 1$ and that $1(1+1)/2 = 1$, so the result holds for the base case.

Induction step – assume for k, show for $k + 1$: Here we have as our induction hypothesis that $S(k) = k(k+1)/2$. We must now show that $S(k+1) = (k+1)(k+2)/2$. The sum $S(k+1)$ can be written as

$$S(k+1) = 1 + \cdots + k + (k+1) = \overbrace{1 + \cdots + k}^{S(k)} + (k+1).$$

Now note that the first k terms of this sum add up to $S(k)$. By virtue of our induction hypothesis we have that $S(k) = k(k+1)/2$, so

$$S(k+1) = \frac{k(k+1)}{2} + (k+1).$$

But then, finding a common denominator, we have

$$S(k+1) = \frac{k(k+1)}{2} + \frac{2(k+1)}{2} = \frac{(k+1)(k+2)}{2},$$

which is what we were supposed to show.

$\square$

Sometimes it is convenient to use a variant of mathematical induction called the *strong principle of induction*. To prove that a claim

For every natural number $k \geq c$ we have that . . .

holds for all k, we do the following.

1. In the base case, we prove the claim for $k = c$.
2. In the step, we assume that the claim holds for all $k' \leq k$ and prove the claim for $k + 1$.

2.2 Logical notation

In the rest of the book we use standard logical notation, albeit in a fairly informal way, that is, we do not fix a particular logic within which we must make our statements.

2.2.1 Boolean connectives

Sometimes we use the Boolean connectives $\wedge$ (and), $\vee$ (or) and $\neg$ (not). The most important thing to remember is that the logical 'or' $\vee$ requires *at least one* of the logical statements that it connects to be true, if the entire statement is to be true. Thus,

$$2 + 2 = 4 \vee 3 + 1 = 4$$

is true, and so is

$$2 + 2 = 5 \vee 2 + 2 = 4,$$

but

$$2 + 2 = 5 \vee 2 + 2 = 3$$

is not.

2.2.2 Quantifiers

We often use the two quantifiers known from predicate logic.

- The *universal quantifier* $\forall$ is used to mean 'for all'. We can then write for instance

$$\forall x.2x = x + x,$$

whose intended meaning is that for all numbers x, $2x$ is equal to $x + x$.
- The *existential quantifier* $\exists$ is used to mean 'there exists'. We can use existential quantifiers to write for instance

$$\exists y.y > 0,$$

whose intended meaning is that there exists a number y which is strictly greater than 0.

We can also *mix quantifiers*, and this allows us to write for instance

$$\forall x.\exists y.y + y = x. \tag{2.1}$$

A moment's thought 2.2   What is the intended meaning of (2.1)?

2.3 Sets

A *set* is an arbitrary collection. One may speak of e.g. the set of all integers, the set of all computer science students or the set of African countries. The members of a set are called its *elements*. In a set every element occurs exactly once.

A set can be described by listing its elements within curly brackets. If x is an element of the set $\mathbf{A}$ we write $x \in \mathbf{A}$. If x is *not* a member of the set $\mathbf{A}$, we write $x \notin \mathbf{A}$.

Example 2.3 $\{1, 2, 42\}$ is a set whose elements are the integers 1, 2 and 42. $\{a, b, 47, \text{Sweden}\}$ is a set whose elements are the letters a and b, the integer 47 and the country Sweden. We have that $1 \in \{1, 2, 42\}$ but also that $3 \notin \{1, 2, 42\}$.

Often one defines a set by defining the universe that its elements should come from and the condition that the elements must satisfy. This is called *set abstraction*.

Example 2.4   Let $\mathbb{N}$ be the set of natural numbers. The set abstraction $\{n \in \mathbb{N} \mid \exists i \in \mathbb{N}.n = i^2\}$ denotes the set of perfect squares.

A moment's thought 2.5   What do we also call the following set?

$$\{n \in \mathbb{N} \mid \forall i \in \mathbb{N} : \text{if } n \neq i, i > 1 \text{ and } n > 1 \text{ then } n/i \notin \mathbb{N}\}.$$

When we use quantifiers, we sometimes restrict our quantification by *quantifying over a set*, so we can write e.g.

$$\forall x \in \mathbb{N}.x + x \geq x. \tag{2.2}$$

A moment's thought 2.6   What is the intended meaning of (2.2)?

In the remainder of this book we shall almost always write sets in **boldface** and starting with an **Uppercase letter**. Elements of sets will never be written in boldface and with a few exceptions in lowercase only. Thus **EnvV** will denote a set whereas env_V is an *element of a set*.

Sets can be compared. The notation $\mathbf{A} \subseteq \mathbf{B}$ says that every element of the set $\mathbf{A}$ also belongs to the set $\mathbf{B}$ ($\mathbf{A}$ is said to be a *subset* of $\mathbf{B}$). More formally: $\mathbf{A} \subseteq \mathbf{B}$ if, for every x, whenever $x \in \mathbf{A}$ then also $x \in \mathbf{B}$.

Two sets $\mathbf{A}$ and $\mathbf{B}$ are equal if they contain the same elements, that is, $x \in \mathbf{A}$ if and only if $x \in \mathbf{B}$. Consequently, $\mathbf{A} = \mathbf{B}$ if and only if $\mathbf{A} \subseteq \mathbf{B}$ and $\mathbf{A} \subseteq \mathbf{B}$.

2.4 Operations on sets

There are some common ways of building new sets from old – these are known as set operations.

2.4.1 Union

Let $\mathbf{A}$ and $\mathbf{B}$ be arbitrary sets. The set $\mathbf{A} \cup \mathbf{B}$ is defined as the set containing exactly the elements that are found in either $\mathbf{A}$ or $\mathbf{B}$, or both:

$$\mathbf{A} \cup \mathbf{B} = \{x \mid x \in A \text{ or } x \in B\}.$$

$\mathbf{A} \cup \mathbf{B}$ is called the *union* of $\mathbf{A}$ and $\mathbf{B}$.

Example 2.7 Let $\mathbf{A} = \{1, 2\}$ and $\mathbf{B} = \{2, 3\}$. Then $\mathbf{A} \cup \mathbf{B} = \{1, 2, 3\}$.

A moment's thought 2.8 Let $\mathbf{A}$ be a finite set with m elements and $\mathbf{B}$ be a finite set with n elements. How many elements are there *at most* in the union $\mathbf{A} \cup \mathbf{B}$?

2.4.2 Intersection

Let $\mathbf{A}$ and $\mathbf{B}$ be sets. The set $\mathbf{A} \cap \mathbf{B}$ is defined as the set containing exactly the elements that are found in both $\mathbf{A}$ and $\mathbf{B}$:

$$\mathbf{A} \cap \mathbf{B} = \{x \mid x \in A \text{ and } x \in B\}.$$

$\mathbf{A} \cap \mathbf{B}$ is called the *intersection* of $\mathbf{A}$ and $\mathbf{B}$.

Example 2.9 Let $\mathbf{A} = \{1, 2\}$ and $\mathbf{B} = \{2, 3\}$. Then $\mathbf{A} \cap \mathbf{B} = \{2\}$.

A moment's thought 2.10 Let $\mathbf{A}$ be a finite set with m elements and $\mathbf{B}$ be a finite set with n elements. How many elements are there *at most* in the intersection $\mathbf{A} \cap \mathbf{B}$?

2.4.3 Power set

Let $\mathbf{A}$ be a set. Then $\mathcal{P}(\mathbf{A})$ is *the set which is the collection of all subsets of* $\mathbf{A}$:

$$\mathcal{P}(\mathbf{A}) = \{C \mid C \subseteq \mathbf{A}\}.$$

$\mathcal{P}(\mathbf{A})$ is called the *power set* of $\mathbf{A}$. Sometimes one sees another notation used for the power set, namely $2^{\mathbf{A}}$. In this book we shall stick to $\mathcal{P}(\mathbf{A})$.

Example 2.11 Let $\mathbf{A} = \{1, 2\}$. Then $\mathcal{P}(\mathbf{A}) = \{\emptyset, \{1\}, \{2\}, \{1, 2\}\}$.

A moment's thought 2.12 Let **A** be a finite set with m elements. Exactly how many elements will $\mathcal{P}(\mathbf{A})$ have?

2.4.4 Cartesian product

Let **A** and **B** be sets. Then $\mathbf{A} \times \mathbf{B}$ denotes *the set of ordered pairs whose first coordinate is an element of* **A** *and whose second coordinate is an element of* **B**:

$$\mathbf{A} \times \mathbf{B} = \{(a, b) \mid a \in \mathbf{A}, b \in \mathbf{B}\}.$$

$\mathbf{A} \times \mathbf{B}$ is called the *Cartesian product* of **A** and **B**.

Example 2.13 Let $\mathbf{A} = \{1, 2\}$ and $\mathbf{B} = \{2, 3\}$. Then

$$\mathbf{A} \times \mathbf{B} = \{(1, 2), (1, 3), (2, 2), (2, 3)\}.$$

One can define Cartesian products of arbitrarily many sets. Let $A_1, \ldots, A_k$ be a family of k sets. Then $A_1 \times \cdots \times A_k$ is the set of all k-tuples whose ith coordinate belongs to A_i:

$$A_1 \times \cdots \times A_k = \{(a_1, \ldots, a_k) \mid a_i \in A_i \text{ for } 1 \leq i \leq k\}.$$

If the sets used to form the product are the same set, we write $\overbrace{\mathbf{A} \times \cdots \times \mathbf{A}}^{k \text{ times}}$ as $\mathbf{A}^k$.

A moment's thought 2.14 Let **A** be a finite set with m elements and let **B** be a finite set with n elements. How many elements are there in $\mathbf{A} \times \mathbf{B}$?

2.5 Relations

A relation is a set of tuples all taken from the same Cartesian product. Let $A_1, \ldots, A_k$ be a family of sets. Then a k-ary relation between $A_1, \ldots, A_k$ is any subset of $A_1 \times \cdots \times A_k$. If $k = 2$, we call the relation a *binary relation*.

Some relations are well known and use infix notation, so that we write e.g. $2 < 3$ and not $(2, 3) \in {<}$.

We now generalize this notation to arbitrary binary relations: if we have a binary relation R and $(a, b) \in R$ we will write aRb instead.

Example 2.15 Let $\mathbf{A} = \{1, 2\}$ and $\mathbf{B} = \{2, 3\}$. Then $R = \{(1, 2), (2, 2)\}$ is a binary relation between **A** and **B**. Here $1R2$ and $2R2$ but it is *not* the case that $1R3$.

We are often interested in a special kind of relation. An *equivalence relation* is any relation that shares certain properties with equality ($=$).

Definition 2.16   Let R be a binary relation over the set $\mathbf{A}$, i.e. $R \subseteq \mathbf{A} \times \mathbf{A}$. R is said to be an *equivalence relation* over $\mathbf{A}$ if

- R is *reflexive*, i.e. xRx whenever $x \in \mathbf{A}$
- R is *symmetric*, i.e. xRy implies yRx whenever $x, y \in \mathbf{A}$
- R is *transitive*, i.e. if xRy and yRz then also xRz, whenever $x, y, z \in \mathbf{A}$

A moment's thought 2.17   Let $\mathbf{A}$ be the set of people. Let p_1 and p_2 be arbitrary persons and say that $p_1 \bowtie p_2$ if p_1 and p_2 have the same parents. Show that $\bowtie$ is an equivalence relation.

A moment's thought 2.18   Let $\mathbf{A}$ be the set of people. Let p_1 and p_2 be arbitrary persons and say that $p_1 \equiv p_2$ if p_1 and p_2 have at least one parent in common. Is $\equiv$ an equivalence relation?

2.6 Functions

A *function* f is a special kind of binary relation. Let $\mathbf{A}$ and $\mathbf{B}$ be sets. Then a function from $\mathbf{A}$ to $\mathbf{B}$ is a binary relation between $\mathbf{A}$ and $\mathbf{B}$ that for every element $a \in \mathbf{A}$ assigns a unique element $b \in \mathbf{B}$.

If f is a function from $\mathbf{A}$ to $\mathbf{B}$ we often simply write $f : \mathbf{A} \to \mathbf{B}$. We sometimes say that f *has type* $\mathbf{A} \to \mathbf{B}$.

If $f : \mathbf{A} \to \mathbf{B}$, we call $\mathbf{A}$ the *domain* of f and call $\mathbf{B}$ the *range* or *codomain* of f. We often write $\mathrm{dom}(f)$ and $\mathrm{ran}(f)$ to denote the domain and the range of f, respectively.

If $f : \mathbf{A} \to \mathbf{B}$ and f assigns the element y to the element x, we write $f(x) = y$. Here x is called the *argument* of the function. Sometimes we leave out the parentheses and simply write $fx = y$.

We often define a function by giving an assignment of values to arguments.

Example 2.19   The relation t defined by the assignment $t(1) = 2$, $t(2) = 3$ and $t(7) = 2$ is a function having $\mathrm{dom}(t) = \{1, 2, 7\}$ and $\mathrm{ran}(t) = \{2, 3\}$.

Example 2.20   The relation t defined by the assignment $t(1) = 7$, $t(1) = 8$ and $t(2) = 7$ is *not* a function, since it does not give us a unique value for every argument; in particular, two distinct values are assigned to the argument 1.

A moment's thought 2.21   Let the relation t be defined by the assignment $t(1) = 1, t(2) = 1, t(3) = 1$. Is t a function from $\{1, 2, 3\}$ to $\{1, 2, 3\}$?

2.6.1 Partial and total functions

In program semantics we often consider function-like objects that satisfy the uniqueness condition for functions but may not assign a value to every argument.

A *partial function* from **A** to **B** is a binary relation f such that for every argument a there is *at most one* value b such that $f(a) = b$. We again call **A** the *domain* of f and **B** the *range* of f. We write that $f : \mathbf{A} \rightharpoonup \mathbf{B}$.

Note that the condition given above implies that some arguments may not yield a value. If a partial function in fact yields a value for every argument in its domain, we call it a *total function*.

Example 2.22 Consider the relation given by the assignment $f(1) = 2$, $f(2) = 3$ and $f(4) = 2$. f is then a partial function from $\{1, 2, 3, 4\}$ to $\{1, 2, 3, 4\}$ since it satisfies the uniqueness condition for values but $f(3)$ is not defined.

A moment's thought 2.23 Find a partial function which is not total and whose domain is the set of real numbers.

A moment's thought 2.24 Are total functions partial?

2.6.2 Defining functions

One often defines a function f by providing an expression that defines how $f(x)$ is found, given argument x.

Example 2.25 The function f where $\mathrm{dom}(f) = \mathbb{N}$ and $\mathrm{ran}(f) = \mathbb{N}$ defined by $f(x) = x + 1$ maps every natural number to its immediate successor.

2.6.3 Function spaces

Let **A** and **B** be sets. Then $\mathbf{A} \to \mathbf{B}$ denotes the set of functions from **A** to **B**:

$$\mathbf{A} \to \mathbf{B} = \{f \mid f : \mathbf{A} \to \mathbf{B}\}.$$

We call this set the *function space from* **A** *to* **B**. Consequently, we might as well write $f \in \mathbf{A} \to \mathbf{B}$ instead of $f : \mathbf{A} \to \mathbf{B}$.

Example 2.26 Assume that $\mathbf{A} = \{1, 2\}$ and $\mathbf{B} = \{2, 3\}$. Then we have that $A \rightarrow B = \{f_1, f_2, f_3, f_4\}$, where

$$f_1(1) = 2, \quad f_1(2) = 2;$$
$$f_2(1) = 3, \quad f_2(2) = 3;$$
$$f_3(1) = 3, \quad f_3(2) = 2;$$
$$f_4(1) = 2, \quad f_4(2) = 3.$$

A moment's thought 2.27   Let $A = \{a, b, c\}$ and $B = \{x, y, z\}$. Find $A \rightarrow B$.

A moment's thought 2.28   Let A be a finite set with m elements and let B be a finite set with n elements. How many elements are there in $A \rightarrow B$?

We can also define *partial function spaces* – if A and B are sets, then $A \rightharpoonup B$ denotes the set of partial functions from A to B:

$$A \rightharpoonup B = \{f \mid f : A \rightharpoonup B\}.$$

A moment's thought 2.29   As before, let $A = \{a, b, c\}$ and $B = \{x, y, z\}$. Find $A \rightharpoonup B$.

PART II
FIRST EXAMPLES

3

The basic principles

In this chapter we encounter our first examples of structural operational semantics, namely big-step and small-step semantics of arithmetic and Boolean expressions. These examples are on a small scale, but they still manage to introduce the principles that we shall be using throughout the remainder of the book.

A structural operational semantics is syntax-directed, and for this reason we first introduce the notion of *abstract syntax*. We use abstract syntax in this chapter to introduce the language **Bims**, which forms the core of almost all of the tiny programming languages considered in this book.

The rest of the chapter is devoted to introducing the basics of structural operational semantics. A central concept is that of a *transition system*. Transition systems are defined using *transition rules*.

The final section of the chapter briefly explores how we may now formulate and prove properties of a structural operational semantics. We shall return to this topic in later chapters.

3.1 Abstract syntax

In order to describe the behaviour of programs we must first present an account of the structure of programs, that is, their syntax. In program semantics we are not interested in syntax analysis – that is part of the theory of parsing. Instead, we are interested in a notion of abstract syntax that will allow us to describe the essential structure of a program. In other words, abstract syntax is not concerned with operator precedence etc.

The abstract syntax of a programming language is defined as follows.

- We assume a collection of *syntactic categories*.
- For each syntactic category we give a finite set of *formation rules* that

define how the inhabitants of the category can be built. These formation rules are given as context-free production rules.

3.1.1 The language Bims and its abstract syntax

Most of the rest of this book considers extensions of a tiny language called **Bims**.[1] **Bims** uses *statements, arithmetic expressions, Boolean expressions, variables* and *numerals*.

Each of these fundamental entities of **Bims** is represented by a *syntactic category* as given in Table 3.1 . To represent an arbitrary element of a syntactic category we use *metavariables*. In Table 3.1 S is the metavariable for statements, b the metavariable for Boolean expressions etc. We speak of *meta*variables to make explicit that e.g. x denotes an *arbitrary* variable as opposed to actual variables such as **y** or **z**. To avoid confusion, we often use indices to distinguish occurrences of variables – b_1, b_2 etc.

We define the structure of the members of a syntactic category by means of a set of *formation rules*. These, too, can be found in Table 3.1. The formation rules are production rules in the style of Backus-Naur Form.

Note that we do not provide formation rules for **Num** and **Var**; we shall assume that elements of **Num** are numerals written using decimal notation and that elements of **Var** are strings of letters from the Latin alphabet. However, we also need a notation that will let us talk about the entities that numerals denote, namely *numbers*. For this reason we shall *underline* numerals in the remainder of this chapter. Thus $\underline{10}$ is a numeral written in decimal notation, whereas 10 is the number ten (corresponding to the number of toes that many people have).

In the formation rule for **Aexp**

$$a ::= n \mid x \mid a_1 \texttt{+} a_2 \mid a_1 \texttt{*} a_2 \mid a_1 \texttt{-} a_2 \mid (a_1)$$

we have several right-hand sides. An arithmetic expression a can be e.g. a numeral n, a variable x or a sum expression $a_1\texttt{+}a_2$. In this rule, the right-hand side n is called a *simple element* of the syntactic category, whereas the right-hand side $a_1\texttt{+}a_2$ is called a *composite element*, as it is built from smaller entities. We call a_1 and a_2 the *immediate constituents* of $a_1\texttt{+}a_2$. Note that we use the indices on metavariables in formation rules only in order to be able to distinguish between distinct occurrences of the same metavariable.

A moment's thought 3.1 (Important)   What are the immediate

---

[1] Basic **im**perative statements.

Syntactic categories

$n \in \mathbf{Num}$ – Numerals
$x \in \mathbf{Var}$ – Variables
$a \in \mathbf{Aexp}$ – Arithmetic expressions
$b \in \mathbf{Bexp}$ – Boolean expressions
$S \in \mathbf{Stm}$ – Statements

Formation rules

$S ::= x{:=}a \mid \mathtt{skip} \mid S_1 ; S_2 \mid \mathtt{if}\ b\ \mathtt{then}\ S_1\ \mathtt{else}\ S_2 \mid$
$\quad \mathtt{while}\ b\ \mathtt{do}\ S$
$b ::= a_1 = a_2 \mid a_1 < a_2 \mid \neg b_1 \mid b_1 \wedge b_2 \mid (b_1)$
$a ::= n \mid x \mid a_1{+}a_2 \mid a_1{*}a_2 \mid a_1{-}a_2 \mid (a_1)$

Table 3.1 *Abstract syntax of* **Bims**

constituents of the following arithmetic expression?

$$(\underline{3}{+}\underline{4}){*}(\underline{14}{+}\underline{9}).$$

Why are they *not* $\underline{3}$, $\underline{4}$, $\underline{14}$ and $\underline{9}$?

Note that, since we distinguish between numbers and numerals, we write $*$ to indicate that this multiplication symbol is a syntactic constructor that can be used to form a composite arithmetic expression and does *not* represent multiplication of numbers.

If a function has a syntactic category as its domain, we use fat brackets to enclose its argument. For instance, in Chapter 14 we shall introduce a function S which as its argument takes an arbitrary member of **Stm**. We then write $S[\![\mathtt{while}\ b\ \mathtt{do}\ S]\!]$ to indicate an application of S.

Bims is a very small programming language, but it is well known that all computable functions can be represented in a language which has only the features found in **Bims** (Jacopini and Böhm, 1966). **Bims** is therefore said to be *Turing-complete*.[2]

---

[2] After the British mathematician Alan Mathison Turing (1912–1954), one of the founders of computability theory. Turing defined the universal model of computation now known as the Turing machine.

3.1.2 Some useful conventions

We introduce some conventions that make it a little easier to write expressions and statements in **Bims**.

- In Boolean expressions we shall use the inequality sign $\neq$, so that we can write $a_1 \neq a_2$. This should be read as a shorthand for $\neg(a_1 = a_2)$.
- In arithmetic expressions we assume the normal operator precedences for $*, +$ and $-$ such that e.g. $x + y * z$ should be read as $x + (y * z)$.
- In statements we assume that the semicolon operator is left-associative. So $S_1; S_2; S_3$ is to be read as $S_1; (S_2; S_3)$, the statement whose immediate constituents are S_1 and $S_2; S_3$.

3.2 Transition systems

A structural operational semantics defines a *transition system.*

A transition system is a particular kind of directed graph. The vertices of the graph are called *configurations.* They correspond to snapshots of the program and its current state. The edges are called *transitions.* They correspond to steps of the program. Some configurations have no transitions leading away from them; a configuration of this kind is called a *terminal configuration.*

A transition is a pair (γ, γ') where (γ, γ') represents that we can reach the configuration γ' from the configuration γ in one step. In other words, the set of transitions forms a binary relation over the set of configurations and we therefore speak of *the transition relation.*

We get the following definition.

Definition 3.2 A *transition system* is a triple $(\Gamma, \rightarrow, T)$ where Γ is a set of *configurations,* $\rightarrow$ is the *transition relation,* which is a subset of $\Gamma \times \Gamma$, and $T \subseteq \Gamma$ is a set of *terminal configurations.*

Example 3.3 Consider the transition system of Figure 3.1 on page 31. Here the components of the transition system are given by

$$\Gamma = \{\gamma_1, \gamma_2, \gamma_3, \gamma_4\}$$
$$\rightarrow = \{(\gamma_1, \gamma_2), (\gamma_1, \gamma_4), (\gamma_2, \gamma_3)\}$$
$$T = \{\gamma_3, \gamma_4\}$$

It is sometimes possible to define a transition system as a picture similar to that of Figure 3.1. However, this is only feasible for transition systems with finitely many configurations. In a typical semantic description of a

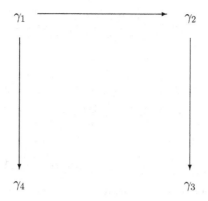

Figure 3.1 A very small transition system

programming language there will be a configuration for every possible intermediate state of every possible program and a transition for every possible program step. In the following section we shall therefore introduce a systematic approach to defining transition systems that describe the behaviour of programming language constructs. This approach makes use of the structure of constructs in the language and therefore gives rise to the name *structural operational semantics*.

3.3 Big-step vs. small-step semantics

There are two kinds of operational semantics, which describe computations in different ways. In a *big-step semantics* a single transition $\gamma \rightarrow \gamma'$ describes the entire computation that starts in configuration γ, and γ' is always a terminal configuration. In a *small-step semantics* a single transition $\gamma \rightarrow \gamma'$ describes a single step of a larger computation, and γ' need not be a terminal configuration.

In this book we shall consider both kinds of semantics, since both have their justifications and advantages. In some cases, a big-step semantics has the advantage of being easier to formulate. In other cases, notably in the case of languages that involve notions of parallelism, a small-step semantics is the most natural option.

3.4 Operational semantics of arithmetic expressions

Our first examples of structural operational semantics deal with arithmetic expressions, that is, the syntactic category **Aexp**.

In this chapter we make the simplifying assumption that arithmetic expressions do not contain variables, that is, that they can be built using the formation rules

$$a ::= n \mid a_1 + a_2 \mid a_1 * a_2 \mid a_1 - a_2 \mid (a_1)$$

In the next chapter we show how to incorporate variables.

3.4.1 A big-step semantics of Aexp

Our first structural operational semantics will be a *big-step semantics*. In our transition system every transition will correspond to the entire evaluation of an arithmetic expression.

Transitions are therefore of the form $a \to v$, where $a \in \mathbf{Aexp}$ and $v \in \mathbb{Z}$.

Here is a first example. Consider the expression $(\underline{2}+\underline{3}) * (\underline{4}+\underline{9})$. To evaluate this expression, we must first evaluate the immediate constituents $(\underline{2}+\underline{3})$ and $(\underline{4}+\underline{9})$ and then multiply these intermediate results.

Since we think of $a \to v$ as '*expression a evaluates to the value v*', we can write

If $a_1 \to v_1$ and $a_2 \to v_2$ then $a_1 + a_2 \to v$ where $v = v_1 + v_2$.

We usually write this in the following way:

$$\frac{a_1 \to v_1 \quad a_2 \to v_2}{a_1 + a_2 \to v} \qquad \text{where } v = v_1 + v_2. \qquad (3.1)$$

The rule (3.1) is our first example of a *transition rule*. The claim $a_1 + a_2 \to v$ is called the *conclusion* of the rule, and the claims $a_1 \to v_1$ and $a_2 \to v_2$ are called the *premises* of the rule. The condition that $v = v_1 + v_2$ is called a *side condition*.

We can now formulate similar transition rules for multiplication expressions, for bracketed expressions and for numerals.

The rules are found in Table 3.2.

In the rule [NUM$_{\text{BSS}}$] for numerals, we assume the existence of a semantic function $\mathcal{N} : \mathbf{Num} \to \mathbb{Z}$ that for every numeral gives us the number that is its value, so e.g. $\mathcal{N}[\![\underline{3}]\!] = 3$ and $\mathcal{N}[\![\underline{-42}]\!] = -42$. Notice that the rule has no premise. A rule of this kind is called an *axiom*.

Together, these rules provide us with a definition of the possible transitions, and the collection of rules therefore defines the transition relation $\to$: it is the case that a evaluates to the value v exactly in the case where it is

$[\text{PLUS}_{\text{BSS}}]$ $\qquad \dfrac{a_1 \to v_1 \quad a_2 \to v_2}{a_1 + a_2 \to v}$ $\qquad$ where $v = v_1 + v_2$

$[\text{MINUS}_{\text{BSS}}]$ $\qquad \dfrac{a_1 \to v_1 \quad a_2 \to v_2}{a_1 - a_2 \to v}$ $\qquad$ where $v = v_1 - v_2$

$[\text{MULT}_{\text{BSS}}]$ $\qquad \dfrac{a_1 \to v_1 \quad a_2 \to v_2}{a_1 * a_2 \to v}$ $\qquad$ where $v = v_1 \cdot v_2$

$[\text{PARENT}_{\text{BSS}}]$ $\qquad \dfrac{a_1 \to v_1}{(a_1) \to v_1}$

$[\text{NUM}_{\text{BSS}}]$ $\qquad n \to v$ if $\mathcal{N}[\![n]\!] = v$

Table 3.2 *Big-step transition rules for* **Aexp**

possible to prove the claim $a \to v$ by starting from the axioms and using the transition rules until we reach the conclusion $a \to v$.

Defining a structural operational semantics

We now have a big-step semantics of **Aexp** given by the transition system $(\Gamma, \to, T)$ where the set of configurations $\Gamma = \textbf{Aexp} \cup \mathbb{Z}$, where the transition relation $\to$ is defined by the rules of Table 3.2 and the set of terminal configurations is $T = \mathbb{Z}$.

This is our first example of a structural operational semantics, and all the examples that we give later on will follow the same pattern. A structural operational semantics assumes that we have given an abstract syntax and then defines a transition system $(\Gamma, \to, T)$ as follows.

- First, determine the format that transitions are supposed to have. All transitions in our transition system must adhere to this format.
- Next, we define the set Γ of *configurations* and define the subset $T \subseteq \Gamma$ of *terminal configurations*.
- Finally, we define the transition relation $\to$ by a set of *transition rules*. A transition exists if and only if it can be proved from the axioms using the transition rules.

Note that our transition rules in Table 3.2 are *syntax-directed* in the sense that for every formation rule in our syntactic category we have a number of transition rules for it. We always make this requirement.

How to build a derivation tree

We can use the rules of Table 3.2 to conclude that there is a transition $(2+3)*(4+9) \to 65$. We do this by using the transition rules to prove its existence. First, we know by the rule [NUM$_{BSS}$] that $\underline{2} \to 2$ and that $\underline{3} \to 3$. From the rule [PLUS$_{BSS}$] we therefore conclude that $\underline{2+3} \to 5$. By the rule [PARENT$_{BSS}$] we have that $(\underline{2+3}) \to 5$. Similarly we know from the rule [NUM$_{BSS}$] that $\underline{4} \to 4$ and that $\underline{9} \to 9$ and thence, using the rule [PLUS$_{BSS}$], we get the transition $\underline{4+9} \to 13$. Then, by applying [PARENT$_{BSS}$] this gives us that $(\underline{4+9}) \to 13$. Finally, by using [MULT$_{BSS}$] we obtain the desired transition $(\underline{2+3})*(\underline{4+9}) \to 65$.

The above proof of the existence of a transition is normally presented in the form of a *derivation tree* such as that of Figure 3.2.

Definition 3.4 (Derivation tree)   Assume given a finite set R of transition rules and let $A \subseteq R$ be the set of axioms. A *derivation tree* is a finite node-labelled tree whose nodes are labelled by transitions as follows.

1. All leaves are labelled by members of A
2. A node labelled by C has descendants labelled $P_1, \ldots, P_n$ if there exists a transition rule in R of the form

$$\frac{P_1, \ldots, P_n}{C}.$$

Derivation trees are normally constructed using a top-down procedure starting from the root, since one is usually interested in determining the result of a transition – in this case, the result of evaluating an arithmetic expression.

As an example, assume that we want to find the result of evaluating $(2+3)*(4+9)$. This is the same as asking whether there is a transition $(2+3)*(4+9) \to v$ for some value v. This in turn is equivalent to asking whether there is a derivation tree whose root is labelled $(\underline{2+3})*(\underline{4+9}) \to v$.

Can such a tree exist? If it exists, we must have used the rule [MULT$_{BSS}$] at the end of the construction to conclude

$$\frac{(\underline{2+3}) \to v_1 \ (\underline{4+9}) \to v_2}{(\underline{2+3})*(\underline{4+9}) \to v} \qquad \text{where } v = v_1 \cdot v_2$$

for some v_1 and some v_2. We must now find v_1 and v_2 and therefore need to construct derivation trees for $(\underline{2+3}) \to v_1$ and $(\underline{4+9}) \to v_2$, where $v = v_1 \cdot v_2$.

If there is a tree whose root is labelled $(\underline{2+3}) \to v_1$, as a final step of its construction we must have used the rule [PARENT$_{BSS}$] with premise $\underline{2+3} \to v_1$ such that

$$\frac{\displaystyle \frac{\underline{2} \to 2 \quad \underline{3} \to 3}{\underline{2}+\underline{3} \to 5} \quad \frac{\underline{4} \to 4 \quad \underline{9} \to 9}{\underline{4}+\underline{9} \to 13}}{\displaystyle \frac{(\underline{2}+\underline{3}) \to 5 \quad (\underline{4}+\underline{9}) \to 13}{(\underline{2}+\underline{3})*(\underline{4}+\underline{9}) \to 65}}$$

Figure 3.2 Derivation tree for a big-step transition for $(\underline{2}+\underline{3})*(\underline{4}+\underline{9}) \to 65$

$$\frac{\underline{2}+\underline{3} \to v_1}{(\underline{2}+\underline{3}) \to v_1}.$$

How can we then find a transition $\underline{2}+\underline{3} \to v_1$? This can be concluded only by using [PLUS$_{\text{BSS}}$]:

$$\frac{\underline{2} \to v_{11} \ \underline{3} \to v_{12}}{\underline{2}+\underline{3} \to v_1} \qquad \text{where } v_1 = v_{11}+v_{12}.$$

But from [NUM$_{\text{BSS}}$] we immediately get that $\underline{2} \to 2$ and also that $\underline{3} \to 3$, so $v_{11} = 2$ and $v_{12} = 3$.

All we need to do now is to construct a derivation tree for $(\underline{4}+\underline{9}) \to v_2$, and this construction is completely similar. The final derivation tree is found in Figure 3.2.

To summarize, the underlying idea of the construction of a derivation tree is to apply the following recursive strategy.

1. Find a transition rule whose syntactic construct in the conclusion matches that of the transition and whose side conditions are true.
2. Construct derivation trees for all premises of the rule, if any such premises exist. If no premises exist (that is, we are looking at an axiom), terminate this branch.
3. If more than one transition rule can match the transition, then try the recursive procedure for all such rules until one succeeds.

Notice that it becomes very important that the rules are structural. In particular, we would like the rules to be *compositional*. A rule is compositional if the premises of the rule make use only of syntactic entities that are immediate constituents of the syntactic construct found in the conclusion.

Example 3.5 The rule

$$\frac{a_2{+}a_1 \to v}{a_1{+}a_2 \to v}$$

is *not* compositional and it would be of no use whatsoever if we tried to apply it.

A moment's thought 3.6 Why would the above rule be useless?

Problem 3.7 Consider the big-step semantics of **Aexp**. Is there a transition $(\underline{4}{+}\underline{3}){*}\underline{8} \to v$? If there is, find it by recursively constructing a derivation tree and determine v in this way.

Problem 3.8 Is there a transition $(\underline{3}{+}\underline{12}){*}(\underline{4}{*}(\underline{5}{*}\underline{8})) \to v$? If there is, find it by recursively constructing a derivation tree and determine v in this way.

A moment's thought 3.9 We do not want transitions such as $\underline{7} \to \underline{7}$. What have we done to ensure that such transitions are ruled out?

3.4.2 A small-step semantics of Aexp

There is another way of defining a structural operational semantics of arithmetic expressions. In this approach a transition represents a single step of the computation. The resulting semantics is therefore called a *small-step semantics*.

Transitions are now either of the form $a \Rightarrow v$ or of the form $a \Rightarrow a'$, where $a \Rightarrow a'$ should be understood as 'in one step, a evaluates to the intermediate result a''. a' is here called an *intermediate configuration*, and v again denotes a terminal configuration.

The presentation becomes a little easier if we can let values appear directly in our intermediate results. We do this by extending the formation rules for **Aexp** such that values become elements of **Aexp**:

$$a ::= n \mid a_1{+}a_2 \mid a_1{*}a_2 \mid a_1{-}a_2 \mid (a_1) \mid v.$$

Our small-step semantics defines the transition system where $\Gamma = \mathbf{Aexp} \cup \mathbb{Z}$, where $\Rightarrow$ is defined by the rules in Table 3.3 and where $T = \mathbb{Z}$.

The difference from the big-step semantics can be illustrated by an example. For instance we now have the transition

$$(\underline{3}{+}\underline{12}){*}(\underline{4}{*}(\underline{5}{*}\underline{8})) \Rightarrow (3{+}\underline{12}){*}(\underline{4}{*}(\underline{5}{*}\underline{8})) \tag{3.2}$$

$[\text{PLUS-1}_{\text{SSS}}]$	$\dfrac{a_1 \Rightarrow a_1'}{a_1 + a_2 \Rightarrow a_1' + a_2}$
$[\text{PLUS-2}_{\text{SSS}}]$	$\dfrac{a_2 \Rightarrow a_2'}{a_1 + a_2 \Rightarrow a_1 + a_2'}$
$[\text{PLUS-3}_{\text{SSS}}]$	$v_1 + v_2 \Rightarrow v \quad \text{where } v = v_1 + v_2$
$[\text{MULT-1}_{\text{SSS}}]$	$\dfrac{a_1 \Rightarrow a_1'}{a_1 * a_2 \Rightarrow a_1' * a_2}$
$[\text{MULT-2}_{\text{SSS}}]$	$\dfrac{a_2 \Rightarrow a_2'}{a_1 * a_2 \Rightarrow a_1 * a_2'}$
$[\text{MULT-3}_{\text{SSS}}]$	$v_1 * v_2 \Rightarrow v \quad \text{where } v = v_1 \cdot v_2$
$[\text{SUB-1}_{\text{SSS}}]$	$\dfrac{a_1 \Rightarrow a_1'}{a_1 - a_2 \Rightarrow a_1' - a_2}$
$[\text{SUB-2}_{\text{SSS}}]$	$\dfrac{a_2 \Rightarrow a_2'}{a_1 - a_2 \Rightarrow a_1 - a_2'}$
$[\text{SUB-3}_{\text{SSS}}]$	$v_1 - v_2 \Rightarrow v \quad \text{where } v = v_1 - v_2$
$[\text{PARENT-1}_{\text{SSS}}]$	$\dfrac{a_1 \Rightarrow a_1'}{(a_1) \Rightarrow (a_1')}$
$[\text{PARENT-2}_{\text{SSS}}]$	$(v) \Rightarrow v$
$[\text{NUM}_{\text{SSS}}]$	$n \Rightarrow v \quad \text{if } \mathcal{N}[\![n]\!] = v$

Table 3.3 *Small-step transition rules for* **Aexp**

and a following transition

$$(3 + \underline{12}) * (\underline{4} * (\underline{5} * \underline{8})) \Rightarrow (3 + 12) * (\underline{4} * (\underline{5} * \underline{8})) \tag{3.3}$$

and the transition

$$(3 + 12) * (\underline{4} * (\underline{5} * \underline{8})) \Rightarrow (15) * (\underline{4} * (\underline{5} * \underline{8})). \tag{3.4}$$

Problem 3.10 Build derivation trees for the transitions (3.2), (3.3) and (3.4).

All in all, this gives us the *transition sequence*

$$(\underline{3} + \underline{12}) * (\underline{4} * (\underline{5} * \underline{8})) \Rightarrow (3 + \underline{12}) * (\underline{4} * (\underline{5} * \underline{8}))$$
$$\Rightarrow (3 + 12) * (\underline{4} * (\underline{5} * \underline{8}))$$
$$\Rightarrow (15) * (\underline{4} * (\underline{5} * \underline{8})).$$

If one is not interested in all the intermediate configurations, one writes

$$(\underline{3+12})*(\underline{4}*(\underline{5}*\underline{8})) \Rightarrow^3 (15)*(\underline{4}*(\underline{5}*\underline{8}))$$

where $\Rightarrow^3$ should be read as 'evaluates in 3 steps to'. We now make this precise by defining the relation $\gamma \Rightarrow^k \gamma'$ inductively on k.

If $k = 0$, nothing much can happen, so $\gamma = \gamma'$. If $k = n + 1$, $\gamma \Rightarrow^{n+1} \gamma'$ implies that we in one step reach a new configuration γ'' and from there in n transition steps reach γ'. This leads to the following formal definition.

Definition 3.11   Let $(\Gamma, \Rightarrow, T)$ be a transition system. *The k-step transition closure* $\Rightarrow^k$ is defined inductively by

$$\gamma \Rightarrow^0 \gamma \quad \text{for all } \gamma$$

$$\gamma \Rightarrow^{k+1} \gamma' \quad \text{if for some } \gamma'' : \gamma \Rightarrow \gamma'' \text{ and } \gamma'' \Rightarrow^k \gamma'.$$

We write $\gamma \Rightarrow^* \gamma'$ if for some k we have that $\gamma \Rightarrow^k \gamma'$.

Problem 3.12   Find a v such that $(\underline{2+3})*(\underline{4+9}) \Rightarrow^* v$. Remember to construct the derivation trees for the individual transitions.

3.5 Proving properties

Because our approach is structural, we can use proof techniques based on mathematical induction to prove properties of a structural operational semantics.

3.5.1 Determinacy

We would like our big-step semantics of Table 3.2 to be *deterministic*, that is,

$$\text{if } a \rightarrow v_1 \text{ and } a \rightarrow v_2 \text{ then } v_1 = v_2, \tag{3.5}$$

for then we would know that evaluation of an arithmetic expression would always produce a unique value.

To prove this, we must show that the claim (3.5) holds *for all transitions*. Since a transition exists if and only if it is the root of some derivation tree, our claim can be shown if we can show that the property (3.5) holds for all roots of derivation trees. Since derivation trees are built using the transition rules, this in turn is equivalent to showing that the property holds for all axioms and is preserved by all other transition rules.

This is in fact just normal mathematical induction on the natural number h, where h is the height of the derivation tree of a transition. The base case

$h = 0$ corresponds to the case where a transition is concluded directly from an axiom, and the inductive step corresponds to the case where a transition was concluded by a rule with a premise.

The proof technique hinted at here is therefore called *transition induction*. We shall return to it in Chapter 5.

Theorem 3.13   *The big-step semantics of Table 3.2 is deterministic.*

We would also like our small-step semantics of Table 3.3 to be deterministic. That is, we want it to be the case that if $a \Rightarrow a_1$ and $a \Rightarrow a_2$ then $a_1 = a_2$. However, this is *not the case*. Consider for example the transitions $\underline{2}+\underline{3} \Rightarrow 2+\underline{3}$ and $\underline{2}+\underline{3} \Rightarrow \underline{2}+3$.

Problem 3.14   Suggest an alternative small-step semantics for **Aexp** that is deterministic.

On the other hand, we can show that our small-step semantics is 'eventually deterministic' in the sense that the eventual value found by an evaluation is unique:

Theorem 3.15   *For the transition system* $(\textbf{\textit{Aexp}} \cup \mathbb{Z}, \Rightarrow, \mathbb{Z})$ *where* $\Rightarrow$ *is defined by the rules in Table 3.3 we have for all* $a \in \textbf{\textit{Aexp}}$ *that if* $a \Rightarrow^* v_1$ *and* $a \Rightarrow^* v_2$ *then* $v_1 = v_2$.

The above theorem tells us that a property holds *for all transition sequences*. One can prove properties of this kind by induction in the length of transition sequences. This is therefore also an application of normal mathematical induction and is another proof technique that we return to later.

3.6 A semantics of Boolean expressions

Let us complete the picture by presenting an operational semantics of **Bexp**. Boolean expressions evaluate to a truth value, that is, either *tt* or *ff*.

We consider a big-step semantics given by the transition system $(\textbf{Bexp} \cup \{\textit{tt}, \textit{ff}\}, \rightarrow_b, \{\textit{tt}, \textit{ff}\})$, where $\rightarrow_b$ is defined by the rules in Table 3.4.

When we evaluate a Boolean expression, we will need to evaluate the arithmetic expressions that may occur in it. Consequently, the semantics of **Bexp** refers to the semantics of **Aexp**; many of the rules refer to the evaluation of arithmetic expressions. To be able to tell transition relations apart, we let $\rightarrow_a$ denote the transition relation for **Aexp** defined in Table 3.2.

[EQUALS-1$_{\text{BSS}}$]	$$\frac{a_1 \to_a v_1 \quad a_2 \to_a v_2}{a_1 = a_2 \to_b \textit{tt}}$$	if $v_1 = v_2$
[EQUALS-2$_{\text{BSS}}$]	$$\frac{a_1 \to_a v_1 \quad a_2 \to_a v_2}{a_1 = a_2 \to_b \textit{ff}}$$	if $v_1 \neq v_2$
[GREATERTHAN-1$_{\text{BSS}}$]	$$\frac{a_1 \to_a v_1 \quad a_2 \to_a v_2}{a_1 < a_2 \to_b \textit{tt}}$$	if $v_1 < v_2$
[GREATERTHAN-2$_{\text{BSS}}$]	$$\frac{a_1 \to_a v_1 \quad a_2 \to_a v_2}{a_1 < a_2 \to_b \textit{ff}}$$	if $v_1 \not< v_2$
[NOT-1$_{\text{BSS}}$]	$$\frac{b \to_b \textit{tt}}{\neg b \to_b \textit{ff}}$$	
[NOT-2$_{\text{BSS}}$]	$$\frac{b \to_b \textit{ff}}{\neg b \to_b \textit{tt}}$$	
[PARENTH-B$_{\text{BSS}}$]	$$\frac{b_1 \to_b v}{(b_1) \to_b v}$$	
[AND-1$_{\text{BSS}}$]	$$\frac{b_1 \to_b \textit{tt} \quad b_2 \to_b \textit{tt}}{b_1 \wedge b_2 \to_b \textit{tt}}$$	
[AND-2$_{\text{BSS}}$]	$$\frac{b_i \to_b \textit{ff}}{b_1 \wedge b_2 \to_b \textit{ff}}$$	$i \in \{1,2\}$

Table 3.4 *Big-step transition rules for* **Bexp**

The rules reflect our intuitive understanding. For instance, rules [NOT-1$_{\text{BSS}}$] and [NOT-2$_{\text{BSS}}$] tell us that if b evaluates to $\textit{tt}$, then $\neg b$ must evaluate to $\textit{ff}$ – and conversely. The rules [AND-1$_{\text{BSS}}$] and [AND-2$_{\text{BSS}}$] tell us that $b_1 \wedge b_2$ evaluates to $\textit{tt}$ exactly when both b_1 and b_2 evaluate to $\textit{tt}$.

Problem 3.16 Suggest *a small-step semantics* of **Bexp**.

3.7 The elements of an operational semantics

In this chapter we have seen the first examples of structural operational semantics. They include a big-step semantics and a small-step semantics for arithmetic expressions.

An operational semantics describes computations in the form of a *transition system*. The transition relation $\to$ is normally defined by a set of

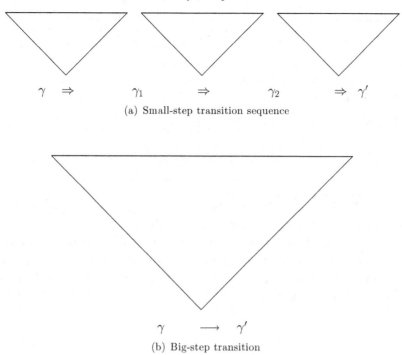

(a) Small-step transition sequence

(b) Big-step transition

Figure 3.3 Comparison between the derivation trees for the individual steps of a small-step transition sequence and that of a big-step transition

transition rules. A transition $\gamma \to \gamma'$ exists exactly when it is possible to find it from the transition rules by constructing a derivation tree.

The difference between a big-step semantics and a small-step semantics lies in the amount of information contained in a single transition. In a big-step semantics a single transition describes the entire computation leading from start configuration γ to terminal configuration γ'. In a small-step semantics, we capture the computation leading from start configuration γ to terminal configuration γ' by a *transition sequence*.

In both cases, we prove the existence of a single transition by construction a derivation tree for it.

Figure 3.3 shows the difference.

In the chapter that follows, we shall see an operational semantics of statements in **Bims** – or rather, there will be both a big-step and a small-step semantics, and as it turns out, they are equivalent in a very precise sense.

To summarize, a structural operational semantics consists of the following.

- A definition of the abstract syntax of the languages with

- a listing of the syntactic categories used in the language
- for each syntactic category, a set of formation rules.

- Definitions of additional sets and auxiliary functions, if needed.
- Definitions of *all* transition systems. For each transition system $(\Gamma, \rightarrow, T)$ there must be

  - a definition of the set of configurations Γ and the set of terminal configurations T
  - a set of syntax-directed transition rules defining the transition relation $\rightarrow$.

Appendix A contains a complete definition of the language **Bip**, which is an extension of **Bims** with blocks and procedures.

In the rest of the book, beginning with the treatment of extensions of **Bims** in Chapter 5, we often extend the syntax of **Bims** in a very simple way that does not influence the constructs known already. In these cases we often describe only the new features.

4

Basic imperative statements

In this chapter we present a big-step semantics and a small-step semantics of statements in **Bims**. In the big-step semantics, a transition represents the execution of an entire statement, while in the small-step semantics a transition will represent a single execution step.

Statements may modify the values of program variables, and for this reason we introduce a simple model of program states.

After the presentation of the two operational semantics we explore their properties. In particular, we formulate two results which together show that the semantics agree in the expected way – namely that the state change represented by a big-step transition corresponds to the state change of a corresponding transition sequence in the small-step semantics. The proof techniques that we shall use to prove this correspondence result are forms of mathematical induction.

4.1 Program states

In our abstract syntax of **Bims** the formation rules for **Aexp** tell us that arithmetic expressions may contain variables:

$$a ::= n \mid x \mid a_1 + a_2 \mid a_1 * a_2 \mid a_1 - a_2 \mid (a_1);$$

and the formation rules for **Stm** tell us that statements may modify variables:

$$S ::= x := a \mid \texttt{skip} \mid S_1; S_2 \mid \texttt{if } b \texttt{ then } S_1 \texttt{ else } S_2 \mid$$
$$\texttt{while } b \texttt{ do } S.$$

Consequently, we need to be able to describe how variables are bound to values. We do this by introducing the notion of a *state* which records the values of the variables that occur.

Definition 4.1 (State)   A state is a partial function[1] $s : \mathbf{Var} \rightharpoonup \mathbb{Z}$.

In other words, a state tells us the values of variables, so if $sx = v$ this means that variable x has value v. (Recall that sx is the application of function s to the argument x.)

In Chapter 6 we shall introduce a more advanced notion of program state that will allow us to describe concepts such as references and procedures. For now, we view variables as bound directly to their values.

A moment's thought 4.2   Why should we think of states as partial and not total functions?

Definition 4.3   The set of states is called **States** and is defined by

$$\mathbf{States} = \mathbf{Var} \rightharpoonup \mathbb{Z}.$$

We often represent a state by listing its contents. Consider for instance the state $s \in \mathbf{States}$ given by $sx = 2$, $sy = 5$ and $sz = 9$. This state can be represented by the list

$$[\mathbf{x} \mapsto 2, \mathbf{y} \mapsto 5, \mathbf{z} \mapsto 9].$$

Definition 4.4 (Update of state)   Let s be a state. The updated state $s[x \mapsto v]$ ('s where x is now bound to v ') is the state s' given by

$$s'y = \begin{cases} sy & \text{if } y \neq x \\ v & \text{if } y = x. \end{cases} \tag{4.1}$$

We are going return to this update notation in other, similar settings in the chapters that follow.

4.1.1 A new big-step operational semantics of Aexp

Now that we have introduced a notion of state we can present a big-step semantics of all of **Aexp**. This semantics is given by the transition system $(\mathbf{Aexp} \cup \mathbb{Z}, \rightarrow_a, \mathbb{Z})$. Here transitions are of the form

$$s \vdash a \rightarrow_a v$$

and should be read as 'in state s the expression a evaluates to the value v'. Table 4.1 contains the new transition rules defining $\rightarrow_a$. The key axiom is $[\text{VAR}_{\text{BSS}}]$, since this is where we look up the value of a variable, and for this we need the state.

---

[1] See Section 2.6 for the definition of a partial function.

$[\text{PLUS}_{\text{BSS}}]$ $\quad\dfrac{s \vdash a_1 \rightarrow_a v_1 \quad s \vdash a_2 \rightarrow_a v_2}{s \vdash a_1 + a_2 \rightarrow_a v}$ $\qquad$ where $v = v_1 + v_2$

$[\text{MINUS}_{\text{BSS}}]$ $\quad\dfrac{s \vdash a_1 \rightarrow_a v_1 \quad s \vdash a_2 \rightarrow_a v_2}{s \vdash a_1 - a_2 \rightarrow_a v}$ $\qquad$ where $v = v_1 - v_2$

$[\text{MULT}_{\text{BSS}}]$ $\quad\dfrac{s \vdash a_1 \rightarrow_a v_1 \quad s \vdash a_2 \rightarrow_a v_2}{s \vdash a_1 * a_2 \rightarrow_a v}$ $\qquad$ where $v = v_1 \cdot v_2$

$[\text{PARENT}_{\text{BSS}}]$ $\quad\dfrac{s \vdash a_1 \rightarrow_a v_1}{s \vdash (a_1) \rightarrow_a v_1}$

$[\text{NUM}_{\text{BSS}}]$ $\qquad s \vdash n \rightarrow_a v \quad$ if $\quad \mathcal{N}[\![n]\!] = v$

$[\text{VAR}_{\text{BSS}}]$ $\qquad s \vdash x \rightarrow_a v \quad$ if $\quad sx = v$

Table 4.1 *Big-step transition rules for **Aexp***

4.1.2 A new big-step operational semantics of Bexp

Similarly, we can now give a big-step semantics of all of **Bexp**, that is, including Boolean expressions that contain variables.

Here we define the transition system $(\textbf{Bexp} \cup \{t\!t, f\!f\}, \rightarrow_b, \{t\!t, f\!f\})$ where transitions are of the form $s \vdash b \rightarrow_b v$, where v is $t\!t$ or $f\!f$. The transition relation $\rightarrow_b$ is defined by the rules in Table 4.2.

4.2 A big-step semantics of statements

We can now present a big-step semantics of statements in **Bims**.

4.2.1 The transition system for Stm

Since a statement can now change the value of a variable, a transition must represent a potential *state change*. The transitions of the big-step semantics therefore have the form

$$\langle S, s \rangle \rightarrow s'$$

and must be interpreted as follows: *if we execute statement S in state s we get the final state s'*. Configurations are therefore either initial configurations $\langle S, s \rangle$ where $S \in \textbf{Stm}, s \in \textbf{States}$ or terminal configurations s where $s \in$ **States**.

[EQUAL-1$_{\text{BSS}}$]	$\dfrac{s \vdash a_1 \rightarrow_a v_1 \quad s \vdash a_2 \rightarrow_a v_2}{s \vdash a_1 = a_2 \rightarrow_b \text{ } t\!t}$	if $v_1 = v_2$
[EQUAL-2$_{\text{BSS}}$]	$\dfrac{s \vdash a_1 \rightarrow_a v_1 \quad s \vdash a_2 \rightarrow_a v_2}{s \vdash a_1 = a_2 \rightarrow_b \textit{ff}}$	if $v_1 \neq v_2$
[GREATHERTHAN-1$_{\text{BSS}}$]	$\dfrac{s \vdash a_1 \rightarrow_a v_1 \quad s \vdash a_2 \rightarrow_a v_2}{s \vdash a_1 < a_2 \rightarrow_b \text{ } t\!t}$	if $v_1 < v_2$
[GREATERTHAN-2$_{\text{BSS}}$]	$\dfrac{s \vdash a_1 \rightarrow_a v_1 \quad s \vdash a_2 \rightarrow_a v_2}{s \vdash a_1 < a_2 \rightarrow_b \textit{ff}}$	if $v_1 \not< v_2$
[NOT-1$_{\text{BSS}}$]	$\dfrac{s \vdash b \rightarrow_b \text{ } t\!t}{s \vdash \neg b \rightarrow_b \textit{ff}}$	
[NOT-2$_{\text{BSS}}$]	$\dfrac{s \vdash b \rightarrow_b \textit{ff}}{s \vdash \neg b \rightarrow_b \text{ } t\!t}$	
[PARENT-B$_{\text{BSS}}$]	$\dfrac{s \vdash b_1 \rightarrow_b v}{s \vdash (b_1) \rightarrow_b v}$	
[AND-1$_{\text{BSS}}$]	$\dfrac{s \vdash b_1 \rightarrow_b \text{ } t\!t \quad s \vdash b_2 \rightarrow_b \text{ } t\!t}{s \vdash b_1 \wedge b_2 \rightarrow_b \text{ } t\!t}$	
[AND-2$_{\text{BSS}}$]	$\dfrac{s \vdash b_i \rightarrow_b \textit{ff}}{s \vdash b_1 \wedge b_2 \rightarrow_b \textit{ff}}$	$i \in \{1, 2\}$

Table 4.2 *Big-step transition rules for* **Bexp**

To summarize, our transition system is $(\Gamma, \rightarrow, T)$ where

$$\Gamma = (\textbf{Stm} \times \textbf{States}) \cup \textbf{States},$$
$$T = \textbf{States}$$

and $\rightarrow$ is defined by the rules in Table 4.3.

It is now time for an informal explanation of each of the transition rules.

The axiom [ASS$_{\text{BSS}}$] tells us that in the start state s the assignment statement $x := a$ will result in a new, modified state $s[x \mapsto v]$ where v is the result of evaluating a in state s.

[SKIP$_{\text{BSS}}$], too, is an axiom. This axiom tells us that the skip statement cannnot modify the state.

Strictly speaking the rule [ASS$_{\text{BSS}}$] is what logicians call an *axiom schema*, that is, a collection of axiom instances of the same form. For [ASS$_{\text{BSS}}$] de-

[ASS$_{\text{BSS}}$]	$\langle x := a, s \rangle \rightarrow s[x \mapsto v]$ where $s \vdash a \rightarrow_a v$
[SKIP$_{\text{BSS}}$]	$\langle \text{skip}, s \rangle \rightarrow s$

[COMP$_{\text{BSS}}$]
$$\frac{\langle S_1, s \rangle \rightarrow s'' \quad \langle S_2, s'' \rangle \rightarrow s'}{\langle S_1 ; S_2, s \rangle \rightarrow s'}$$

[IF-TRUE$_{\text{BSS}}$]
$$\frac{\langle S_1, s \rangle \rightarrow s'}{\langle \text{if } b \text{ then } S_1 \text{ else } S_2, s \rangle \rightarrow s'} \quad \text{if } s \vdash b \rightarrow_b tt$$

[IF-FALSE$_{\text{BSS}}$]
$$\frac{\langle S_2, s \rangle \rightarrow s'}{\langle \text{if } b \text{ then } S_1 \text{ else } S_2, s \rangle \rightarrow s'} \quad \text{if } s \vdash b \rightarrow_b ff$$

[WHILE-TRUE$_{\text{BSS}}$]
$$\frac{\langle S, s \rangle \rightarrow s'' \quad \langle \text{while } b \text{ do } S, s'' \rangle \rightarrow s'}{\langle \text{while } b \text{ do } S, s \rangle \rightarrow s'} \quad \text{if } s \vdash b \rightarrow_b tt$$

[WHILE-FALSE$_{\text{BSS}}$] $\quad \langle \text{while } b \text{ do } S, s \rangle \rightarrow s \text{ if } s \vdash b \rightarrow_b ff$

Table 4.3 *Big-step transition rules for* **Stm**

scribes that *for every* assignment statement a certain state change will occur. For instance we have from [ASS$_{\text{BSS}}$] that $\langle \text{x} := 7, s \rangle \rightarrow s[\text{x} \rightarrow 7]$. In fact, all the axioms and transition rules that we shall consider are schemata in this sense.

The rule [COMP$_{\text{BSS}}$] describes the effect of the sequential composition of S_1 and S_2 when executed in start state s. First we execute S_1 in start state s. This results in a new state s'', which is the start state when control is passed on to the statement S_2. The result of executing S_2 in state s'' gives us the state s', which is the result of the entire composite statement.

The rule [IF-FALSE$_{\text{BSS}}$] expresses the following: in state s we must evaluate the Boolean condition b. If b evaluates to ff, the effect of evaluating if b then S_1 else S_2 is the effect of executing S_2 in state s. Similarly, the rule [IF-TRUE$_{\text{BSS}}$] expresses that we must evaluate the Boolean condition b in state s and that the effect of executing the statement is then that of executing S_1 in start state s.

Likewise, there are two rules describing the effect of a while-statement. The rule [WHILE-FALSE$_{\text{BSS}}$] expresses that if the condition b evaluates to ff in state s, then while b do S gives us the final state s – we never enter the loop.

All rules found in Table 4.3 are structural, since they are syntax-directed. Moreover, every rule that we have described so far is compositional in the sense of page 35, that is, the transitions in the premise make use only of the immediate constituents of the piece of syntax mentioned in the conclusion. In other words, with rules of this kind, we can find the state change of a composite statement by finding the state changes made by the immediate constituents of the statement.

However, the rule [WHILE-TRUE$_{\text{BSS}}$] fails to be compositional. This is due to the fact that the premise has an occurrence of while b do S. The reason for this is that our semantic description of the execution of a while-loop is *recursive* by nature – we execute the loop by first evaluating the condition. If b evaluates to true, we execute the loop body and then re-enter the loop.

4.2.2 On building derivation trees

The big-step transition rules describe the intended behaviour of an arbitrary **Bims** statement, and in fact the derivation tree of a transition $\langle S, s \rangle \rightarrow s'$ contains all information concerning the execution of the statement S in start state s.

A large example

We shall now go through a large example which is meant to illustrate the construction of a derivation tree for a transition. As always, it is a good idea to have pencil and paper ready when reading the text.

We consider the statement

$$S = \text{i:=6; while i} \neq 0 \text{ do (x:= x + i;i := i-2)}$$

and let s be the state given by $sx = 5$. Is there a transition $\langle S, s \rangle \rightarrow s'$? If so, what is s'? By constructing a derivation tree we can find s'. Along the way we discover all the intermediate states of the computation, as we shall now see.

We have defined the transition relation $\rightarrow$ as exactly those transitions that can be concluded from the transition rules by starting from the axioms. So if there is a transition $\langle S, s \rangle \rightarrow s'$, this *by definition* tells us that there must be a derivation tree whose root is labelled by the transition

$$\langle \text{i:=6; while i} \neq 0 \text{ do (x:= x + i;i := i-2)}, s \rangle \rightarrow s'.$$

We shall now construct this derivation using the top-down recursive strategy outlined previously.

Since our transition rules are syntax-directed, the root transition must have been concluded using the rule [COMP$_{BSS}$], because the statement S is a sequential composition.

$$\frac{\langle \texttt{i:=6}, s \rangle \rightarrow s'' \quad \langle \texttt{while i} \neq \texttt{0 do (x:= x + i;i := i-2)}, s'' \rangle \rightarrow s'}{\langle \texttt{i :=6; while i} \neq \texttt{0 do (x:= x + i;i := i-2)}, s \rangle \rightarrow s'},$$

where s'' is a new intermediate state to be found. How can we have arrived at the following transitions?

$$\langle \texttt{i:=6}, s \rangle \rightarrow s'', \tag{4.2}$$

$$\langle \texttt{while i} \neq \texttt{0 do (x:= x + i;i := i-2)}, s'' \rangle \rightarrow s'. \tag{4.3}$$

Again by definition there must be two derivation trees whose roots are labelled by these transitions.

From the big-step semantics for **Aexp** we see that there is a transition $s \vdash 6 \rightarrow_a 6$, and the axiom [ASS$_{BSS}$] therefore tells us that

$$\langle \texttt{i :=6}, s \rangle \rightarrow s[\texttt{i} \mapsto 6].$$

So $s'' = s[\texttt{i} \mapsto 6]$. We are now a little closer to finding the state s'. Since our transition rules are syntax-directed, (4.3) must have been concluded using either [WHILE-TRUE$_{BSS}$] or [WHILE-FALSE$_{BSS}$]. So here we must examine the side conditions of the two rules. From the big-step semantics of **Bexp** we see that $s'' \vdash \texttt{i} \neq \texttt{0} \rightarrow_b tt$ and therefore the rule must have been [WHILE-TRUE$_{BSS}$]:

$$\frac{\langle \texttt{x:= x + i;i := i-2}, s'' \rangle \rightarrow s^{(3)}}{\langle \texttt{while i} \neq \texttt{0 do (x:= x + i;i := i-2)}, s^{(3)} \rangle \rightarrow s'}{\langle \texttt{while i} \neq \texttt{0 do (x:= x + i;i := i-2)}, s'' \rangle \rightarrow s'},$$

where $s^{(3)}$ is another intermediate state to be found. We have now reduced our problem to that of finding derivation trees for the transitions

$$\langle \texttt{x:= x + i;i := i-2}, s'' \rangle \rightarrow s^{(3)} \tag{4.4}$$

and

$$\langle \texttt{while i} \neq \texttt{0 do (x:= x + i;i := i-2)}, s^{(3)} \rangle \rightarrow s'. \tag{4.5}$$

The transition (4.4) must have been concluded using [COMP$_{BSS}$]:

$$\frac{\langle \texttt{x:= x + i}, s'' \rangle \rightarrow s^{(4)} \quad \langle \texttt{i := i-2}, s^{(4)} \rangle \rightarrow s^{(3)}}{\langle \texttt{x:= x + i; i := i-2}, s'' \rangle \rightarrow s^{(3)}},$$

where $s^{(4)}$ is yet another intermediate state to be found. But the big-step semantics for **Aexp** allows us to find the right-hand side of the first assignment statement – we get that $s'' \vdash \mathtt{x} + \mathtt{i} \to_a 11$ (check that this is indeed the case!). So using the axiom [ASS$_{\mathrm{BSS}}$] we then get that

$$\langle \mathtt{x:= x + i}, s'' \rangle \to s''[\mathtt{x} \mapsto 11]$$

and from this we now see that $s^{(4)} = s''[\mathtt{x} \mapsto 11] = s[\mathtt{i} \mapsto 6, \mathtt{x} \mapsto 11]$. Using our new knowledge of $s^{(4)}$, we get from [ASS$_{\mathrm{BSS}}$] and the big-step semantics of **Aexp**, which tells us that $s^{(4)} \vdash \mathtt{i-2} \to_a 4$, that

$$\langle \mathtt{i := i-2}, s^{(4)} \rangle \to s^{(4)}[\mathtt{i} \mapsto 4]$$

and consequently that $s^{(3)} = s^{(4)}[\mathtt{i} \mapsto 4] = s[\mathtt{i} \mapsto 4, \mathtt{x} \mapsto 11]$.

We now look at the transition (4.5); this transition must have been concluded using [WHILE-TRUE$_{\mathrm{BSS}}$] or [WHILE-FALSE$_{\mathrm{BSS}}$]. Here the big-step semantics of **Bexp** tells us that $s^{(3)} \vdash \mathtt{i} \neq 0 \to_b t\!t$ and therefore we know that we must have applied [WHILE-TRUE$_{\mathrm{BSS}}$]:

$$\frac{\langle \mathtt{x:= x + i; i := i-2}, s^{(3)} \rangle \to s^{(5)} \quad \langle \mathtt{while\ i} \neq 0\ \mathtt{do\ (x:= x + i; i := i-2)}, s^{(5)} \rangle \to s'}{\langle \mathtt{while\ i} \neq 0\ \mathtt{do\ (x:= x + i; i := i-2)}, s^{(3)} \rangle \to s'}.$$

So now we must determine how the transitions

$$\langle \mathtt{x:= x + i; i := i-2}, s^{(3)} \rangle \to s^{(5)} \tag{4.6}$$

and

$$\langle \mathtt{while\ i} \neq 0\ \mathtt{do\ (x := x + i; i:= i-2)}, s^{(5)} \rangle \to s', \tag{4.7}$$

were concluded. First, we consider (4.6). This transition must have been concluded using [COMP$_{\mathrm{BSS}}$]:

$$\frac{\langle \mathtt{x:= x + i}, s^{(3)} \rangle \to s^{(6)} \quad \langle \mathtt{i := i-2}, s^{(6)} \rangle \to s^{(5)}}{\langle \mathtt{x:= x + i;\ i := i-2}, s^{(3)} \rangle \to s^{(5)}},$$

where $s^{(6)}$ is a new intermediate state to be found. The two premises must both have been concluded using [ASS$_{\mathrm{BSS}}$] and the big-step semantics of **Aexp**, so we first get that

$$\langle \mathtt{x:= x + i}, s^{(3)} \rangle \to s^{(3)}[\mathtt{x} \mapsto 15],$$

from which we see that $s^{(6)} = s^{(3)}[\mathtt{x} \mapsto 15]$ and next discover that

$$\langle \mathtt{i := i-2}, s^{(6)} \rangle \to s^{(6)}[\mathtt{i} \mapsto 2].$$

We get $s^{(5)} = s^{(6)}[\mathtt{i} \mapsto 2] = s^{(3)}[\mathtt{x} \mapsto 15, \mathtt{i} \mapsto 2] = s[\mathtt{x} \mapsto 15, \mathtt{i} \mapsto 2]$. Here we used our knowledge of $s^{(3)}$.

Next, we consider (4.7). This transition must have been concluded using [WHILE-TRUE$_{BSS}$] or [WHILE-FALSE$_{BSS}$]. Here the big-step semantics of **Bexp** tells us that $s^{(5)} \vdash$ i $\neq$ 0 $\rightarrow_b$ *tt*, so again we must be dealing with an application of [WHILE-TRUE$_{BSS}$]:

$$\frac{\langle \text{x:= x + i; i := i-2}, s^{(5)} \rangle \rightarrow s^{(7)} \quad \langle \text{while i} \neq \text{0 do (x:= x + i; i := i-2)}, s^{(7)} \rangle \rightarrow s'}{\langle \text{while i} \neq \text{0 do (x:= x + i; i := i-2)}, s^{(5)} \rangle \rightarrow s'}.$$

This time we have to find derivation trees for the transitions

$$\langle \text{x:= x + i; i := i-2}, s^{(5)} \rangle \rightarrow s^{(7)} \tag{4.8}$$

and

$$\langle \text{while i} \neq \text{0 do (x:= x + i; i := i-2)}, s^{(7)} \rangle \rightarrow s'. \tag{4.9}$$

As before, we first consider (4.8). In this case, too, we are looking at a transition that must have been concluded using [COMP$_{BSS}$]. Here we have that

$$\frac{\langle \text{x:= x+i}, s^{(5)} \rangle \rightarrow s^{(8)} \quad \langle \text{i:= i-2}, s^{(8)} \rangle \rightarrow s^{(7)}}{\langle \text{x:= x+i; i:= i-2}, s^{(5)} \rangle \rightarrow s^{(7)}},$$

where $s^{(8)}$ is an intermediate state. From [ASS$_{BSS}$] and the big-step semantics of **Aexp**, which tells us that $s^{(5)} \vdash$ x+i $\rightarrow_a$ 17, we see that

$$\langle \text{x:= x+i}, s^{(5)} \rangle \rightarrow s^{(5)}[\text{x} \mapsto 17]$$

and from this, since we can now conclude that $s^{(8)} \vdash$ i-2 $\rightarrow_a$ 0, we see that

$$\langle \text{i:= i-2}, s^{(8)} \rangle \rightarrow s^{(8)}[\text{i} \mapsto 0]$$

and hence $s^{(7)} = s^{(5)}[\text{x} \mapsto 17, \text{i} \mapsto 0]$. Now consider the transition (4.9). Since here $s^{(7)} \vdash$ i $\neq$ 0 $\rightarrow_b$ *ff*, the transition (4.9) must have been concluded using [WHILE-FALSE$_{BSS}$]. This lets us conclude that

$$\langle \text{while i} \neq \text{0 do (x:= x + i; i := i-2)}, s^{(7)} \rangle \rightarrow s^{(7)}.$$

In other words, $s' = s^{(7)}$ and therefore $s' = s^{(5)}[\text{x} \mapsto 17, \text{i} \mapsto 0] = s[\text{x} \mapsto 17, \text{i} \mapsto 0]$. This concludes the construction of the derivation tree and we thus have the transition

$$\langle S, s \rangle \rightarrow s[\text{x} \mapsto 17, \text{i} \mapsto 0].$$

Problem 4.5 (Important!) Draw the derivation tree that we have just constructed. Where do the states appear?

The example just given illustrates some important points.

First, note that the construction of a derivation tree can be done using a straightforward algorithm – we inspect the structure of S and then consider all the rules whose conclusion contains a statement having the same structure as S. The choice between the rules is made by checking the side condition. To do this, we need to evaluate the side conditions of each candidate rule.

Next, note that in the construction of the derivation tree for $\langle S, s \rangle \to s'$ we do not know s' initially. However, eventually we discover what s' is. In some cases, as for instance in the above example, we introduce transitions with *intermediate states* that we then need to find. This is then done by finding the derivation trees for the new goals. This, in turn, will introduce more intermediate states,

The construction of a derivation tree is easily implemented, and the resulting algorithm can therefore be thought of as an *interpreter*.

Problem 4.6 (Important!)   Let the state s be given by $sx = 3$ and $sy = 4$. Construct a derivation tree for the transition $\langle S, s \rangle \to s'$ where $S = $ x := y; y := 3; x := x + 3, finding s'. Do not bother with derivation trees for any **Aexp**-transitions $s \vdash a \to_a v$ that may be involved.

Problem 4.7 (Important!)   Let $S = $ i := 1; while ($\neg$x = 0) do (i := i * x; x := x-1). Construct a derivation tree for the transition $\langle S, s \rangle \to s'$ where $sx = 3$, finding s'.

Termination in the big-step semantics

Given our big-step semantics, we can now define the formal counterparts of two informal notions used by programmers.

We say that the execution of statement S *terminates from start state s* if there exists a state s' such that $\langle S, s \rangle \to s'$. Moreover, we say that S *loops forever on s* if there does not exist a state s' such that $\langle S, s \rangle \to s'$.

We say that S *always terminates* if S terminates for all $s \in$ **States** and that S *always loops forever* if S loops forever for all $s \in$ **States**.

Problem 4.8 (Important!)   Let $S = $ while 0=0 do skip. Show that S always loops forever. *Hint:* Let s be an arbitrary state and show by induction that for all $n \geq 0$ it is the case that $\langle S, s \rangle \to s'$ has no derivation tree of height n.

[ASS$_{\text{SSS}}$]	$\langle x := a, s \rangle \Rightarrow s[x \mapsto v]$ where $s \vdash a \rightarrow_a v$
[SKIP$_{\text{SSS}}$]	$\langle \texttt{skip}, s \rangle \Rightarrow s$

[COMP-1$_{\text{SSS}}$] $\dfrac{\langle S_1, s \rangle \Rightarrow \langle S_1', s' \rangle}{\langle S_1; S_2, s \rangle \Rightarrow \langle S_1'; S_2, s' \rangle}$

[COMP-2$_{\text{SSS}}$] $\dfrac{\langle S_1, s \rangle \Rightarrow s'}{\langle S_1; S_2, s \rangle \Rightarrow \langle S_2, s' \rangle}$

[IF-TRUE$_{\text{SSS}}$] $\langle \texttt{if } b \texttt{ then } S_1 \texttt{ else } S_2, s \rangle \Rightarrow \langle S_1, s \rangle$
                 where $s \vdash b \rightarrow_b \mathit{tt}$

[IF-FALSE$_{\text{SSS}}$] $\langle \texttt{if } b \texttt{ then } S_1 \texttt{ else } S_2, s \rangle \Rightarrow \langle S_2, s \rangle$
                 where $s \vdash b \rightarrow_b \mathit{ff}$

[WHILE$_{\text{SSS}}$] $\langle \texttt{while } b \texttt{ do } S, s \rangle \Rightarrow$
          $\langle \texttt{if } b \texttt{ then } (S; \texttt{while } b \texttt{ do } S) \texttt{ else skip}, s \rangle$

Table 4.4 *Small-step transition rules for **Stm***

4.3 A small-step semantics of statements in Bims

We shall now consider a very different operational semantics of **Bims**, namely a small-step semantics. Here, a transition will describe *a single execution step*.

There are now two kinds of transitions: $\langle S, s \rangle \Rightarrow s'$ and $\langle S, s \rangle \Rightarrow \langle S', s' \rangle$. The first kind of transition will represent termination in a single step, whereas the second kind of transition expresses that we will, by executing a single step of statement S, reach the intermediate configuration $\langle S', s' \rangle$ where we still have to execute S' and the variables have the values described by state s'.

We define the transition system $(\Gamma, \Rightarrow, T)$ where

$$\Gamma = (\textbf{Stm} \times \textbf{States}) \cup \textbf{States},$$
$$T = \textbf{States}$$

and $\Rightarrow$ is defined by the transition rules of Table 4.4.

The difference between the small-step semantics and the big-step semantics becomes very obvious in the transition rules for a sequential composition $S_1; S_2$. [COMP-1$_{\text{SSS}}$] says the following: if the result of executing the first step of $\langle S_1, s \rangle$ is $\langle S_1', s' \rangle$, then the resulting configuration is $\langle S_1'; S_2, s' \rangle$. [COMP-2$_{\text{SSS}}$] describes what happens when S_1 runs to completion within a single step – control is then transferred to S_2 in state s'.

The axioms [IF-TRUE$_{\text{SSS}}$] and [IF-FALSE$_{\text{SSS}}$] show that the first step of executing a conditional statement consists in testing its Boolean condition.

The [WHILE$_{\text{SSS}}$]-rule describes that we execute a while-loop by first *unfolding* it to a conditional statement. The test of the loop condition happens as the first step of the new conditional statement.

Note that derivation trees for transitions in our small-step semantics are very low.

Problem 4.9 Find all transitions (if there are any) in the transition sequence starting from $\langle S, s \rangle$, where

$$S = \text{if } x > 3 \text{ then } (x := 3\text{+}x; y := 4) \text{ else skip}$$

and state s is given by $sx = 4$. You should construct a derivation tree for each transition in the sequence.

Termination in the small-step semantics

In Problem 4.8 we saw that the statement while 0=0 do skip always loops forever, that is, does not give rise to a transition in the big-step semantics. In our small-step semantics nontermination shows up in a different way: for any state s our statement will lead to *an infinite transition sequence*.

$$\langle \text{while } 0\text{=}0 \text{ do skip}, s \rangle \Rightarrow^3 \langle \text{while } 0\text{=}0 \text{ do skip}, s \rangle \ldots \tag{4.10}$$

Problem 4.10 (Important!) Show, by constructing derivation trees for each transition in the sequence, that we do indeed get the transition sequence postulated in (4.10).

Consequently, in our small-step semantics we shall say that S *terminates from start state* s if there exists a state s' such that $\langle S, s \rangle \Rightarrow^* s'$. Likewise we say that S *loops forever on* s if there exists an infinite transition sequence

$$\langle S, s \rangle \Rightarrow \langle S_1, s_1 \rangle \cdots$$

and that S *always loops forever* if S loops forever for every start state. Conversely, S *always terminates* if S terminates from every start state.

Our example hints at a connection between the big-step semantics and the small-step semantics, namely that nontermination in the big-step semantics coincides with nontermination in the small-step semantics. In fact, in the following section we show an even stronger result, namely that our two semantics are equivalent.

4.4 Equivalence of the two semantics

In this section we shall formulate and prove a collection of theorems that together establish a precise correspondence between our big-step and our small-step semantics for **Bims**.

At the same time our proofs will demonstrate the power of two important inductive proof techniques.

Our first result says that our small-step semantics for **Bims** is at least as strong as our big-step semantics. Put differently, our small-step semantics can simulate our big-step semantics.

Theorem 4.11 *Let $S \in$ **Stm** and $s \in$ **States**. If $\langle S, s \rangle \rightarrow s'$ then $\langle S, s \rangle \Rightarrow^*$ s'.*

Before we can prove this theorem, we need the following lemma about our small-step semantics.

Lemma 4.12 *Let $S_1, S_2 \in$ **Stm** and $s \in$ **States**. If $\langle S_1, s \rangle \Rightarrow^* s'$ then we have that $\langle S_1; S_2, s \rangle \Rightarrow^* \langle S_2, s' \rangle$.*

Proof If $\langle S_1, s \rangle \Rightarrow^* s'$ we know that there exists a k such that $\langle S_1, s \rangle \Rightarrow^k s'$. We therefore show that for all $k \in \mathbb{N}$ we have that if $\langle S_1, s \rangle \Rightarrow^k s'$ then $\langle S_1; S_2, s \rangle \Rightarrow^k \langle S_2, s' \rangle$. The proof proceeds by induction on k. This proof strategy is known as *induction on the length of transition sequences*.

$k = 0$: Since there are no transition sequences of length 0, our lemma holds vacuously.

Assume for k, show for $k + 1$: We now consider an arbitrary transition sequence $\langle S_1, s \rangle \Rightarrow^{k+1} s'$ and must show that we then have $\langle S_1; S_2, s \rangle \Rightarrow^{k+1} \langle S_2, s' \rangle$. Our transition sequence $\langle S_1, s \rangle \Rightarrow^{k+1} s'$ can be written out as $\langle S_1, s \rangle \Rightarrow \langle S_1', s'' \rangle \Rightarrow^k s'$ for some statement S_1' and some state s''. By virtue of our induction hypothesis we have that $\langle S_1'; S_2, s'' \rangle \Rightarrow^k \langle S_2, s' \rangle$. By applying [COMP-1$_{\text{SSS}}$] with premise $\langle S_1, s \rangle \Rightarrow \langle S_1', s'' \rangle$ we get that $\langle S_1; S_2, s \rangle \Rightarrow \langle S_1'; S_2, s'' \rangle$. As a consequence we obtain the transition sequence

$$\langle S_1; S_2, s \rangle \Rightarrow \langle S_1'; S_2, s'' \rangle \Rightarrow^k \langle S_2, s' \rangle$$

whose length is $k + 1$ as requested. $\square$

We can now prove our theorem.

Proof of Theorem 4.11 We must show that the claim of the theorem is true *for all transitions* in our big-step semantics. Since a transition exists if and only if it has a derivation tree, we must prove that our claim holds for all roots of derivation trees. This is then tantamount to showing that the claim holds for all simple derivation trees, that is, those built directly from axioms and is preserved whenever we apply a transition rule. This is the proof principle known as *transition induction*; it is in fact equivalent to induction on k, where k is the height of our derivation tree.

The proof now proceeds by considering each transition rule.

[ass$_{bss}$] Assume that $\langle S, s \rangle \rightarrow s'$ was concluded directly from the axiom [ASS$_{BSS}$]. Then we must have that S is $x := a$, that $s \vdash a \rightarrow_a v$ for some value v and that $\langle S, s \rangle \rightarrow s[x \mapsto v]$. But then the small-step rule [ASS$_{SSS}$] tells us that $\langle S, s \rangle \Rightarrow s[x \mapsto v]$.

[skip$_{bss}$] Assume that $\langle S, s \rangle \rightarrow s'$ was concluded directly from the axiom [SKIP$_{BSS}$]. Then we must have that S is skip and that $\langle S, s \rangle \rightarrow s$. From the rule [SKIP$_{SSS}$] we now see that $\langle S, s \rangle \Rightarrow s$.

[comp$_{bss}$] Assume that $\langle S_1; S_2, s \rangle \rightarrow s''$ was concluded using the rule

$$\frac{\langle S_1, s \rangle \rightarrow s' \quad \langle S_2, s' \rangle \rightarrow s''}{\langle S_1; S_2, s \rangle \rightarrow s''}.$$

By virtue of our induction hypothesis, the claim of the theorem holds for the premises of the rule. That is,

$$\langle S_1, s \rangle \Rightarrow^* s' \text{ and } \langle S_2, s' \rangle \Rightarrow^* s''.$$

By applying Lemma 4.12 we get that

$$\langle S_1; S_2, s \rangle \Rightarrow^* \langle S_2, s' \rangle$$

and consequently we have that $\langle S_1; S_2, s \rangle \Rightarrow^* s''$.

[if-false$_{bss}$] Assume that $\langle \text{if } b \text{ then } S_1 \text{ else } S_2, s \rangle \rightarrow s'$ was concluded using the rule

$$\frac{\langle S_1, s \rangle \rightarrow s'}{\langle \text{if } b \text{ then } S_1 \text{ else } S_2, s \rangle \rightarrow s'},$$

where $s \vdash b \rightarrow_b \mathit{ff}$. The rule [IF-FALSE$_{SSS}$] tells us that

$$\langle \text{if } b \text{ then } S_1 \text{ else } S_2, s \rangle \Rightarrow \langle S_2, s \rangle.$$

By virtue of our induction hypothesis, the claim holds for the premise of the rule, so we must have that $\langle S_2, s \rangle \Rightarrow^* s'$, and we now get the transition sequence $\langle \text{if } b \text{ then } S_1 \text{ else } S_2, s \rangle \Rightarrow^* s'$.

[if-true$_{bss}$] Similar to the previous case.

[**while-true$_{bss}$**] Assume that $\langle \text{while } b \text{ do } S, s \rangle \rightarrow s'$ was concluded using the rule

$$\frac{\langle S, s \rangle \rightarrow s'' \quad \langle \text{while } b \text{ do } S, s'' \rangle \rightarrow s'}{\langle \text{while } b \text{ do } S, s \rangle \rightarrow s'},$$

where $s \vdash b \rightarrow_b t\!t$. By virtue of our induction hypothesis, the claim of the theorem holds for the premises of the rule, so we get that

$$\langle S, s \rangle \Rightarrow^* s'' \text{ and } \langle \text{while } b \text{ do } S, s'' \rangle \Rightarrow^* s'$$

and again we can apply Lemma 4.12, this time giving us

$$\langle S; \text{while } b \text{ do } S, s \rangle \Rightarrow^* s'.$$

But because $s \vdash b \rightarrow_b t\!t$ we can use the rules [IF-TRUE$_{SSS}$] and [WHILE$_{SSS}$] to extend this to the transition sequence

$$\langle \text{while } b \text{ do } S, s \rangle \Rightarrow^* \langle \text{if } b \text{ then } (S; \text{ while } b \text{ do } S) \text{ else skip}, s \rangle$$
$$\Rightarrow \langle S; \text{while } b \text{ do } S, s \rangle$$
$$\Rightarrow^* s'.$$

[**while-false$_{bss}$**] Assume that $\langle \text{while } b \text{ do } S, s \rangle \rightarrow s$ was concluded because $s \vdash b \rightarrow_b f\!f$. But then from [WHILE$_{SSS}$] and [IF-FALSK$_{SSS}$] we get the transition sequence

$$\langle \text{while } b \text{ do } S, s \rangle \Rightarrow^* \langle \text{if } b \text{ then } (S; \text{ while } b \text{ do } S) \text{ else skip}, s \rangle$$
$$\Rightarrow \langle \text{skip}, s \rangle$$
$$\Rightarrow s.$$

□

Our second result tells us that our big-step semantics for **Bims** is able to describe all terminating transition sequences in our small-step semantics.

Theorem 4.13 *Let $S \in \textbf{Stm}$ and $s \in \textbf{States}$. If $\langle S, s \rangle \Rightarrow^* s'$ then $\langle S, s \rangle \rightarrow s'$.*

Again we need a lemma.

Lemma 4.14 *For all $S_1, S_2 \in \textbf{Stm}, s, s'' \in \textbf{States}$ we have that if $\langle S_1; S_2 \rangle \Rightarrow^k s''$ then there exist $s' \in \textbf{States}$ and k_1, k_2 such that $\langle S_1, s \rangle \Rightarrow^{k_1} s'$ and $\langle S_2, s' \rangle \Rightarrow^{k_2} s''$ with $k = k_1 + k_2$*

A moment's thought 4.15 Think about the statement made in the above lemma. What does it tell us from the point of view of programming intuition?

Proof of Lemma 4.14   Induction on the length of the transition sequence $\langle S_1; S_2, s \rangle \Rightarrow^k s''$, that is, induction on k.

$k = 0$: There are no transition sequences of length 0, so the claim of the lemma holds vacuously in this case.

Assume for n, show for $n + 1$: Assume that $\langle S_1; S_2, s \rangle \Rightarrow^{n+1} s''$. Then there exists a configuration γ such that $\langle S_1; S_2, s \rangle \Rightarrow \gamma \Rightarrow^n s''$. The transition $\langle S_1; S_2, s \rangle \Rightarrow \gamma$ must have been concluded using either [COMP-1SSS] or [COMP-2SSS], that is, *either* it can be of the form $\langle S_1; S_2, s \rangle \Rightarrow \langle S_1'; S_2, s''' \rangle$, with $\gamma = \langle S_1'; S_2, s''' \rangle$, *or* it can be of the form $\langle S_1; S_2, s \rangle \Rightarrow \langle S_2, s''' \rangle$ with $\gamma = \langle S_2, s''' \rangle$.

In the first case we would use the rule [COMP-1SSS]:

$$\frac{\langle S_1, s \rangle \Rightarrow \langle S_1', s''' \rangle}{\langle S_1; S_2, s \rangle \Rightarrow \langle S_1'; S_2, s''' \rangle};$$

and in this case we have that $\langle S_1'; S_2, s''' \rangle \Rightarrow^n s''$. The induction hypothesis now gives us that there exist k_{11}, k_{21} and a state s' such that $n = k_{11} + k_{21}$ and $\langle S_1', s''' \rangle \Rightarrow^{k_{11}} s'$ and $\langle S_2, s' \rangle \Rightarrow^{k_{21}} s''$. But since $\langle S_1, s \rangle \Rightarrow \langle S_1', s''' \rangle$ we get that $\langle S_1, s \rangle \Rightarrow^{k_{11}+1} s'$. Now we can choose $s' = s'$ and $k_1 = k_{11} + 1, k_2 = k_{22}$.

For the other case we used the rule [COMP-2SSS]:

$$\frac{\langle S_1, s \rangle \Rightarrow s'''}{\langle S_1; S_2, s \rangle \Rightarrow \langle S_2, s''' \rangle}.$$

But this means that $\langle S_2, s''' \rangle \Rightarrow^n s''$ and here we can choose $s' = s'''$ and $k_1 = 1, k_2 = n$.

□

Proof of Theorem 4.13   Again we are dealing with a claim of the type 'for all finite transition sequences it is the case that ...', so we must prove that for all natural numbers k we have that $\langle S, s \rangle \Rightarrow^k s'$ implies $\langle S, s \rangle \rightarrow s'$. In other words, we are again using induction on the length of transition sequences. This time we shall use the strong principle of induction: we assume that our claim holds for *all* $k' \leq k$ and show the claim for $k + 1$.

$k = 0$: There are no transition sequences of length 0, so the claim of the lemma holds vacuously in this case.

Assume for $k' \leq k$, show for $k + 1$: We are now considering a transition sequence of length $k + 1$

$$\langle S, s \rangle \Rightarrow^{k+1} s', \tag{4.11}$$

which is in fact of the form $\langle S, s \rangle \Rightarrow \langle S', s'' \rangle \Rightarrow^k s'$. The rest of the proof depends on the exact nature of the transition $\langle S, s \rangle \Rightarrow \langle S', s'' \rangle$, and here in particular on the transition rule used to conclude this initial transition.

We show only two cases here.

The first case is that $\langle S, s \rangle \Rightarrow \langle S', s'' \rangle$ could have been concluded using [COMP-2$_{SSS}$]. But then we have that $S = S_1; S_2$ and $S' = S_2$. By applying Lemma 4.14 to the transition sequence (4.11) we conclude that there exist natural numbers k_1, k_2 and a state s''' such that $k + 1 = k_1 + k_2$ and

$$\langle S_1, s \rangle \Rightarrow^{k_1} s'' \text{ and } \langle S_2, s'' \rangle \Rightarrow^{k_2} s'.$$

We can now apply the induction hypothesis, and it gives us that

$$\langle S_1, s \rangle \rightarrow s'' \text{ and } \langle S_2, s'' \rangle \rightarrow s'.$$

All that remains now is for us to use [COMP$_{BSS}$].

The second case that we consider is the one where $\langle S, s \rangle \Rightarrow \langle S', s'' \rangle$ was concluded using the rule [WHILE$_{SSS}$]. The transition sequence (4.11) then looks as follows:

$$\langle \texttt{while } b \texttt{ do } S, s \rangle \Rightarrow \langle \texttt{if } b \texttt{ then } (S; \texttt{ while } b \texttt{ do } S) \texttt{ else skip}, s \rangle$$
$$\Rightarrow^k s''.$$

We can now apply the induction hypothesis to the last part of the transition sequence, since it is of length k. Here we get

$$\langle \texttt{if } b \texttt{ then } (S; \texttt{ while } b \texttt{ do } S) \texttt{ else skip}, s \rangle \rightarrow s''.$$

The further analysis depends on the value of b. First consider the case where $s \vdash b \rightarrow_b \textit{ff}$. In the small-step semantics [IF-FALSE$_{SSS}$] says that

$$\langle \texttt{if } b \texttt{ then } (S; \texttt{ while } b \texttt{ do } S) \texttt{ else skip}, s \rangle \Rightarrow \langle \texttt{skip}, s \rangle.$$

In the big-step semantics we get from [IF-FALSE$_{BSS}$] that

$$\frac{\langle \texttt{skip}, s \rangle \rightarrow s''}{\langle \texttt{if } b \texttt{ then } (S; \texttt{ while } b \texttt{ do } S) \texttt{ else skip}, s \rangle \rightarrow s''}$$

and [SKIP$_{BSS}$] now tells us that in fact $s'' = s$. So here we have that if $\langle \texttt{while } b \texttt{ do } S, s \rangle \Rightarrow s''$ then $\langle \texttt{while } b \texttt{ do } S, s \rangle \rightarrow s''$.

Next, consider the case $s \vdash b \to_b t\!\!t$. In the small-step semantics we get from [IF-TRUE$_{\mathrm{SSS}}$] that

$$\langle \texttt{if } b \texttt{ then } (S\texttt{; while } b \texttt{ do } S) \texttt{ else skip}, s\rangle$$
$$\Rightarrow \langle(S\texttt{; while } b \texttt{ do } S), s\rangle$$

and the transition sequence

$$\langle(S\texttt{; while } b \texttt{ do } S), s\rangle \Rightarrow^{(k-1)} s''.$$

By virtue of our induction hypothesis we now know that there exists a big-step transition

$$\langle(S\texttt{; while } b \texttt{ do } S), s\rangle \to s''.$$

The derivation tree of this transition must have been concluded using [COMP$_{\mathrm{BSS}}$], so we have that

$$\langle S, s\rangle \to s''' \quad \text{and} \quad \langle\texttt{while } b \texttt{ do } S, s'''\rangle \to s''$$

and since we are assuming that $s \vdash b \to_b t\!\!t$, the rule [WHILE-TRUE$_{\mathrm{BSS}}$] tells us that

$$\langle\texttt{while } b \texttt{ do } S, s\rangle \to s''$$

as desired.

$\square$

4.5 Two important proof techniques

In this chapter we have encountered two important proof techniques often used in structural operational semantics. They are as follows.

Transition induction We use this technique, if we want to prove a claim of the form *'For all transitions P holds'*, where P is some property. We then proceed as follows.

- For each axiom show that P holds.
- For each transition rule show that P is preserved by the rule, that is, show that if we assume that P holds for all premises in the rule, then P will also hold for its conclusion.

As we saw earlier, this is in fact induction on k, where k is the height of our derivation tree.

Induction on the length of transition sequences We use this technique for a small-step semantics, if we want to prove a claim of the form *'For all transition sequences P holds'*. This, too, is an induction in the normal sense, in that we show the claim *'For all k it is the case that P holds for every transition sequence of length k'* by induction on k.

Problem 4.16 Prove the remaining cases of Theorem 4.13.

A moment's thought 4.17 Why is induction on the length of transition sequences not a very useful proof technique for properties of a big-step semantics?

Problem 4.18 Prove, using a suitable proof technique, that the big-step semantics of statements is *deterministic*, that is, that for any statement S and state s we have that if $\langle S, s \rangle s'$ and $\langle S, s \rangle s''$ then $s' = s''$. (You may assume that the big-step semantics of arithmetic and Boolean expressions are deterministic.)

Problem 4.19 Describe what it means for a *small-step semantics* to be deterministic. Then prove, using a suitable proof technique, that the small-step semantics of statements is deterministic.

The equivalence results that we have shown in this chapter are reassuring; our big-step semantics and our small-step semantics are in agreement in a very precise sense. This allows us to choose freely between the two semantics whenever we want to reason about **Bims**. However, one must not forget that these are results that are particular to the semantics presented in this chapter. We are not dealing with a result which states that every big-step semantics will be equivalent to every small-step semantics for the same language. Such a result cannot be true.

Problem 4.20 Define a 'pathological' big-step semantics for **Bims** with the property that it is not equivalent to the small-step semantics for **Bims** presented in this chapter.

Rather, our result should be thought of as a goal that has been reached: we have given two descriptions of the behaviour of **Bims** statements which agree in a well-defined sense. In general, this is a reasonable requirement of a language-design effort.

PART III
LANGUAGE CONSTRUCTS

5

Control structures

In this chapter we investigate some additional control structures in the setting of **Bims**.

First, we consider two well-known loop constructs, namely repeat-loops and for-loops, and their big-step semantics. Then we have a look at nondeterminism and concurrency. Here it turns out that the difference between big-step and small-step semantics becomes all-important.

In the case of nondeterminism, a big-step semantics captures so-called *angelic nondeterminism* and a small-step semantics captures *demonic nondeterminism*.

In the case of concurrency, we have little choice: a big-step semantics will be of no use.

Another difference between the two styles of operational semantics becomes clear when we consider *nonterminating* computations. These can be described directly in a small-step semantics but not in a big-step semantics.

An important concept that we use throughout this chapter is that of *semantic equivalence*, which provides a formal mathematical understanding of the informal notion of 'having the same behaviour'.

5.1 Some general assumptions

The control structures considered in the following are all extensions of the syntactic category **Stm** of statements in **Bims**. In each case, the new big-step semantics assumes a transition system $(\Gamma, \rightarrow, T)$ where

$$\Gamma = (\mathbf{Stm} \times \mathbf{States}) \cup \mathbf{States},$$
$$T = \mathbf{States}$$

and $\rightarrow$ is defined by the transition rules of Table 4.3 together with new rules for the control structure that has been added.

Similarly, in our small-step semantics we consider a transition system $(\Gamma, \Rightarrow, T)$ where

$$\Gamma = (\mathbf{Stm} \times \mathbf{States}) \cup \mathbf{States},$$

$$T = \mathbf{States}$$

and $\Rightarrow$ is defined by the transition rules of Table 4.4 together with new rules for the control structure that has been added.

5.2 Loop constructs

In this section we shall describe the semantics of two well-known loop constructs found in imperative programming languages: repeat-loops and for-loops.

5.2.1 Repeat-loops

First, we consider an extension of **Bims** with repeat-loops. We add the following to our formation rules for **Stm**:

$$S ::= \cdots \mid \mathtt{repeat}\ S\ \mathtt{until}\ b.$$

The informal semantics of $\mathtt{repeat}\ S\ \mathtt{until}\ b$ is straightforward: the loop body S is executed, and only then is the condition b checked. If b evaluates to true, we leave the loop. If b evaluates to false, the loop is executed again.

We can capture this informal description by the big-step transition rules of Table 5.1. Notice the side conditions, $s' \vdash b \rightarrow_b \mathit{tt}$ in [REPEAT-TRUE$_{\mathrm{BSS}}$] and $s' \vdash b \rightarrow_b \mathit{ff}$ in [REPEAT-FALSE$_{\mathrm{BSS}}$]. The presence of the state s' resulting from the execution of S captures the intuition that we check the condition b *after* the execution of the body of the loop.

Problem 5.1   Build a derivation tree – and thereby find the final state s' – for the transition

$$\langle \mathtt{repeat\ y:=y*x;\ x:=x-1\ until\ x=1}, s \rangle \rightarrow s',$$

where the initial state s is given by $sx = 4$, $sy = 1$.

Strictly speaking, repeat-loops are not needed. Readers with some programming experience will probably notice that one might just as well write $S; \mathtt{while}\ \neg b\ \mathtt{do}\ S$ instead of $\mathtt{repeat}\ S\ \mathtt{until}\ b$. In fact, the following theorem holds.

Theorem 5.2   *For all* $s \in \mathbf{States}$ *we have* $\langle \mathtt{repeat}\ S\ \mathtt{until}\ b, s \rangle \rightarrow s'$ *if and only if* $\langle S; \mathtt{while}\ \neg b\ \mathtt{do}\ S, s \rangle \rightarrow s'$.

$[\text{REPEAT-TRUE}_{\text{BSS}}]$	$\dfrac{\langle S, s \rangle \to s'}{\langle \texttt{repeat } S \texttt{ until } b, s \rangle \to s'}$

if $s' \vdash b \to_b t\!t$

$[\text{REPEAT-FALSE}_{\text{BSS}}]$	$\dfrac{\langle S, s \rangle \to s' \;\; \langle \texttt{repeat } S \texttt{ until } b, s' \rangle \to s''}{\langle \texttt{repeat } S \texttt{ until } b, s \rangle \to s''}$

if $s' \vdash b \to_b f\!f$

Table 5.1 *Big-step transition rules for repeat-loops*

Proof To prove this, we must prove each of the two implications separately. In both cases we shall use transition induction. Here, this is most easily thought of as induction on the height of the derivation tree.

Only if: We show that, if we have a transition $\langle \texttt{repeat } S \texttt{ until } b, s \rangle \to s'$, then we can also find a transition $\langle S; \texttt{while } \neg b \texttt{ do } S, s \rangle \to s'$. Let n be the height of the derivation tree for $\langle \texttt{repeat } S \texttt{ until } b, s \rangle \to s'$. We now proceed by induction on n.

> $n = 0$: The only derivation trees of height 0 are the ones that can be obtained by an application of one of the axioms $[\text{ASS}_{\text{BSS}}]$, $[\text{SKIP}_{\text{BSS}}]$ or $[\text{WHILE-FALSE}_{\text{BSS}}]$. None of these are derivation trees for the transition
>
> $$\langle \texttt{repeat } S \texttt{ until } b, s \rangle \to s'.$$
>
> Consequently, the claim holds vacuously in this case.
>
> **Assume for $n' \leq n$, show for $n + 1$:** Now assume that the transition $\langle \texttt{repeat } S \texttt{ until } b, s \rangle \to s'$ has a derivation tree of height $n+1$. The only rules that can be used to complete this derivation tree are $[\text{REPEAT-TRUE}_{\text{BSS}}]$ and $[\text{REPEAT-FALSE}_{\text{BSS}}]$. First consider $[\text{REPEAT-TRUE}_{\text{BSS}}]$. Here we have
>
> $$\dfrac{\langle S, s \rangle \to s'}{\langle \texttt{repeat } S \texttt{ until } b, s \rangle \to s'} \quad \text{where } s' \vdash b \to_b t\!t.$$
>
> From this we get that $s' \vdash \neg b \to_b f\!f$, and by applying the rule $[\text{WHILE-FALSE}_{\text{BSS}}]$ we now get that
>
> $$\langle \texttt{while } \neg b \texttt{ do } S, s' \rangle \to s'.$$

Then, by applying [COMP$_{\mathrm{BSS}}$] we obtain

$$\langle S; \texttt{while } \neg b \texttt{ do } S, s \rangle \rightarrow s'.$$

Next, consider [REPEAT-FALSE$_{\mathrm{BSS}}$]. Here we have

$$\frac{\langle S, s \rangle \rightarrow s' \quad \langle \texttt{repeat } S \texttt{ until } b, s' \rangle \rightarrow s''}{\langle \texttt{repeat } S \texttt{ until } b, s \rangle \rightarrow s''} \quad \text{where } s' \vdash b \rightarrow_b \textit{ff}.$$

From this we get $s' \vdash \neg b \rightarrow_b \textit{tt}$. The derivation tree for

$$\langle \texttt{repeat } S \texttt{ until } b, s' \rangle \rightarrow s''$$

has height n. By virtue of our induction hypothesis we therefore get that

$$\langle S; \texttt{while } \neg b \texttt{ do } S, s' \rangle \rightarrow s''.$$

The derivation tree for this transition must have been concluded by a final application of [COMP$_{\mathrm{BSS}}$], so in the premises
of this rule occurrence we must have had the transitions

$$\langle S, s' \rangle \rightarrow s''' \quad \langle \texttt{while } \neg b \texttt{ do } S, s''' \rangle \rightarrow s''.$$

Since $s' \vdash \neg b \rightarrow_b \textit{tt}$, we can now use these two transitions as
premises of [WHILE-TRUE$_{\mathrm{BSS}}$] and get

$$\langle \texttt{while } \neg b \texttt{ do } S, s' \rangle \rightarrow s''.$$

This transition and $\langle S, s \rangle \rightarrow s'$ can be used as premises of
[COMP$_{\mathrm{BSS}}$], and we obtain

$$\langle S; \texttt{while } \neg b \texttt{ do } S, s \rangle \rightarrow s''$$

as desired.

If: Here, we show that, if we have a transition $\langle S; \texttt{while } \neg b \texttt{ do } S, s \rangle \rightarrow s'$,
then there is a transition $\langle \texttt{repeat } S \texttt{ until } b, s \rangle \rightarrow s'$. Let n be the
height of the derivation tree for $\langle S; \texttt{while } \neg b \texttt{ do } S, s \rangle \rightarrow s'$. The
proof now proceeds by induction on n.

$n = 0$: The only derivation trees of height 0 are those found by
an application of one of the axioms [ASS$_{\mathrm{BSS}}$], [SKIP$_{\mathrm{BSS}}$] or
[WHILE-FALSE$_{\mathrm{BSS}}$]. However, none of these give us deriva-
tion trees for the transition $\langle S; \texttt{while } \neg b \texttt{ do } S, s \rangle \rightarrow s'$. Consequently, this case is vacuously true.

Assume for $n' \leq n$, show for $n + 1$: Now we assume that $\langle S; \texttt{while } \neg b \texttt{ do } S, s \rangle \rightarrow s'$ has a derivation tree of height $n + 1$. The only rule that can be used to conclude the construction of this derivation tree is [COMP$_{\text{BSS}}$]. Then we have

$$\frac{\langle S, s \rangle \rightarrow s'' \quad \langle \texttt{while } \neg b \texttt{ do } S, s'' \rangle \rightarrow s'}{\langle S; \texttt{while } \neg b \texttt{ do } S, s \rangle \rightarrow s'}.$$

The rest of the proof depends on the truth value of b. First, assume that $s'' \vdash b \rightarrow_b f\!f$. Then we have that $s'' \vdash \neg b \rightarrow_b t\!t$ and therefore the transition $\langle \texttt{while } \neg b \texttt{ do } S, s'' \rangle \rightarrow s'$ must be concluded by an application of [WHILE-TRUE$_{\text{BSS}}$], and we must have

$$\frac{\langle S, s'' \rangle \rightarrow s''' \quad \langle \texttt{while } \neg b \texttt{ do } S, s''' \rangle \rightarrow s'}{\langle \texttt{while } \neg b \texttt{ do } S, s'' \rangle \rightarrow s'}.$$

By applying the rule [COMP$_{\text{BSS}}$] with premises $\langle S, s'' \rangle \rightarrow s'''$ and $\langle \texttt{while } \neg b \texttt{ do } S, s''' \rangle \rightarrow s'$ we obtain

$$\langle S; \texttt{while } \neg b \texttt{ do } S, s'' \rangle \rightarrow s'.$$

But since the derivation tree for this transition has height n, by virtue of our induction hypothesis we have the transition

$$\langle \texttt{repeat } S \texttt{ until } b, s'' \rangle \rightarrow s'.$$

We already know that $\langle S, s \rangle \rightarrow s''$ and have found that $\langle \texttt{repeat } S \texttt{ until } b, s'' \rangle \rightarrow s'$ when assuming $s'' \vdash b \rightarrow_b f\!f$. As a consequence, we can apply [REPEAT-FALSE$_{\text{BSS}}$] and get that $\langle \texttt{repeat } S \texttt{ until } b, s \rangle \rightarrow s'$.

The other case is that of $s'' \vdash b \rightarrow_b t\!t$. Here, we must have concluded the transition $\langle \texttt{while } \neg b \texttt{ do } S, s'' \rangle \rightarrow s'$ using the rule [WHILE-FALSE$_{\text{BSS}}$], so here $s' = s''$. This means that we can apply [REPEAT-TRUE$_{\text{BSS}}$] to the premise $\langle S, s \rangle \rightarrow s'$, and we get

$$\langle \texttt{repeat } S \texttt{ until } b, s \rangle \rightarrow s'$$

as desired.

□

A moment's thought 5.3 In the above proof we sometimes used a particular fact, namely that $s \vdash b \rightarrow_b f\!f$ if and only if $s \vdash \neg b \rightarrow_b t\!t$. How do we know that this is the case?

5.3 Semantic equivalence

Theorem 5.2 is an example of a result about *semantic equivalence* of statements. Often one is interested in proving that two programs have the same behaviour, and this is where the notion of semantic equivalence becomes important. Here are some situations where the need will arise.

- We have two different implementations of the same underlying algorithm, written in the same programming language. If the two implementations have the same behaviour, we have more reason to believe that the algorithm has been correctly implemented.
- We have an old version of a program and a new, optimized version of the program. Here, too, we want the two programs to have the same behaviour.
- We have a program written in some high-level language and a machine-code version obtained by compiling our high-level program. If our compiler is correct, these two programs must have the same behaviour.

Semantic equivalence is a formal version of the notion of 'same behaviour'. Intuitively, two statements have the same behaviour according to a big-step semantics if they always result in the same final state when they are run from the same initial state. This is captured by the following definition.

Definition 5.4 (Big-step semantic equivalence)   Let $(\Gamma, \rightarrow, T)$ be the transition system for our big-step semantics of **Bims**. We say that S_1 and S_2 are *semantically equivalent* in the big-step semantics, written $S_1 \sim_{bss} S_2$, if for all $s \in$ **States** we have

$$\langle S_1, s \rangle \rightarrow s' \text{ if and only if } \langle S_2, s \rangle \rightarrow s'.$$

In the following chapters, we will sometimes refer to other notions of semantic equivalence. In Section 8.5 we introduce the important notion of bisimulation equivalence.

Theorem 5.2 tells us that `repeat S until b` $\sim_{bss}$ `S;while ¬b do S`. The rest of this chapter will provide some more examples of statements that are semantically equivalent as well as some that are not.

As the name implies, semantic equivalence is an *equivalence relation*.

Theorem 5.5 $\sim_{bss}$ *is an equivalence relation over* **Stm**.

Proof   We must show that our relation $\sim_{bss}$ satisfies the three conditions of Definition 2.16.

- It is obvious that for every statement S and for every state s we have that $\langle S, s \rangle \rightarrow s'$ if and only if $\langle S, s \rangle \rightarrow s'$. This proves that $\sim_{bss}$ is *reflexive*.

- Next, assume that $S_1 \sim_{bss} S_2$. By definition, this means that for every state s we have that $\langle S_1, s \rangle \to s'$ if and only if $\langle S_2, s \rangle \to s'$. This immediately tells us that $\langle S_2, s \rangle \to s'$ if and only if $\langle S_1, s \rangle \to s'$, that is, that $S_2 \sim_{bss} S_1$. This proves that $\sim_{bss}$ is *symmetric*.
- Finally, assume that $S_1 \sim_{bss} S_2$ and that $S_2 \sim_{bss} S_3$. We then have for every state s that $\langle S_1, s \rangle \to s'$ if and only if $\langle S_2, s \rangle \to s'$ and that $\langle S_2, s \rangle \to s'$ if and only if $\langle S_3, s \rangle \to s'$. Again it is easy to see that this implies that $\langle S_1, s \rangle \to s'$ if and only if $\langle S_3, s \rangle \to s'$, that is, that $S_1 \sim_{bss} S_3$. This proves that $\sim_{bss}$ is *transitive*.

$\square$

One can also define a notion of semantic equivalence for a small-step semantics. The intuition is as before, namely that two statements have the same behaviour if they yield the same final state when given the same initial state. Here, though, we have to consider *terminating transition sequences*, that is, sequences of the form $\langle S, s \rangle \Rightarrow^* s'$.

Definition 5.6 (Small-step semantic equivalence)   Let $(\Gamma, \Rightarrow, T)$ be the transition system given by the small-step semantics for **Bims**. We say that S_1 and S_2 are *semantically equivalent* in the small-step semantics, written $S_1 \sim_{sss} S_2$, if for all $s \in$ **States** we have

$$\langle S_1, s \rangle \Rightarrow^* s' \text{ if and only if } \langle S_2, s \rangle \Rightarrow^* s'.$$

Problem 5.7   Prove that $\sim_{sss}$ is an equivalence relation.

Problem 5.8   Give a small-step semantics of repeat-loops and show that in your semantics we have that **repeat** S **until** $b \sim_{sss} S;$ **while** $\neg b$ **do** S.

Problem 5.9   Some programming languages have a general loop construct **loop** S_1; **exit on** b; S_2 **end** whose intended meaning is as follows. First execute S_1, then check the truth value of b. If b evaluates to true, then leave the loop. If b evaluates to false, then execute S_2 and execute the loop again. Give a big-step semantics for this loop construct. Suggest some reasonable results about semantic equivalence that relate our new loop construct to the repeat-construct and to the while-construct.

5.3.1 For-loops

Unlike repeat- and while-loops, for-loops provide a notion of bounded iteration. Our abstract syntax adds the formation rule below to those for **Stm**:

$$S ::= \cdots \mid \mathtt{for}\ x := n_1\ \mathtt{to}\ n_2\ \mathtt{do}\ S.$$

[FOR-1$_{\text{BSS}}$] $\dfrac{\langle S, s[x \mapsto v_1]\rangle \rightarrow s'' \quad \langle \texttt{for } x := n_1' \texttt{ to } n_2 \texttt{ do } S, s''\rangle \rightarrow s'}{\langle \texttt{for } x := n_1 \texttt{ to } n_2 \texttt{ do } S, s\rangle \rightarrow s'}$

  if $v_1 \leq v_2$ where $v_1 = \mathcal{N}[\![n_1]\!], v_2 = \mathcal{N}[\![n_2]\!]$
  and $n_1' = \mathcal{N}^{-1}(v_1 + 1)$

[FOR-2$_{\text{BSS}}$] $\langle \texttt{for } x := n_1 \texttt{ to } n_2 \texttt{ do } S, s\rangle \rightarrow s[x \mapsto v_1]$

  if $v_1 > v_2$ where $v_1 = \mathcal{N}[\![n_1]\!], v_2 = \mathcal{N}[\![n_2]\!]$

Table 5.2 *Big-step transition rules for for-loops*

The intuition behind this loop construct is that the initial value of x is set to v_1, the value of numeral n_1. If $v_1 \leq v_2$, where v_2 is the value of n_2, we execute the loop body S and increment the value of x by 1. We continue in this way until $v_1 > v_2$. Immediately after the for-loop has terminated, the variable x has the value $v_2 + 1$.

In our big-step semantics we make use of the function $\mathcal{N} : \textbf{Num} \rightarrow \mathbb{Z}$ that returns the number corresponding to a numeral, and of its inverse, $\mathcal{N}^{-1} : \mathbb{Z} \rightarrow \textbf{Num}$, that returns the numeral corresponding to a given number.

We could of course also give a small-step semantics of for-loops, extending our small-step semantics of **Bims**.

Problem 5.10   Do this; give small-step transition rules for for-loops.

Problem 5.11   One can imagine a more general version of for-loops with the syntax for $x := a_1$ to a_2 do S. Think about what a loop construct of this form should do and define big-step and small-step transition rules for this version.

Problem 5.12   In the previous problem, one could choose either to evaluate the bounds of the for-loop prior to the execution of the loop or to evaluate the bounds following each traversal of the loop body. Give big-step semantics for both of these options.

5.4 Abnormal termination

Sometimes one may wish to describe that a program terminates unsuccessfully. We can capture this by introducing a new statement, abort, whose intended behaviour is that, given an initial state, no final state is returned.

Our formation rules for **Stm** are now extended to

$$S ::= \cdots \mid \texttt{abort}.$$

With our extension we can then write the following (assuming an extension of **Bims** which allows integer division):

$$\texttt{if } \neg(\texttt{x=0}) \texttt{ then x} := \texttt{1/x else abort}.$$

Intuitively, there will be no transitions from a configuration of the form $\langle \texttt{abort}, s \rangle$. This is very easy to capture both in our big-step and in our small-step semantics, since we know by definition that a transition exists if and only if it can be concluded using the transition rules. Consequently, *there are no transition rules for* ***abort***.

Given this, it is clear that it *cannot* be the case that $\texttt{abort} \sim_{bss} \texttt{skip}$ or that $\texttt{abort} \sim_{sss} \texttt{skip}$.

A moment's thought 5.13   Why not?

We have already seen other examples of statements that have no transitions in our big-step semantics of **Bims**. An example is $\texttt{while 0=0 do skip}$. From this we conclude that $\texttt{while 0=0 do skip} \sim_{bss} \texttt{abort}$. Thus, our big-step semantics does not distinguish between abnormal termination and infinite loops. In our small-step semantics the same equivalence holds, that is, $\texttt{while 0=0 do skip} \sim_{sss} \texttt{abort}$.

A moment's thought 5.14   Why does this hold?

On the other hand, the two sources of nontermination are captured differently in the small-step semantics. $\texttt{while 0=0 do skip}$ gives rise to an infinite transition sequence starting from s, while the only transition sequence from $\langle \texttt{abort}, s \rangle$ is one of length 0, namely $\langle \texttt{abort}, s \rangle \Rightarrow^0 \langle \texttt{abort}, s \rangle$.

This means that if we use a different notion of semantic equivalence, where individual transitions of one statement must be matched by individual transitions by the other statement, we can distinguish between abnormal termination and infinite loops. Notions of bisimulation equivalence (see Section 8.5) will allow us to do this.

5.5 Nondeterminism

Another extension is that of *nondeterminism*. Here, nondeterminism should be thought of as the ability to choose freely between different branches of execution. If a branch is not chosen, then it simply disappears. In **Bims** we

[OR-1$_{BSS}$]	$$\frac{\langle S_1, s \rangle \rightarrow s'}{\langle S_1 \text{ or } S_2, s \rangle \rightarrow s'}$$
[OR-2$_{BSS}$]	$$\frac{\langle S_2, s \rangle \rightarrow s'}{\langle S_1 \text{ or } S_2, s \rangle \rightarrow s'}$$

Table 5.3 *Big-step transition rules for the* or-*statement*

can introduce nondeterminism as an or-statement:

$$S ::= \cdots \mid S_1 \text{ or } S_2.$$

S_1 or S_2 should then be read as 'the program can choose to execute either S_1 or S_2'. This is known as *bounded nondeterminism*, as the number of potential choices within a single transition step is bounded.

Nondeterminism is a language construct not usually found in programming languages, since it is difficult to implement. For how does one implement a truly free choice? In actual implementations bounded nondeterminism can be implemented as 'flipping a coin' using a random-number generator. On the other hand, nondeterminism is useful in *specifications* of algorithms, and in some formalisms for parallel computation such as CSP (Hoare, 1988) and CCS (Milner, 1989) it is a central feature.

Giving an operational semantics of nondeterminism is straightforward. Table 5.3 contains big-step transition rules for the or-statement.

The rules of Table 5.3 capture the intution that the effect of executing S_1 or S_2 will be either the effect of executing S_1 or that of executing S_2.

Example 5.15   We have the transitions

$$\langle \text{x:= 1 or (x:=2; x:= x+3)}, s \rangle \rightarrow s[\text{x} \mapsto 1]$$

and

$$\langle \text{x:= 1 or (x:=2; x:= x+3)}, s \rangle \rightarrow s[\text{x} \mapsto 5].$$

We can also give a small-step semantics of nondeterminism. Here the idea is that the first step of executing S_1 or S_2 consists in choosing between S_1 and S_2. The rules are shown in Table 5.4.

Example 5.16   According to our small-step semantics we get the transition sequences

$$\langle \text{x:= 1 or (x:=2; x:= x+3)}, s \rangle \Rightarrow^* s[\text{x} \mapsto 1]$$

[OR-1$_{\text{SSS}}$]	$\langle S_1 \text{ or } S_2, s \rangle \Rightarrow \langle S_1, s \rangle$
[OR-2$_{\text{SSS}}$]	$\langle S_1 \text{ or } S_2, s \rangle \Rightarrow \langle S_2, s \rangle$

Table 5.4 *Small-step transition rules for the **or**-statement*

and

$$\langle \texttt{x:= 1 or (x:=2; x:= x+3)}, s \rangle \Rightarrow^* s[\texttt{x} \mapsto 5].$$

The two semantics provide different accounts of nondeterminism. Consider the statement $(\texttt{x := 1})$ or $\texttt{while (0=0) do skip}$. Since there is no transition $\langle \texttt{while (0=0) do skip}, s \rangle \to s'$ for any $s, s' \in \textbf{States}$, the only rule applicable is [OR-1$_{\text{BSS}}$] and we therefore have the transition

$$\langle (\texttt{x := 1}) \text{ or while } \texttt{(0=0) do skip}, s \rangle \to s[\texttt{x} \mapsto 1].$$

Our big-step semantics can therefore be said to suppress infinite loops, that is, unfortunate choices do not result in a transition. This is called *angelic nondeterminism*.

The small-step semantics does not suppress infinite loops. Here we have two transition sequences. One is

$$\langle (\texttt{x := 1}) \text{ or while } \texttt{(0=0) do skip}, s \rangle \Rightarrow \langle \texttt{x := 1}, s \rangle \Rightarrow s[\texttt{x} \mapsto 1].$$

The other is the infinite sequence

$$\langle (\texttt{x := 1}) \text{ or while } \texttt{(0=0) do skip}, s \rangle \Rightarrow \langle \texttt{while (0=0) do skip}, s \rangle \Rightarrow \cdots.$$

Thus, unfortunate choices also give rise to transitions in our small-step semantics. This is called *demonic nondeterminism*.

So a very real question is: What do we want to describe in our semantics? In some programming languages and under some circumstances infinite loops may be very desirable. For instance one may think of an operating system as a computation that should never terminate.

If one wants to reason about the properties of nonterminating computations, this then implies that one must be able to describe the existence of such computations.

Problem 5.17 Introduce the statement $\texttt{morph}(x)$ into **Bims**. This statement leads to a version of *unbounded nondeterminism*; upon completion, the value of the variable x will be an arbitrary integer. Give a big-step and a small-step semantics of the **morph** statement. Is the statement a necessary addition, if we already have the **or**-statement available in **Bims**?

5.6 Concurrency

As our final example we shall have a brief look at non-communicating parallelism – as opposed to the kind of channel-based concurrency that is found in e.g. CSP (Hoare, 1988) and CCS (Milner, 1989) and is the focus of Chapter 8. In **Bims** we can introduce the **par**-statement as follows:

$$S ::= \cdots \mid S_1 \text{ par } S_2.$$

The intended meaning of S_1 **par** S_2 is that S_1 and S_2 are executed in parallel.

By this we mean that the executions of the two statements are *interleaved*. This means that the statement

$$\texttt{x:=1 par (x:=2; x:= x+3)}$$

may give us three distinct values of x, namely 1, 4 and 5. If we first execute the statement x:=1, we eventually get that the value of x is 5. If, on the other hand, we execute x:= 2, then x:=1 and finally x:= x+3, we get 4.

A moment's thought 5.18   How can we get 1 as the final value of x?

We can capture this by the small-step transition rules of Table 5.5. The rules [PAR-1$_{SSS}$] and [PAR-2$_{SSS}$] cover the case where the parallel component on the left, S_1, makes a step. If the component terminates in one step, it disappears. The rules [PAR-3$_{SSS}$] and [PAR-4$_{SSS}$] are analogous, applying to the component on the right.

Example 5.19   We can use the rules of Table 5.5 to find the transition sequences

$$\langle \texttt{x:= 1 par (x:=2; x:= x+3)}, s \rangle \Rightarrow \langle \texttt{(x:=2; x:= x+3)}, s[\texttt{x} \mapsto 1] \rangle$$
$$\Rightarrow \langle \texttt{x:= x+3}, s[\texttt{x} \mapsto 2] \rangle$$
$$\Rightarrow s[\texttt{x} \mapsto 5]$$

and

$$\langle \texttt{x:= 1 par (x:=2; x:= x+3)}, s \rangle \Rightarrow \langle \texttt{x:= 1 par (x:= x+3)}, s[\texttt{x} \mapsto 2] \rangle$$
$$\Rightarrow \langle \texttt{x:= x+3}, s[\texttt{x} \mapsto 1] \rangle$$
$$\Rightarrow s[\texttt{x} \mapsto 4]$$

and

$$\langle \texttt{x:= 1 par (x:=2; x:= x+3)}, s \rangle \Rightarrow \langle \texttt{x:= 1 par (x:= x+3)}, s[\texttt{x} \mapsto 2] \rangle$$
$$\Rightarrow \langle \texttt{x:= 1}, s[\texttt{x} \mapsto 5] \rangle$$
$$\Rightarrow s[\texttt{x} \mapsto 1].$$

[PAR-1$_{\text{SSS}}$]
$$\frac{\langle S_1, s \rangle \Rightarrow \langle S_1', s' \rangle}{\langle S_1 \text{ par } S_2, s \rangle \Rightarrow \langle S_1' \text{ par } S_2, s' \rangle}$$

[PAR-2$_{\text{SSS}}$]
$$\frac{\langle S_1, s \rangle \Rightarrow s'}{\langle S_1 \text{ par } S_2, s \rangle \Rightarrow \langle S_2, s' \rangle}$$

[PAR-3$_{\text{SSS}}$]
$$\frac{\langle S_2, s \rangle \Rightarrow \langle S_2', s' \rangle}{\langle S_1 \text{ par } S_2, s \rangle \Rightarrow \langle S_1 \text{ par } S_2', s' \rangle}$$

[PAR-4$_{\text{SSS}}$]
$$\frac{\langle S_2, s \rangle \Rightarrow s'}{\langle S_1 \text{ par } S_2, s \rangle \Rightarrow \langle S_1, s' \rangle}$$

Table 5.5 *Small-step semantics of the **par**-statement*

[PAR-1$_{\text{BSS}}$]
$$\frac{\langle S_1, s \rangle \rightarrow s' \quad \langle S_2, s' \rangle \rightarrow s''}{\langle S_1 \text{ par } S_2, s \rangle \rightarrow s''}$$

[PAR-2$_{\text{BSS}}$]
$$\frac{\langle S_2, s \rangle \rightarrow s' \quad \langle S_1, s' \rangle \rightarrow s''}{\langle S_1 \text{ par } S_2, s \rangle \rightarrow s''}$$

Table 5.6 *An attempt at big-step transition rules for the **par**-statement*

What would a big-step semantics of the parallel operator look like? One attempt is to use the transition rules of Table 5.6.

However, something is missing here! There is now no way to describe the interleaving of individual steps. The rules of Table 5.6 tell us that either we first execute *all of* S_1 before executing S_2 or vice versa. This is due to the fact that the atomic steps of a big-step semantics correspond to the execution of an entire statement. In other words, a big-step semantics will be of no use if we want to describe parallel computations.

Problem 5.20 Consider the new statement **atomic** S **end** whose intuitive meaning is that S is to be executed indivisibly, that is, that the execution of S is not allowed to be interleaved with the execution of any other command.

For instance the command

$$(x:= 1) \text{ par atomic } (x:=2; \ x:= x+3) \text{ end}$$

can now only give rise to either 1 or 5 as the final value of x. Provide the atomic-statement with a small-step semantics *without* invoking the big-step semantics of **Bims** and *without* referring to the transitive closure $\Rightarrow^*$ in your new rules. *Hint:* Try to capture a definition of $\Rightarrow^*$ in your new rules.

Of course our understanding of parallel computation as mere interleaving has its limitations, since it simply states that *we reduce parallel computation to nondeterminism.* If we had both **par** and **or** in **Bims**, we would have that

$$x:= 1 \text{ par } (x:=2; \ x:= x+3) \sim_{sss}$$

$$(x:=1;x:=2;x:=x+3)$$
$$\text{or } (x:=2;x:=1;x:=x+3)$$
$$\text{or } (x:=2;x:=x+3;x:=1).$$

Note, however, that we cannot always explain away parallel compositions in this way. To see this, consider e.g. the command

$$(\text{while } b_1 \text{ do } S_1) \text{ par } (\text{while } b_2 \text{ do } S_2).$$

A moment's thought 5.21   Use the ideas hinted at above to try to find a statement with or-constructs but no **par**-constructs that is semantically equivalent to

$$(\text{while } (0 = 0) \text{ do } x := x + 4) \text{ par } (\text{while } (17 = 17) \text{ do } y := y + 3).$$

What do you observe?

Problem 5.22   Suggest an alternative small-step semantics of the **par**-statement that will allow parallel components to make simultaneous steps. Discuss how updates of shared variables should be dealt with.

6

Blocks and procedures (1)

In this chapter we look at **Bip**,[1] an extension of **Bims** with blocks and procedures, and define a big-step semantics of the language. The semantics will depend on our choice of scope rules, and for this reason we need to introduce a more refined notion of program states. We therefore introduce the *environment–store model* and the notion of *procedure environment*. In Chapter 10 we shall describe how to give a small-step semantics of **Bip**.

6.1 Abstract syntax of Bip

The syntactic categories of **Bims** are also found in **Bip**; however, we now introduce three additional categories:

- **Pnames** – the category of *procedure names*
- **DecV** – the category of *variable declarations*
- **DecP** – the category of *procedure declarations*

We denote elements of **Pnames** by $p, q \ldots$, elements of **DecV** by D_V and elements of **DecP** by D_P. The formation rules of **Aexp** and **Bexp** are as in **Bims**. The formation rules of **Stm**, **DecV** and **DecP** are as given below. Here ϵ denotes both the empty variable declaration and the empty procedure declaration[2].

$$S ::= x := a \mid \mathbf{skip} \mid S_1; S_2 \mid \mathbf{if}\ b\ \mathbf{then}\ S_1\ \mathbf{else}\ S_2 \mid$$
$$\mathbf{while}\ b\ \mathbf{do}\ S \mid \mathbf{begin}\ D_V\ D_P\ S\ \mathbf{end} \mid \mathbf{call}\ p$$
$$D_V ::= \mathbf{var}\ x := a; D_V \mid \epsilon$$
$$D_P ::= \mathbf{proc}\ p\ \mathbf{is}\ S; D_P \mid \epsilon$$

---

[1] Bims incorporating procedures.
[2] In what follows, the actual meaning of ϵ will always be clear from the context.

There are thus two new statements in **Bip**.

- A *block* is of the form `begin` D_V D_P S `end`. A block is a statement with declarations of local variables, D_V, declarations of local procedures, D_P, and a body, S.
- A *procedure call*, `call` p, invokes a procedure named p.

The intention is that variables and procedures declared in a block should be available only within the block itself. Notice that all variables are assigned an initial value, namely the value of an arithmetic expression a, when declared.

The meaning of a procedure call will depend on the *scope rules*, that is, which variables and procedures are known during the execution of the procedure.

In this chapter, procedures will have no parameters, as parameter passing is not the focus of the development here. We treat parameter passing in Chapter 7.

6.2 The environment–store model

We now introduce a more refined description of a program state. The idea originally arose in the work of Scott and Strachey on denotational semantics (Strachey, 1966, 1967; Scott, 2000).

In Chapter 4 we presented a first model of variable bindings, the simple state model where a state s is a partial function $s : \textbf{Var} \rightharpoonup \mathbb{Z}$. However, this model does not describe that variables are actually bound to storage cells in the computer memory. For this reason, the simple state model will be inadequate when we need to give a concise description of phenomena such as side effects or program constructs such as references.

The environment–store model describes how variables are actually bound during a program execution: each variable is bound to a storage cell, and the content of a storage cell is the value of the variable.

Thus, in the environment–store model a program state describes to which storage locations variables are bound and which values are found in the individual cells.

- The *variable environment* is a function that for each variable tells us to which storage location it is bound. In other words, a variable environment corresponds to a *symbol table*.
- The *store* is a function that for each storage location tells us which value is found at the location. In other words, a store corresponds to a complete description of the contents of the memory.

In the environment–store model, storage cells are called *locations*. The set of locations is called **Loc**. We let l denote an arbitrary element of **Loc**. In the following we always assume that **Loc** $= \mathbb{N}$, that is, that locations are natural numbers.

Since we would like to describe that new locations may be allocated to new variables, we introduce a special pointer, next, which is bound to the next available location.

Summing up, we obtain the following definition.

Definition 6.1 The set of variable environments is the set of partial functions from variables to locations:

$$\textbf{EnvV} = \textbf{Var} \cup \{\text{next}\} \rightharpoonup \textbf{Loc}.$$

We let env_V denote an arbitrary member of **EnvV**.

A moment's thought 6.2 Why should variable environments be *partial* functions?

Moreover, we shall assume the existence of a function

$$\text{new} : \textbf{Loc} \rightarrow \textbf{Loc}$$

that for every location returns its successor (no matter whether this successor location is available or not).

Since we are assuming that **Loc** $= \mathbb{N}$, we can define new by

$$\text{new } l = l + 1.$$

In our model, values are integers, so we have the following definition.

Definition 6.3 The set of stores is the set of partial functions from locations to values:

$$\textbf{Sto} = \textbf{Loc} \rightharpoonup \mathbb{Z}.$$

We let *sto* denote an arbitrary element of **Sto**.

We again introduce a notation for updating environments and stores. For environments, we write $env_V[x \mapsto l]$ to denote the environment env'_V given by

$$env'_V y = \begin{cases} env_V y & \text{if } y \neq x \\ l & \text{if } y = x. \end{cases} \tag{6.1}$$

A moment's thought 6.4 Define the update notation $sto[l \mapsto v]$ for stores.

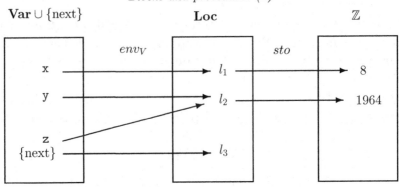

Figure 6.1 Example of a variable environment and a store

Example 6.5 Figure 6.1 shows an example of a variable environment and a store. We here have three variables, **x**, **y** and **z**. env_V is the function described by the arrows between $\mathbf{Var} \cup \{next\}$ and **Loc**. From these arrows we see the following: **x** is bound to the location l_1. The variables **y** and **z** are both bound to the location l_2 – so if one of these two variables is updated, so is the other one. The next free location is l_3. No other variables are bound to any location.

sto is the function described by the arrows between **Loc** and $\mathbb{Z}$. This function tells us that the content of location l_1 is 8 and that the content of l_2 is 1964. The contents of all other locations are undefined.

A moment's thought 6.6   What is the value of the variable **x** in Example 6.5? What is the value of **z** ?

It is straightforward to relate the environment–store model to the simple state model from Chapter 4. This was the model where a state is a function $s : \mathbf{Var} \rightharpoonup \mathbb{Z}$.

Here, every pair (env_V, sto) gives rise to a state given by the function composition $sto \circ env_V$; the value v of the variable x can be found as $v = sto(env_V\ x)$.

So far, we have defined only a model of variable bindings. We will also need a notion of procedure environments that will allow us to describe the binding of procedures. However, the model of procedure bindings will depend on the scope rules that we chose, so the definition of procedure environments is postponed to Section 6.6.

6.3 Arithmetic and Boolean expressions

The semantics of statements and declarations both depend on the semantics of arithmetic expressions, and arithmetic expressions may contain variables. So, since we have a new model of variable bindings, we need to redefine our semantics of arithmetic and Boolean expressions.

In what follows, we shall define a big-step semantics of arithmetic expressions. Our transition system for arithmetic expressions is $(\mathbf{Aexp} \cup \mathbb{Z}, \rightarrow_a, \mathbb{Z})$, where $\rightarrow_a$ is defined by the rules of Table 6.1. All transitions are of the form $env_V, sto \vdash a \rightarrow_a v$ and must be read as 'given the variables known by env_V and the storage content of sto the arithmetic expression a evaluates to the value v'.

The essential difference from the semantics of **Aexp** given in Chapter 4 lies in the rule [VAR-BIP$_{\mathrm{BSS}}$], since we now find the value of a variable by first finding its location and then determining the content of the location.

A moment's thought 6.7   We shall also need a new semantics of Boolean expressions. Why?

Problem 6.8   Give a new big-step semantics of Boolean expressions under the environment–store model that makes use of the new semantics of **Aexp**.

[PLUS-BIP$_{\mathrm{BSS}}$]
$$\frac{env_V, sto \vdash a_1 \rightarrow_a v_1 \quad env_V, sto \vdash a_2 \rightarrow_a v_2}{env_V, sto \vdash a_1 + a_2 \rightarrow_a v}$$

where $v = v_1 + v_2$

[MINUS-BIP$_{\mathrm{BSS}}$]
$$\frac{env_V, sto \vdash a_1 \rightarrow_a v_1 \quad env_V, sto \vdash a_2 \rightarrow_a v_2}{env_V, sto \vdash a_1 - a_2 \rightarrow_a v}$$

where $v = v_1 - v_2$

[MULT-BIP$_{\mathrm{BSS}}$]
$$\frac{env_V, sto \vdash a_1 \rightarrow_a v_1 \quad env_V, sto \vdash a_2 \rightarrow_a v_2}{env_V, sto \vdash a_1 * a_2 \rightarrow_a v}$$

where $v = v_1 \cdot v_2$

[PARENT-BIP$_{\mathrm{BSS}}$]
$$\frac{env_V, sto \vdash a_1 \rightarrow_a v_1}{env_V, sto \vdash (a_1) \rightarrow_a v_1}$$

[NUM-BIP$_{\mathrm{BSS}}$] $env_V, sto \vdash n \rightarrow_a v$ if $\mathcal{N}[\![n]\!] = v$

[VAR-BIP$_{\mathrm{BSS}}$] $env_V, sto \vdash x \rightarrow_a v$ if $env_V \ x = l$ and $sto \ l = v$

Table 6.1 *Big-step operational semantics of **Aexp** using the environment–store model*

6.4 Declarations

The execution of a block begin D_V D_P S end starts with the declaration of variables in D_V and procedures in D_P before S can be executed. So we need to define an operational semantics of **DecV** and **DecP**.

6.4.1 Declaring variables

Any non-empty variable declaration will modify the variable environment, since new variables will be bound to new locations. However, a variable declaration will also modify the store, since the new locations will be initialized to contain the initial values of the new variables.

The transition relation describing variable declarations, $\rightarrow_{DV}$, defines a big-step semantics. This is reasonable, since we know that the allocation of new address space for newly declared variables is an *indivisible* operation – a compiler will allocate addresses to all program variables in one go.

Our semantics of variable declarations is given by the transition system $(\Gamma_{DV}, \rightarrow_{DV}, T_{DV})$ whose configurations are defined by

$$\Gamma_{DV} = (\mathbf{DecV} \times \mathbf{EnvV} \times \mathbf{Sto}) \cup (\mathbf{EnvV} \times \mathbf{Sto}),$$
$$T_{DV} = \mathbf{EnvV} \times \mathbf{Sto}.$$

Transitions here have the format $\langle D_V, env_V, sto \rangle \rightarrow_{DV} (env_V', sto')$. The rules defining the transition relation $\rightarrow_{DV}$ are given in Table 6.2.

We now explain the rules defining $\rightarrow_{DV}$. The rule [VAR-DECL-BIP$_{\mathrm{BSS}}$] expresses that we perform the variable declaration var $x := a$; D_V relative to env_V and sto by first finding the value v of the expression a. Then we update the variable bindings found in env_V by binding x to l, where l is

---

[VAR-DECL$_{\mathrm{BSS}}$]
$$\frac{\langle D_V, envv'', sto[l \mapsto v] \rangle \rightarrow_{DV} (env_V', sto')}{\langle \text{var } x := a; D_V, env_V, sto \rangle \rightarrow_{DV} (env_V', sto')}$$

where $env_V, sto \vdash a \rightarrow_a v$
and $l = env_V$ next
and $envv'' = env_V[x \mapsto l][\text{next} \mapsto \text{new } l]$

[EMPTY-VAR$_{\mathrm{BSS}}$] $\quad \langle \epsilon, env_V, sto \rangle \rightarrow_{DV} (env_V, sto)$

Table 6.2 *Big-step semantics of variable declarations*

the next available location, and bind the next-pointer to the location following l. This location is determined by an application of the new-function to next. Finally, *sto* gets updated by letting the location l contain the value v. The rule [EMPTY-VAR$_{\text{BSS}}$] expresses that the empty declaration will change neither the variable environment nor the store.

6.4.2 Procedure declarations

A procedure declaration updates our procedure environment. A procedure environment holds information about the bindings of procedure names. As in the case of variable declaration, declarations should be thought of as indivisible operations, so again we give a big-step semantics.

Our semantics is given by the transition system $(\Gamma_{DP}, \rightarrow_{DP}, T_{DP})$ whose configurations are defined by

$$\Gamma_{DP} = (\textbf{DecP} \times \textbf{EnvP}) \cup \textbf{EnvP},$$
$$T_{DP} = \textbf{EnvP}.$$

Transitions are of the form $env_V \vdash \langle D_P, env_P \rangle \rightarrow_{DP} env'_P$; we need to assume this format, since some kinds of scope rules will require us to retrieve information about the variable bindings that were known when a procedure was declared. In these cases the result of a procedure declaration will depend on the variable environment known.

We defer the transition rules defining $\rightarrow_{DP}$ to Section 6.6, since they depend upon our definition of procedure environments, and this definition turns out to depend on the scope rules that we choose.

6.5 Statements

We can now present a big-step semantics of all statements in our language apart from procedure calls. The semantics of procedure calls depends on our choice of scope rules and will be presented in Section 6.6.

The effect of a statement is that the store may change. This is the case, since a statement may modify the values of variables involved through assignments. On the other hand, a statement should not modify the variable environment.

A moment's thought 6.9 Why should a statement not modify the variable environment?

So here we define the transition system $((\textbf{Stm} \times \textbf{Sto}) \cup \textbf{Sto}, \rightarrow, \textbf{Sto})$.

Transitions are of the form

$$env_V, env_P \vdash \langle S, sto \rangle \rightarrow sto'$$

and should be interpreted as follows: 'given the variable bindings env_V and the procedure bindings env_P, the execution of statement S will modify the store sto to the new store sto''. The rules for all statements (except procedure calls) are shown in Table 6.3

Let us now explain the intended meaning of the transition rules.

The rule [ASS-BIP$_{BSS}$] captures how variables are updated in the environment-store model: we execute $x := a$ by evaluating a to obtain its value v and then, by a lookup in the variable environment, find the location associated with x. Finally, we update the contents of l to v.

The rule [BLOCK-BIP$_{BSS}$] describes the execution of a block. Notice how the premises invoke several other transition relations. The first premise, $\langle D_V, env_V, sto \rangle \rightarrow_{DV} (env'_V, sto'')$, captures that we perform the variable declarations of D_V and thereby update our variable environment and our store. The second premise, $env'_V \vdash \langle D_P, env_P \rangle \rightarrow_{DP} env'_P$, describes that we perform the procedure declarations in D_P and thereby update our procedure environment. The third and final premise, $env'_V, env'_P \vdash \langle S, sto'' \rangle \rightarrow sto'$, describes the execution of the block body S given the new bindings.

A moment's thought 6.10   How does the rule [BLOCK-BIP$_{BSS}$] capture that the bindings provided by the locally declared variables and procedures are truly local, that is, are known only within the block body S?

6.6 Scope rules

The environment–store model provides us with a nice way of explaining the different kinds of scope rules.

In **Bip**, the scope rules tell us *which bindings are in effect during the execution of a procedure call*. There are two kinds of scope rules. *Dynamic scope rules* employ the bindings known when the procedure is *called*, whereas *static scope rules* employ the bindings known when the procedure was *declared*. Most programming languages today use some variation of static scope rules, but a few (such as Emacs Lisp and some other dialects of Lisp) stick to dynamic scope rules.

Different scope rules give rise to different interpretations of the same piece of code. Consider the example statement of Figure 6.2.

If we assume *fully dynamic scope rules*, that is, dynamic scope rules for both variables and procedures, this implies that during the execution of

[ASS-BIP$_{\text{BSS}}$]	$env_V, env_P \vdash \langle x := a, sto \rangle \rightarrow sto[l \mapsto v]$
	where $env_V, sto \vdash a \rightarrow_a v$ and $env_V\, x = l$
[SKIP-BIP$_{\text{BSS}}$]	$env_V, env_P \vdash \langle \texttt{skip}, sto \rangle \rightarrow sto$

[COMP-BIP$_{\text{BSS}}$]
$$\frac{env_V, env_P \vdash \langle S_1, sto \rangle \rightarrow sto'' \quad env_V, env_P \vdash \langle S_2, sto'' \rangle \rightarrow sto'}{env_V, env_P \vdash \langle S_1; S_2, sto \rangle \rightarrow sto'}$$

[IF-TRUE-BIP$_{\text{BSS}}$]
$$\frac{env_V, env_P \vdash \langle S_1, sto \rangle \rightarrow sto'}{env_V, env_P \vdash \langle \texttt{if } b \texttt{ then } S_1 \texttt{ else } S_2, sto \rangle \rightarrow sto'}$$

if $env_V, sto \vdash b \rightarrow_b tt$

[IF-FALSE-BIP$_{\text{BSS}}$]
$$\frac{env_V, env_P \vdash \langle S_2, sto \rangle \rightarrow sto'}{env_V, env_P \vdash \langle \texttt{if } b \texttt{ then } S_1 \texttt{ else } S_2, sto \rangle \rightarrow sto'}$$

if $env_V, sto \vdash b \rightarrow_b ff$

[WHILE-TRUE-BIP$_{\text{BSS}}$]
$$\frac{env_V, env_P \vdash \langle S, sto \rangle \rightarrow sto'' \quad env_V, env_P \vdash \langle \texttt{while } b \texttt{ do } S, sto'' \rangle \rightarrow sto'}{env_V, env_P \vdash \langle \texttt{while } b \texttt{ do } S, sto \rangle \rightarrow sto'}$$

if $env_V, sto \vdash b \rightarrow_b tt$

[WHILE-FALSE-BIP$_{\text{BSS}}$] $\quad env_V, env_P \vdash \langle \texttt{while } b \texttt{ do } S, sto \rangle \rightarrow sto$

if $env_V, sto \vdash b \rightarrow_b ff$

[BLOCK-BIP$_{\text{BSS}}$]
$$\frac{\langle D_V, env_V, sto \rangle \rightarrow_{DV} (env_V', sto'') \quad env_V' \vdash \langle D_P, env_P \rangle \rightarrow_{DP} env_P' \quad env_V', env_P' \vdash \langle S, sto'' \rangle \rightarrow sto'}{env_V, env_P \vdash \langle \texttt{begin } D_V\ D_P\ S \texttt{ end}, sto \rangle \rightarrow sto'}$$

Table 6.3 *Big-step transition rules for* **Bip** *statements (except procedure calls)*

```
begin
        var x:= 0;
        var y:= 42

        proc p is x:= x+3;
        proc q is call p;

        begin
                var x:= 9;
                proc p is x:= x+1;

                call q;
                y:=x

        end

end
```

Figure 6.2 An example **Bip** statement whose behaviour is dependent on the choice of scope rules

procedure q we know the variables and procedures that were known then q was called. The variable y therefore ends up having the value 10.

If we assume *dynamic scope rules for variables and static scope rules for procedures*, then during the execution of q we know the variables that exist when q was called but the procedures that were known when q was declared. Here, the final value of y will be 12.

If we assume *fully static scope rules*, that is, static scope rules for both variables and procedures, this means that during the execution of q we know only the variables and procedures that were known when q was declared. Here, the final value of y becomes 9.

A moment's thought 6.11   What is the final value of y if we assume the other version of mixed scope rules, i.e. *static scope rules for variables but dynamic scope rules for procedures?*

A moment's thought 6.12   What are the advantages and disadvantages of static and dynamic scope rules, respectively? Why do you think most programming languages today have static scope rules?

In the remainder of this section we describe how the operational semantics of **Bip** will change according to different choices of scope rules. The only visible differences lie in the rules for declaration and call of procedures and consequently also involve different definitions of procedure environments.

6.6.1 Fully dynamic scope rules

When we assume fully dynamic scope rules, only the bindings known at the time of invocation matter. So when a procedure is declared, we need to remember only the body of the procedure. Consequently, the definition of the set of possible procedure environments **EnvP** is given by

$$\textbf{EnvP} = \textbf{Pnames} \rightharpoonup \textbf{Stm}. \tag{6.2}$$

The transition rules for procedure declaration are given in Table 6.4.

[PROC-BIP$_{\text{BSS}}$]
$$\frac{env_V \vdash \langle D_P, env_P[p \mapsto S] \rangle \rightarrow_{DP} env'_P}{env_V \vdash \langle \textbf{proc } p \textbf{ is } S \text{ ; } D_P, env_P \rangle \rightarrow_{DP} env'_P}$$

[PROC-EMPTY-BIP$_{\text{BSS}}$] $env_V \vdash \langle \epsilon, env_P \rangle \rightarrow_{DP} env_P$

Table 6.4 *Transition rules for procedure declarations (assuming fully dynamic scope rules)*

When we call a procedure p, we execute the body of p using the current bindings. We retrieve the body of p by looking it up in our procedure environment. The rule for `call p` is therefore that of Table 6.5.

[CALL-DYN-DYN$_{\text{BSS}}$]
$$\frac{env_V, env_P \vdash \langle S, sto \rangle \rightarrow sto'}{env_V, env_P \vdash \langle \textbf{call } p, sto \rangle \rightarrow sto'}$$
where $env_P p = S$

Table 6.5 *Transition rule for procedure calls (assuming fully dynamic scope rules)*

Problem 6.13 Apply the big-step semantics to the statement of Figure 6.2 and thereby conclude that the rules of Tables 6.4 and 6.5 yield the expected result.

6.6.2 Mixed scope rules

One can of course imagine a mix of dynamic and static scope rules. In this section we consider the case where we have dynamic scope rules for variables and static scope rules for procedures. Here we must perform the call of a procedure p using the variable bindings known at call time and the procedure bindings known when p was declared.

$$\mathbf{EnvP} = \mathbf{Pnames} \rightharpoonup \mathbf{Stm} \times \mathbf{EnvP} \tag{6.3}$$

The transition rules for $\rightarrow_{DP}$ describe how procedure environments are created from procedure declarations and can be found in Table 6.6.

[PROC-BIP$_{\text{BSS}}$] $$\dfrac{env_V \vdash \langle D_P, env_P[p \mapsto (S, env_P)]\rangle \rightarrow_{DP} env'_P}{env_V \vdash \langle\ \texttt{proc}\ p\ \texttt{is}\ S\ ;D_P, env_P\rangle \rightarrow_{DP} env'_P}$$

[PROC-EMPTY-BIP$_{\text{BSS}}$] $env_V \vdash \langle \epsilon, env_P\rangle \rightarrow_{DP} env_P$

Table 6.6 *Transition rules for procedure declarations assuming mixed scope rules (dynamic for variables, static for procedures)*

We now describe the behaviour of a procedure call. Since we assume dynamic scope rules for variables, we must execute the body of a procedure named p using the variable bindings known at call time but with the procedure bindings that were in effect when p was declared. The body of p and the bindings that were in effect at the time of declaration can be found by a lookup in the procedure environment. The rule for $\texttt{call}\ p$ is shown in Table 6.7.

Please notice that the body S of procedure p may contain occurrences of $\texttt{call}\ p$. However, during the execution of S we can make use only of the procedure bindings env'_P that were in effect *immediately before* p was declared. Consequently, procedure calls *cannot* be recursive.

In Section 7.3 we will consider recursive procedure calls and show how they can be expressed within our setting.

Problem 6.14   Apply the big-step transition rules for statements to the statement of Figure 6.2 and thereby show that the rules of Table 6.6 and 6.7 yield the expected result.

$$[\text{CALL-DYN-STAT}_{\text{BSS}}] \quad \frac{env_V, env_P' \vdash \langle S, sto \rangle \rightarrow sto'}{env_V, env_P \vdash \langle \texttt{call } p, sto \rangle \rightarrow sto'}$$

$$\text{where } env_P\, p = (S, env_P')$$

Table 6.7 *Transition rules for procedure calls assuming mixed scope rules (dynamic for variables, static for procedures)*

On recursively defined sets

The definition (6.3) defining the set **EnvP** of procedure environments is a *recursive* definition, since **EnvP** is defined in terms of itself. It is not immediately obvious that such definitions make sense. Is there even a set **EnvP** that will satisfy this defining equation? For some defining equations this appears to be impossible. To see this, we need to look at a little bit of set theory.

In set theory, the *cardinality of a set* denotes the size of the set. A set B is said to have strictly greater cardinality than some other set A if there exists a bijection between A and a proper subset of B but no bijection between A and B exists. If A and B are finite sets, this is the case when B has more elements than A.

Now consider the following equation defining a set D:

$$D = D \rightharpoonup D. \tag{6.4}$$

By using the proof technique called *diagonalization* (see e.g. Sipser (2005)) one can show that, for any choice of D, the set $D \rightharpoonup D$ will have *strictly greater cardinality* than the set D, and this is of course a contradiction. A treatment of equations such as (6.4) will therefore require a new interpretation of equality, sets and function spaces.

The resulting mathematical theory originated from insights by Dana Scott (Scott, 1976) and is called *domain theory*. Domain theory is highly interesting but also beyond the scope of this book. See e.g. Gierz *et al.* (2003) and Amadio and Curien (1998)

Fortunately, the definition in (6.3) is not problematic, since **EnvP** appears only on the right-hand side of $\rightharpoonup$ and since we consider only procedure environments with *finite support*, that is, ones that are partial functions that are defined only for finitely many argument values.

We shall return to recursive definitions in Chapter 15.

6.6.3 Fully static scope rules

When we use fully static scope rules, the execution of a procedure call `call` p can use only the variable bindings and procedure bindings known when p was declared.

This then implies that these bindings must be remembered by the procedure environment, and so the set **EnvP** is defined by

$$\mathbf{EnvP} = \mathbf{Pnames} \rightharpoonup \mathbf{Stm} \times \mathbf{EnvV} \times \mathbf{EnvP}. \tag{6.5}$$

Again we notice that **EnvP** is recursively defined.

The transition rules for $\rightarrow_{DP}$, the transition relation for procedure declarations, are given in Table 6.8.

[PROC-BIP$_{\mathrm{BSS}}$]
$$\frac{env_V \vdash \langle D_P, env_P[p \mapsto (S, env_V, env_P)] \rangle \rightarrow_{DP} env'_P}{env_V \vdash \langle \mathtt{proc}\ p\ \mathtt{is}\ S\ ;D_P, env_P \rangle \rightarrow_{DP} env'_P}$$

[PROC-EMPTY-BIP$_{\mathrm{BSS}}$] $env_V \vdash \langle \epsilon, env_P \rangle \rightarrow_{DP} env_P$

Table 6.8 *Transition rules for procedure declarations assuming fully static scope rules*

When we use fully static scope rules we must then, when calling procedure p, execute the body S of p using the variable bindings and procedure declarations known when p was declared. However, *another important modification is needed.* The next pointer must now point to the next location which is free *at the time of invocation*; otherwise, if there are procedure declarations inside S, we run the risk of overwriting the contents of locations used by global variables that were declared later than p.

A moment's thought 6.15   Give a simple example that shows why we need to modify next in this way.

The body of p and the bindings known at the time p was declared can once again be found by a lookup in the procedure environment. The transition rule for `call` p is given in Table 6.9.

Problem 6.16   Apply the big-step semantics to the statement of Figure 6.2 and thereby show that the rules of Tables 6.8 and 6.9 yield the expected result.

Problem 6.17   There is another possible choice of mixed scope rules which

$$[\text{CALL-STAT-STAT}_{\text{BSS}}] \quad \frac{env'_V\,[\text{next} \mapsto l], env'_P \vdash \langle S, sto \rangle \rightarrow sto'}{env_V, env_P \vdash \langle \text{call } p, sto \rangle \rightarrow sto'}$$

where $env_P\, p = (S, env'_V, env'_P)$
and $l = env_V\,\text{next}$

Table 6.9 *Transition rules for procedure calls assuming fully static scope rules*

we have not considered. Give a big-step semantics for a version of **Bip** with *static scope rules for variables and dynamic scope rules for procedures.*

Problem 6.18 Extend **Bip** with references (pointers). Describe the extended abstract syntax and a suitable big-step semantics.

7

Parameters

In this chapter we turn our attention to parameter passing. We add procedures with a single parameter to **Bip** and and show how to modify the big-step semantics of the previous chapter to handle three kinds of parameter passing: *call-by-reference, call-by-value* and *call-by-name*. The common underlying programming language will be called **Bump**.[1]

We also consider another phenomenon that we might just as well have considered in the previous chapter, but which typically arises when parameter passing is used, namely *recursive procedures*.

7.1 The language Bump

The language **Bump** is a small extension of **Bip**; the only difference is that procedures always have one parameter. We consider three variations of **Bump** with slight modifications of the syntax depending on our choice of parameter mechanism.

7.1.1 Syntax of Bump

Let us here start with the version of **Bump** that we shall consider in the next section, namely the one where we consider call-by-reference.

$$S ::= x := a \mid \text{skip} \mid S_1; S_2 \mid \text{if } b \text{ then } S_1 \text{ else } S_2 \mid$$
$$\text{while } b \text{ do } S \mid \text{begin } D_V \ D_P \ S \text{ end} \mid \text{call } p(y)$$
$$D_V ::= \text{var } x := a; D_V \mid \epsilon$$
$$D_P ::= \text{proc } p(\text{var } x) \text{ is } S; D_P \mid \epsilon$$

---

[1] Bip using monadic parameters.

The only differences among the three versions of **Bump** are found in the syntax of procedure declarations D_P and procedure calls.

The terminology is the same, irrespective of our choice of parameter mechanism: in a procedure declaration **proc** $p(\text{var } x)$ **is** S we say that x is the *formal parameter* and in the procedure call **call** $p(y)$ we say that y is the *actual parameter*. A *parameter mechanism* describes the association between the formal and the actual parameter.

7.1.2 Basic assumptions about our semantics

Throughout, we shall assume the environment-store model which describes a program state as a pair of two mappings: a variable environment env_V taken from the set

$$\mathbf{EnvV} = \mathbf{Var} \cup \{\text{next}\} \rightharpoonup \mathbf{Loc}$$

and a store *sto* taken from the set

$$\mathbf{Sto} = \mathbf{Loc} \rightharpoonup \mathbb{Z}.$$

In order not to complicate matters too much, we consider only procedures that have *one parameter*. It is completely straightforward to generalize the account given in this chapter to procedures with multiple parameters.

When we declare a procedure, we need to remember the name of the formal parameter in order to make this association. Therefore, our procedure environments should be defined as follows:

$$\mathbf{EnvP} = \mathbf{Pnames} \rightharpoonup \mathbf{Stm} \times \mathbf{Var} \times \mathbf{EnvV} \times \mathbf{EnvP}.$$

Here, the **Var** component represents the formal parameter.

Given this new definition of the set of procedure environments we also need to modify our semantics of procedure declarations.

The transition rules for $\rightarrow_{DP}$ that describe how declarations build procedure environments can be found in Table 7.1.

It is important to note that our definition of **EnvP** is completely independent of our choice of parameter mechanism and reflects only our choice of scope rules and that the name of the formal parameter must be remembered.

Our big-step semantics will be an extension of the version of the **Bip** big-step semantics having *fully static scope rules*. The rules for procedure declarations will be changed; this change is uniform and applies to all three parameter mechanisms.

For statements, the semantics of procedure calls is dependent on our

[PROC$_{BSS}$]
$$\frac{env_V \vdash \langle D_P, env_P[p \mapsto (S, x, env_V, env_P)]\rangle \rightarrow_{DP} env'_P}{env_V \vdash \langle \textbf{proc } p(\textbf{var } x) \textbf{ is } S \,;\, D_P, env_P\rangle \rightarrow_{DP} env'_P}$$

[PROC-EMPTY$_{BSS}$] $env_V \vdash \langle \epsilon, env_P\rangle \rightarrow_{DP} env_P$

Table 7.1 *Rules for declaring procedures with a single parameter assuming static scope rules*

choice of parameter mechanism. For each of the three choices that we consider in this chapter, we show how to modify the rule for procedure calls, [CALL-STAT-STAT$_{BSS}$]. All other transition rules are left unchanged.

Our transition systems for statements will be of the form $(\Gamma, \rightarrow, T)$ where

$$\Gamma = (\textbf{Stm} \times \textbf{Sto}) \cup \textbf{Sto},$$
$$T = \textbf{Sto}.$$

7.2 Call-by-reference

The call-by-reference parameter mechanism is known from several programming languages, including Pascal, C, C++, and C# – but *not* Java, which uses call-by-value.

The underlying idea of call-by-reference is that *the formal parameter is a reference to the address of the actual parameter.* This then implies that the actual parameter must be a *variable.*

Consider as an example the procedure declaration

```
proc var x is x := x+1
```

and the subsequent call **call** $p(y)$. When the call has been completed, the value of y will have been incremented by 1. This means that the formal parameter x denotes a variable which *has the same address* as y. In the setting of the environment-store model, this then implies that x and y must be *bound to the same location.*

The call-by-reference parameter mechanism therefore associates the formal parameter with the location of the actual parameter.

The new big-step semantics of statements is different from that of **Bip** only insofar as a single rule is concerned, namely the call rule [CALL-R$_{BSS}$]. (But recall that the semantics of procedure declarations is also redefined as described in the previous section.)

$$[\text{CALL-R}_{\text{BSS}}] \quad \frac{env'_V [x \mapsto l][\text{next} \mapsto l'], env'_P \vdash \langle S, sto \rangle \rightarrow sto'}{env_V, env_P \vdash \langle \text{call } p(y), sto \rangle \rightarrow sto'}$$

where $env_P \ p = (S, x, env'_V, env'_P)$,
and $l = env_V \ y$
and $l' = env_V \ \text{next}$

Table 7.2 *Transition rule for calling a call-by-reference procedure*

The new call rule is shown in Table 7.2. It describes the following. We first perform a lookup in env_P under p; in this way, we find the procedure body S, the environments env'_V and env'_P known at declaration time and the formal parameter x. Then we retrieve the location of the actual parameter y by a lookup in env_V. Finally, we execute the body S in the declaration time environment env'_V – but we must remember to update it such that x is now associated with l, which is the location of y, and such that the next free location is the next free location of env_V.

7.3 On recursive and non-recursive procedure calls

The transition rule of Table 7.2 does not allow p to call itself recursively. For any occurrence of **call** p within the body p will refer to some other procedure called p. Remember that the procedure body S is being executed in the procedure environment env'_P, which knows only the procedures that were known immediately prior to the declaration of p.

Consider the example statement of Figure 7.1. Here the procedure named f contains a procedure call **call f(z)**. If we tried to use [CALL-R$_{\text{BSS}}$] to find a transition in this case, we would run into problems, since the side condition requires that the name f must be known in env'_P – which is not the case.

Problem 7.1 (Important) Let S_1 denote the statement found in Figure 7.1 and let env_V and env_P be empty environments; i.e. for all $x \in$ **Var** we have that $env_V x = \underline{\text{undef}}$ and for all $p \in$ **Pnames** we have that $env_P \ p = \underline{\text{undef}}$. Try to build a derivation tree for the transition

$$env_V, env_P \vdash \langle S_1, sto \rangle \rightarrow sto'.$$

Proceed only as far as the part of the construction that reaches the first call of f within the body of f.

```
begin

    var y:= 0;
    var x:=1

    proc f(var x) is

    begin
        var z:= x-1;
        y:= y*x;

        if   x > 1 then
            call f(z)
        else
            skip
    end

    y:=4;
    call f(y);
    z:= y

end
```

Figure 7.1 A **Bump** statement with recursive calls

Fortunately, the solution is simple: we add a binding for p to env'_p such that p is associated with the information needed to call the correct version of p. This is captured in [CALL-R-REC$_{\text{BSS}}$] in Table 7.3.

Problem 7.2 (Important) Again consider the statement found in Figure 7.1 and let env_V and env_P be empty environments but now assume that the transition rule for procedure calls is [CALL-R-REC$_{\text{BSS}}$]. Try to build a derivation tree for the transition

$$env_V, env_P \vdash \langle S_1, sto \rangle \rightarrow sto'.$$

Again, proceed as far as the part of the construction that reaches the first call of f within the body of f.

Here it is important to note that *because we insist on static scope rules for procedures we need to modify the rule for procedure calls*. If we had chosen dynamic scope rules for procedures, no modification would be necessary. All calls of p within the body of p would automatically become recursive calls.

A moment's thought 7.3 Why are calls of p within the body of p always recursive when we assume dynamic scope rules for procedures?

[CALL-R-REC$_{BSS}$] $$\frac{env'_V[x \mapsto l][\text{next} \mapsto l'], env''_P \vdash \langle S, sto \rangle \rightarrow sto'}{env_V, env_P \vdash \langle \text{call } p(y), sto \rangle \rightarrow sto'}$$

where $env_P\ p = (S, x, env'_V, env'_P), env_V\ y = l$
and $l' = env_V$ next
and $env''_P = env_P[p \mapsto (S, x, env'_V, env'_P)]$

Table 7.3 *Revised transition rule for procedure calls that allow recursive calls*

7.4 Call-by-value

Another well-known parameter mechanism is *call-by-value*. Here, the syntax of **Bump** becomes

$$S ::= x := a \mid \text{skip} \mid S_1; S_2 \mid \text{if } b \text{ then } S_1 \text{ else } S_2 \mid$$
$$\text{while } b \text{ do } S \mid \text{begin } D_V\ D_P\ S \text{ end} \mid \text{call } p(a)$$
$$D_V ::= \text{var } x := a; D_V \mid \epsilon$$
$$D_P ::= \text{proc } p(x) \text{ is } S; D_P \mid \epsilon$$

The actual parameter is now an arithmetic expression a. The formal parameter x is then considered a local variable in the body of the procedure, and in a procedure call $\text{call } p(a)$, the initial value of x is the value of the actual parameter a.

Consider as an example the procedure $\text{proc } p(x) \text{ is } x := x + 1$ and the subsequent call $\text{call } p(y + 2)$. Here, we must first find the value of $y + 2$; this value then becomes the initial value of x in the execution of the body of p.

The semantics of procedure declarations is identical to that used for call-by-reference. Again, the only change to the total semantics is that the rule for procedure call is modified.

Table 7.4 contains both versions of the rule – one for which no calls of p can be recursive and another, for which all calls of p within p become recursive.

The side conditions are common to both rules. From a lookup in env_P we discover that p is bound to (S, x, env'_V, env'_P). First, we must evaluate the actual parameter a to obtain the value v. Next, we find the next available location, l. This location will then be assigned to the formal parameter x. In the location l we now place the value v. *Please notice* that since we here update next, we do not need to further modify next in the way that was necessary for the versions of the call rule that we have considered earlier. Finally, we can execute the procedure body S using the bindings known at declaration time.

Problem 7.4 The transition rules in Table 7.4 express that we consider the formal parameter as a local variable. It is therefore possible to assign new values to the formal parameter within the body of the procedure. How can we change our model of program states to give a semantics to the version of call-by-value where there the formal parameter is considered an immutable *local constant*? What would the resulting operational semantics look like? *Hint:* First find out how to introduce declared constants into the **Bump** language.

Problem 7.5 The parameter mechanism *call-by-value-result* lies between call-by-value and call-by-reference. Here, a new location is allocated to the formal parameter (as is the case for call-by-value) and the content of the cell is initialized to hold the value of the actual parameter. However, upon completion of the procedure call, the location of the actual parameter is then updated to hold the final value found in the location of the formal parameter (as is the case for call-by-reference). Describe a transition rule for procedure calls for this parameter mechanism. *Hint:* First, you will need to agree on the syntax. What can the actual parameter be?

Problem 7.6 In **Bip** procedures are not mutually recursive (why not?) Modify the big-step semantics of **Bip** such that mutual recursion becomes possible. Illustrate your idea with a suitable example. *Hint:* It is a good idea to define an extension of the environment update notation that allows you to express that the bindings of several procedures can be updated simultaneously.

7.5 Call-by-name

The ALGOL 60 language (see also Section 1.2.1) has a lot to answer for. It was a clear improvement over FORTRAN, which was the dominant programming language at the time. Moreover, ALGOL 60 was the first programming language whose syntax was defined by a context-free grammar. Backus–Naur Form (BNF) is named after John Backus and Peter Naur, the editors of the ALGOL 60 report (Backus and Naur, 1963). Various successor languages – including Algol W, Algol 68, Pascal, Modula and most recently Oberon – are all based directly on ideas from ALGOL 60, and several other languages are heavily inspired by features of the ALGOL family.

[CALL-V$_{\text{BSS}}$]

$$\frac{env'_V[x \mapsto l][\text{next} \mapsto \text{new } l], env'_P \vdash \langle S, sto[l \mapsto v]\rangle \to sto'}{env_V, env_P \vdash \langle \text{call } p(a), sto\rangle \to sto'}$$

where $env_P\ p = (S, x, env'_V, env'_P)$, $env_V, sto \vdash a \to_a v$ and $l = env_V$ next

[CALL-V-REC$_{\text{BSS}}$]

$$\frac{env'_V[x \mapsto l][\text{next} \mapsto \text{new } l], env'_P[p \mapsto (S, x, env'_V, env'_P)] \vdash \langle S, sto[l \mapsto v]\rangle \to sto'}{env_V, env_P \vdash \langle \text{call } p(a), sto\rangle \to sto'}$$

where $env_P\ p = (S, x, env'_V, env'_P)$, $env_V, sto \vdash a \to_a v$ and $l = env_V$ next

Table 7.4 *Transition rules for procedure calls using call-by-value*

ALGOL 60 has two parameter mechanisms, call-by-value and call-by-name. In this section we consider call-by-name and derive its formal description as a structural operational semantics along the lines of what we have seen so far.

7.5.1 The informal description of call-by-name

At the time of the ALGOL 60 report, the authors did not have access to the methods of formal semantics. As we saw in Chapter 1, denotational semantics only arrived on the scene in the late 1960s and structural operational semantics was almost two decades away. Consequently, the ALGOL 60 report had to resort to using English. Below is what Naur and his colleagues gave as their semantics of call-by-name:

The effect of [a procedure invocation] will be equivalent to the effect of performing the following operations on the program at the time of execution of the procedure [invocation]: Any formal [name parameter identifier] is replaced, throughout the procedure body, by the corresponding actual parameter, after enclosing the latter in parentheses if it is an expression but not [an expression occurring on the left-hand side on an assignment]. Possible conflicts between identifiers inserted through this process and other identifiers already present within the procedure body will be avoided by suitable systematic changes of the formal or local identifiers involved. Finally, the procedure body, modified as above, is inserted in place of the procedure [invocation] and executed. If the procedure is called from a place outside the scope of any [free identifier] of the procedure body, the conflicts between the identifiers inserted through this process of body replacement and the identifiers whose declarations are valid at the place of the procedure statement will be avoided through suitable systematic changes of the latter identifiers. (Backus and Naur, 1963)

Confused? Let us introduce call-by-name into **Bump** and give a structural operational semantics of this relic of the 1960s in such a way that we follow the requirements of the ALGOL 60 report.

Our abstract syntax is now

$$S ::= x := a \mid \texttt{skip} \mid S_1; S_2 \mid \texttt{if } b \texttt{ then } S_1 \texttt{ else } S_2 \mid$$
$$\texttt{while } b \texttt{ do } S \mid \texttt{begin } D_V \, D_P \, S \texttt{ end} \mid \texttt{call } p(a)$$
$$D_V ::= \texttt{var } x := a; D_V \mid \epsilon$$
$$D_P ::= \texttt{proc } p(\texttt{name } x) \texttt{ is } S; D_P \mid \epsilon$$

The underlying idea is that in a procedure invocation $\texttt{call } p(a)$ we *syntactically replace* every occurrence of the formal parameter x inside the body of p by the actual parameter a (having put a in brackets, following Backus and Naur (1963)). We write this as $S[x \mapsto a]$. Note that this is something *entirely different from* the update notation for environments and stores. Syntactic substitution, to be defined shortly, is an operator on statements. By performing a syntactic substitution on a statement we get a modified statement where all free occurrences of x have been replaced by the arithmetic expression a.

Thus, the call-by-name parameter mechanism makes the association between the formal and the actual parameter *at the syntactic level*, whereas the parameter mechanism that we have considered previously made the association *at the semantic level*.

7.5.2 A strong parameter mechanism

Notice that we may never need to find the value of the actual parameter when we use call-by-name as our parameter mechanism. A simple example of this is proc p(name x) is skip. If p had used call-by-value, we would have to evaluate the actual parameter. However, since we use call-by-name we only need to evaluate the actual parameter where it will appear after substitution – and here the formal parameter is absent in the body of p.

Another interesting consequence is that we can exploit the fact that every occurrence of the actual parameter must be evaluated separately. In Figure 7.2 we use this to compute $\sum_{i=1}^{10} i^2$, the sum of the squares of the first 10 positive integers. The trick here is that the formal parameter temp is replaced by i*i. Every time the main loop of the procedure findsum is traversed, i*i is evaluated anew.

This programming technique is known as *Jensen's device*, named after its inventor, the Danish programming pioneer Jørn Jensen.

7.5.3 Scope rules

We must first determine whether we should have static or dynamic scope rules. Let us have another look at the excerpt from the Algol 60 report:

Finally, the procedure body, modified as above, is inserted in place of the procedure [invocation] and executed. If the procedure is called from a place outside the scope of any [free identifier] of the procedure body, the conflicts between the identifiers inserted through this process of body replacement and the identifiers whose declarations are valid at the place of the procedure statement will be avoided through suitable systematic changes of the latter identifiers. (Backus and Naur, 1963)

Here, there is no explicit mention of which bindings should be in effect during the execution of a procedure call. On the one hand, it is required that the body of the procedure is inserted in place of the invocation, and

```
begin
      var lo := 1;
      var i := lo;
      var sum := 0;

      proc findsum (name term) is
           var hi := 10;
           var temp := 0;
             begin
               while not (i > hi) do
                   begin
                        temp := temp + term;
                        i := i+1
                   end;
                sum := temp
             end;

      call findsum (i*i)
end
```

Figure 7.2 Exploiting call-by-name for computing the sum $\sum_{i=1}^{10} i^2$

this, taken on its own, would indicate dynamic scope rules. On the other hand, the description also requires that any conflicts between identifiers (i.e. procedure names and variables) that would arise must be dealt with by systematic renaming of the identifiers that are available at the place of invocation. This indicates that we should assume *static scope rules.*

As was the case for the other parameter mechanisms, we must remember the name of the formal parameter and consequently the set of procedure environments is defined by

$$\textbf{EnvP} = \textbf{Pnames} \rightharpoonup \textbf{Stm} \times \textbf{Var} \times \textbf{EnvV} \times \textbf{EnvP}.$$

The rules for procedure declarations can be found in Table 7.5.

The new rule for procedure calls is given in Table 7.6; note that only non-recursive calls are possible according to this rule.

7.5.4 Defining syntactic substitution

All that is now missing is a precise definition of how to replace the formal parameter by the actual parameter, i.e. a definition of $S[x \mapsto a]$. This definition turns out to be fairly involved.

$$[\text{PROC}_{\text{BSS}}] \quad \frac{env_V \vdash \langle D_P, env_P[p \mapsto (S, x, env_V, env_P)]\rangle \rightarrow_{DP} env'_P}{env_V \vdash \langle \texttt{proc } p(\texttt{name } x) \texttt{ is } S \, ; D_P, env_P\rangle \rightarrow_{DP} env'_P}$$

$$[\text{PROC-EMPTY}_{\text{BSS}}] \quad env_V \vdash \langle \epsilon, env_P\rangle \rightarrow_{DP} env_P$$

Table 7.5 *Transition rules for declaration of call-by-name procedures assuming fully static scope rules*

$$[\text{CALL-N}_{\text{BSS}}] \quad \frac{env'_V, env'_P \vdash \langle S[x \mapsto a], sto\rangle \rightarrow sto'}{env_V, env_P \vdash \langle \texttt{call } p(a), sto\rangle \rightarrow sto'}$$

$$\text{where } env_P \, p = (S, x, env'_V, env'_P)$$

Table 7.6 *Transition rules for procedure calls using call-by-name*

Arithmetic and Boolean expressions

Since arithmetic and Boolean expressions may contain occurrences of the formal parameter and may appear in statements, we first need to define syntactic substitution for these two syntactic categories.

The underlying idea is straightforward: $a'[x \mapsto a]$ is the result obtained by replacing all occurrences of x in a' by a, where a is now *enclosed in parentheses*. If a' is the variable x, the result will be a. If a' is some other variable or a numeral, nothing is changed, and the result is a'. If a' is a composite expression, we replace x by a in each immediate constituent. In other words, the definition of substitution will be recursive in the structure of a' and will not depend on the structure of a. The complete definition can be found in Definition 7.7.

The substitution operators in the present section are all postfix operators: when a substitution acts on a composite term, we sometimes place vertical bars $\|$ around the term to which the substitution is applied. Thus $\|a_1 + a_2\|[y \mapsto a]$ should be read as an application of the substitution to the *entire* expression $a_1 + a_2$.

Definition 7.7 (Substitution in arithmetic expressions) Syntactic substitution is defined compositionally for **Aexp** by

$$x[y \mapsto a] = \begin{cases} (a) & \text{if } x = y, \\ x & \text{if } x \neq y \end{cases}$$

$$n[y \mapsto a] = n,$$
$$(a_1)[y \mapsto a] = (a_1[y \mapsto a])$$
$$\|a_1 + a_2\|[y \mapsto a] = a_1[y \mapsto a] + a_2[y \mapsto a]$$
$$\|a_1 * a_2\|[y \mapsto a] = a_1[y \mapsto a] * a_2[y \mapsto a]$$
$$\|a_1 - a_2\|[y \mapsto a] = a_1[y \mapsto a] - a_2[y \mapsto a].$$

Example 7.8   We have that

$$\|\texttt{(2+x)-z}\|[\texttt{z} \mapsto \texttt{(3+x)}] = \|\texttt{(2+x)}\|[\texttt{z} \mapsto \texttt{(3+x)}]\texttt{-z}[\texttt{z} \mapsto \texttt{(3+x)}]$$
$$= \texttt{(2+x)}[\texttt{z} \mapsto \texttt{(3+x)})]\texttt{-(3+x)}$$
$$= \texttt{(2+x)-(3+x)}.$$

A moment's thought 7.9   What is $\|\texttt{y+((4-9)*x)}\|[\texttt{x} \mapsto \texttt{(x-3)}]$? (Apply the definition!)

We can use Definition 7.7 to define syntactic substitution for Boolean expressions.

Definition 7.10 (Substitution in Boolean expressions)   Syntactic substitution of arithmetic expressions is defined compositionally for **Bexp** by

$$\|a_1 = a_2\|[y \mapsto a] = a_1[y \mapsto a] = a_2[y \mapsto a]$$
$$(a_1)[y \mapsto a] = (a_1[y \mapsto a])$$
$$\|a_1 < a_2\|[y \mapsto a] = a_1[y \mapsto a] < a_2[y \mapsto a]$$
$$\|b_1 \wedge b_2\|[y \mapsto a] = b_1[y \mapsto a] \wedge b_2[y \mapsto a]$$
$$\|\neg b_1\|[y \mapsto a] = \neg b_1[y \mapsto a].$$

Statements and declarations

We finally come to the definition of substitution in statements. Since statements can contain declarations, we also need to define how substitution acts on declarations.

The definition of substitution is more involved here, since we need to take the following part of the ALGOL 60 definition into account:

Possible conflicts between identifiers inserted through this process and other identifiers already present within the procedure body will be avoided by suitable systematic changes of the formal or local identifiers involved. (Backus and Naur, 1963)

This part of the definition is intended to avoid introducing name clashes. A name clash will occur if a local variable declared within a procedure shares its name with a global variable occurring in the actual parameter. Figure 7.3 gives an example of this phenomenon. Here the procedure p contains a locally declared variable y bearing the same name as a variable y found in the surrounding block. Moreover, the procedure contains a locally declared procedure whose formal parameter is also called x.

Consider the following example, where the body of p is the statement

```
begin

    var y := 3;
    var z := 2;

    proc q (name x) is
        begin
            y := x+2;
        end;

    z := (z+x)*y;
    call q(z)

end
```

What is the result of performing the substitution $S[x \mapsto y+4]$? We cannot perform this substitution in the naïve way. If we did, we would get

```
begin

    var y := 3;
    var z := 2;

    proc q (name x) is
        begin
            y := (y+4)+2
        end;

    z := (z+(y+4))*y;
```

```
begin

     var y:=2;
     proc p(name x) is

          begin
                var y:= 3;
                var z := 2;

                proc q(name x) is begin y:= x+2 end;

                z := (z+x)*y;
                call q(z);

          end

     call p(y+4)

end
```

Figure 7.3 A **Bump** statement showing where name clashes could occur as a result of an incorrectly defined substitution

```
     call q(z)

end
```

But this introduces a *name clash*: we no longer distinguish between the global y and the local y, and we erroneously instantiate the parameter x of the local procedure q (which has not yet been invoked).

The way out of this problem is to require that *all variables and parameters must be uniquely named*. After all, the importance lies in what the variables denote. In fact, variables (and procedures) do not need names at all. We might just as well designate a variable by an index which describes in which block it occurs. The innermost y in Figure 7.3 could be given the index 11 (first variable declared in the first block at level 2), whereas the outermost y would get the index 1 (first variable declared at the outermost level). This indexing principle is called *de Bruijn indexing* after the Dutch logician W. de Bruijn. However, in our treatment we shall not take this route.

When we define syntactic substitution on statements, it is important to notice that some statements, namely blocks **begin** D_V D_P S **end**, contain declarations. We substitute y by a in the block **begin** D_V D_P S **end** by substituting y by a in the variable declaration D_V, substituting y by a in the procedure declarations D_P and finally substituting y by a in the block body S.

Substitution of y by a in a variable declaration consists of replacing y by a on the right-hand side of each single declaration. This, then, requires that we avoid name clashes – if the block contains the declaration of a local variable called y, we must rename this local y to a fresh name z and then replace y by z in the remainder of the block. This kind of systematic renaming of bound variable occurrences is known in the literature as *alpha-conversion*.

We shall return to alpha-conversion in Section 8.6 in the setting of the π-calculus and in Section 12.3 in the setting of the λ-calculus, since the same problem of name clashes also appears in those contexts.

Definition 7.11 (Substitution in variable declarations)   Syntactic substitution in variable declarations **DecV** is defined inductively by

$$\|\mathsf{var}\ x := a'; D_V\|[y \mapsto a] = \begin{cases} \mathsf{var}\ x := a'[y \mapsto a]; D_V[y \mapsto a] & \text{if } x \neq y \\ \mathsf{var}\ z := a'[y \mapsto a]; D_V[y \mapsto z]) & \text{if } x = y \end{cases}$$
$$\epsilon[y \mapsto a] = \epsilon$$

where z is a fresh variable name.

Problem 7.12   In this section we assume that all variables in a block are pairwise distinct. This need not be the case. How should we modify the definitions to reflect this?

Substitution of y by a in a procedure declaration also consists of replacing y by a in each procedure that is being declared, and this is the other place where we need to prevent name clashes: if a procedure p has a parameter called y, we should *not* perform the replacement in the body of p.

Notice that the following definition assumes that substitution is defined for statements; this is done below.

Definition 7.13 (Substitution in procedure declarations)   Syntactic substitution of arithmetic expressions is for procedure declarations **DecP** defined inductively by

$$\|\text{proc } p(\text{name } x) \text{ is } S; D_P\|[y \mapsto a] = \begin{cases} \text{proc } p(\text{name } y) \text{ is} \\ S; D_P[y \mapsto a] \\ \\ \text{if } x = y \\ \\ \text{proc } p(\text{name } x) \text{ is} \\ S[y \mapsto a]; D_P[y \mapsto a] \\ \\ \text{if } x \neq y \end{cases}$$

$$\epsilon[y \mapsto a] = \epsilon.$$

We are now finally able to define substitution for statements. The definition of substituting a for y is also fairly delicate; if a locally declared variable shares its name with a variable occurring in the expression a, we must rename the local variable. However, we must remember to do this *throughout the block* and therefore there will be two clauses in the definition for blocks, depending on whether or not a local variable of the same name occurs.

Definition 7.14 (Substitution in statements)   Syntactic substitution is defined compositionally for statements as in Table 7.7.

7.6 A comparison of parameter mechanisms

In this chapter we have seen three distinct parameter mechanisms.

The semantics of call-by-name is a lot more complicated than that of call-by-reference or call-by-value, since we need to associate actual parameters with formals at the level of syntax and therefore need to define a notion of syntactic substitution which avoids name clashes.

On the other hand, call-by-name is a much more powerful parameter mechanism than the other two. Procedure calls sometimes succeed under call-by-name, whereas they would result in a run-time error if either of the other two parameter mechanisms had been assumed.

Consider again the procedure **proc** $p(\text{name } x)$ **is skip**. The procedure call **call** $p(1/0)$ will not lead to a run-time error, since 1/0 will never be evaluated. This would happen, had we taken call-by-name as our parameter mechanism.

Moreover, what we have considered here are the complications that arise in languages with *binding constructs*. Programming languages are by no means the only such languages.

$\|x := a'\|[y \mapsto a] = x := a'[y \mapsto a]$

$\text{skip}[y \mapsto a] = \text{skip}$

$\|S_1; S_2\|[y \mapsto a] = S_1[y \mapsto a]; S_2[y \mapsto a]$

$\|\text{if } b \text{ then } S_1 \text{ else } S_2\|[y \mapsto a] = \text{if } b[y \mapsto a] \text{ then } S_1[y \mapsto a] \text{ else } S_2[y \mapsto a]$

$\|\text{while } b \text{ do } S\|[y \mapsto a]) = \text{while } b[y \mapsto a] \text{ do } S[y \mapsto a]$

$\|\text{begin var } x := a';\ D_V\ D_P\ S \text{ end}\|[y \mapsto a] = \text{begin var } z := a'[y \mapsto a]\ ;\ D'_V\ D'_P\ S' \text{ end}$

where z is fresh and D'_V, D'_P and S' are given by

$\text{begin } D'_V\ D'_P\ S' \text{ end}$

$= \|\text{begin } D_V[x \mapsto z]\ D_P[x \mapsto z]\ S[x \mapsto z]\ \text{end}\|[y \mapsto a]$

if $x = y$ or x occurs in a

$\|\text{begin var } x := a';\ D'_V\ D'_P\ S' \text{ end}\|[y \mapsto a] = \text{begin } x := a'\ D'_V\ D'_P\ S \text{ end}$

where D'_V, D'_P and S' are given by

$\text{begin } D'_V\ D'_P\ S' \text{ end}$

$= \|\text{begin } D_V\ D_P\ S \text{ end}\|[y \mapsto a]$

if $x \neq y$ and x does not occur in the block

$\|\text{begin } \epsilon\ D_P\ S \text{ end}\|[y \mapsto a] = \text{begin } \epsilon\ D_P[y \mapsto a]\ S[y \mapsto a]\ \text{end}$

$\|\text{call } p(a')\|[y \mapsto a] = \text{call } p(a'[y \mapsto a])$

Table 7.7 *Substitution in statements*

We know similar examples from the realm of ordinary mathematical notation. A well-known binding construct is the differential dx in an integral such as

$$\int_0^{\frac{\pi}{2}} \sqrt{y} \sin^2 x \, dx.$$

Here, the differential dx states that we must perform integration w.r.t. x and that y is a free variable.

Another example of the rôle played by binding constructs in mathematics is that of the quantifiers $\exists$ and $\forall$ from predicate logic (see Section 2.2.2) that allow us to write formulae such as

$$\forall x . x + y = 4.$$

In a formal treatment of predicate logic, all definitions of substitions within formulae must avoid name clashes in a way which is entirely similar to that presented in this chapter for call-by-name.

A moment's thought 7.15   Give other examples of binding constructs in mathematics, programming languages and elsewhere.

8

Concurrent communicating processes

In Chapter 5 we saw how one can describe parallel programs using structural operational semantics. Concurrenct behaviour is explained as the nondeterministic interleaving of the steps of the individual parallel components, so to describe this we employ a *small-step semantics.*

However, the language constructs considered in Chapter 5 allowed parallel components to communicate only by reading and modifying the values of shared variables. In this chapter we take a look at other paradigms for communication between concurrent processes.

The first language that we shall consider in Section 8.1 is very reminiscent of the process calculi CSP (Hoare, 1988) and CCS (Milner, 1989). The languages considered in later sections are all variants of this language.

Section 8.5 of the chapter is devoted to a short introduction to the area of behavioural equivalences for concurrent processes, and in particular to the notion of bisimulation.

CSP and CCS are early examples of *process calculi,* and the idea of bisimulation equivalence has become prominent here. A process calculus is a simple notation designed with the aim of being able to describe and reason about the behaviour of concurrent processes. The last section of the chapter describes a more recent and very important process calculus which has given rise to a large body of research. This process calculus, the π-calculus, is an expressive yet simple process calculus that allows one to describe phenomena such as references and the transfer of reference.

8.1 Channel-based communication – Cab

We first extend **Bims** with concurrent processes that communicate over channels – the resulting language is called **Cab**.[1]

---

[1] Channels added to Bims.

A program now consists of a collection of parallel processes (which are statements) that can communicate using *channels*. A process can use a channel to emit or receive values.

The syntactic categories of **Cab** are those of **Bims** together with the category **Proc** of programs and the category **Channels** of channels. We let the metavariable c range over elements of **Channels** and let p range over **Proc**.

The abstract syntax of **Cab** extends that of **Bims** as follows:

$$p ::= \mathbf{par}(S_1, \ldots, S_n)$$
$$S ::= \ldots \mid c?x \mid c!a$$

Here, we assume that in a parallel composition $\mathbf{par}(S_1, \ldots, S_n)$, any two parallel components S_i and S_j (for $1 \leq i, j \leq k$ and $i \neq j$) are *variable-independent*. By this we mean that none of the variables in one occurs in the other. This will ensure that parallel components can execute without interfering with each other.

Also note that the syntax allows us to express the parallel composition of an arbitrary number of processes.

There are two new statements for channel-based communication: $c?x$ denotes that a value is received on channel c and bound to x; $c!a$ denotes that the value of the arithmetic expression a is sent out on the channel c.

8.2 Global and local behaviour

In the following sections we describe variations of **Cab** and their semantics. Common to all the semantics is a two-level view of the operational semantics which is completely independent of our choice of communication.

It is probably easiest to understand the two-level semantics via a metaphor taken from the realm of chemistry. A program can be thought of as a 'solution' comprised of 'molecules' that react by means of rendezvous.[2] This chemistry metaphor was originally proposed by Gerard Berry and Gerard Boudol in their work on the so-called *Chemical Abstract Machine* (Berry and Boudol, 1992), and the following account is inspired by central ideas in their work.

We can therefore think of two levels of behaviour.

Local behaviour: At the local level we describe the behaviour of a single process, i.e. a 'molecule'. A molecule exhibits local (molecular) be-

---

[2] From French *rendez–vous!* - 'present yourselves'.

haviour whenever its behaviour is independent of other molecules. Here, only a single molecule is affected.

Global behaviour: At the global level we describe the interaction between processes. A molecule (process) exhibits global behaviour when it 'reacts' with another molecule; the 'solution' is changed. Here, more than one molecule is affected.

In order not to complicate the presentation, we shall here return to the simple model of program states, i.e. we consider states $s : \textbf{Var} \rightharpoonup \mathbb{Z}$.

8.3 Synchronous communication in Cab

Our first semantics uses *synchronous communication* – both processes involved in a communication must be ready for the exchange. In other words, a communication between processes p_1 and p_2 can take place if p_1 is able to send v on channel c and p_2 is able to receive a value on channel c. This is called a *rendezvous*.

8.3.1 Local behaviour

In our transition system for the local level $(\Gamma_l, \Rightarrow, T)$ the set of configurations is defined by $\Gamma_l = (\textbf{Stm} \times \textbf{States}) \cup \textbf{States}$ and the terminal configurations are given by $T = (\textbf{Stm} \times \textbf{States}) \cup \textbf{States}$.

As for **Bims**, our transitions are of the forms $\langle S, s \rangle \Rightarrow_l \langle S', s' \rangle$ and $\langle S, s \rangle \Rightarrow_l s'$. The rules defining $\Rightarrow_l$ are shown in Table 8.1 and are completely similar to the rules of the small-step semantics of **Bims**.

8.3.2 Global behaviour – semantics of programs

We are now almost ready to describe the behaviour at the global level, including rendezvous. As we saw above, a rendezvous can occur if two processes agree to use a channel for exchanging a value. Our semantics must therefore be able to describe the communication capabilites of individual processes.

A capability semantics

We describe the communication capabilities of a process by means of a *labelled transition system*.

Definition 8.1 (Labelled transition system)   A labelled transition system is a triple $\mathcal{G} = (\Gamma, A, \stackrel{a}{\rightarrow})$, where Γ is a set of *configurations*, A is a set

[ASS$_{\text{L-SSS}}$]	$\langle x := a, s \rangle \Rightarrow_l s[x \mapsto v]$ where $s \vdash a \rightarrow_a v$

[SKIP$_{\text{L-SSS}}$] $\langle \text{skip}, s \rangle \Rightarrow_l s$

[COMP-1$_{\text{L-SSS}}$] $$\frac{\langle S_1, s \rangle \Rightarrow_l \langle S_1', s' \rangle}{\langle S_1; S_2, s \rangle \Rightarrow_l \langle S_1'; S_2, s' \rangle}$$

[COMP-2$_{\text{L-SSS}}$] $$\frac{\langle S_1, s, \rangle \Rightarrow_l s'}{\langle S_1; S_2, s \rangle \Rightarrow_l \langle S_2, s' \rangle}$$

[IF-TRUE$_{\text{L-SSS}}$] $\langle \text{if } b \text{ then } S_1 \text{ else } S_2, s \rangle \Rightarrow_l \langle S_1, s \rangle$

if $\mathcal{B}[\![b]\!]s = \mathbf{tt}$

[IF-FALSE$_{\text{L-SSS}}$] $\langle \text{if } b \text{ then } S_1 \text{ else } S_2, s \rangle \Rightarrow_l \langle S_2, s \rangle$

if $\mathcal{B}[\![b]\!]s = \mathbf{ff}$

[WHILE$_{\text{L-SSS}}$] $\langle \text{while } b \text{ do } S, s \rangle \Rightarrow_l$
$\langle \text{if } b \text{ then } (S; \text{while } b \text{ do } S) \text{ else skip}, s \rangle$

Table 8.1 *Transition rules defining local transitions*

of *labels* and $\rightarrow \subseteq \Gamma \times A \times \Gamma$ is the *labelled transition relation*. Whenever $(\gamma_1, a, \gamma_2) \in \rightarrow$, we write $\gamma_1 \xrightarrow{a} \gamma_2$.

Problem 8.2 (Important)   Finite-state automata and pushdown automata can be viewed as labelled transition systems. Why? What are the configurations and the transition relations?

In our capability semantics, the labelled transition semantics is given by the labelled transition system $(\Gamma_c, A, \xrightarrow{a})$. The set of labels is $A = \mathbf{Channels} \times \mathbb{Z}$; so here a label denotes a communication capability. Our configurations are $\Gamma_c = (\mathbf{Stm} \times \mathbf{States}) \cup \mathbf{States}$ and transitions are of the forms $\langle S, s \rangle \xrightarrow{c?v} \langle S', s' \rangle$ and $\langle S, s \rangle \xrightarrow{c!v} \langle S', s' \rangle$.

We should read $\langle S, s \rangle \xrightarrow{c?v} \langle S', s' \rangle$ as follows: 'From the configuration $\langle S, s \rangle$ we can reach the configuration $\langle S', s' \rangle$ by receiving the value v on channel c'. Similarly, we should read $\langle S, s \rangle \xrightarrow{c!v} \langle S', s' \rangle$ as follows: 'From the configuration $\langle S, s \rangle$ we can reach the configuration $\langle S', s' \rangle$ by sending the value v on channel c'.

[INPUT$_{\text{C-SSS}}$]	$\langle c?x, s\rangle \xrightarrow{c?v} \langle\texttt{skip}, s[x \mapsto v]\rangle$	for all $v \in \mathbb{Z}$
[OUTPUT$_{\text{C-SSS}}$]	$\langle c!a, s\rangle \xrightarrow{c!v} \langle\texttt{skip}, s\rangle$	where $s \vdash a \rightarrow_a v$
[COMP$_{\text{C-SSS}}$]	$\dfrac{\langle S_1, s\rangle \xrightarrow{\alpha} \langle S_1', s'\rangle}{\langle S_1; S_2, s\rangle \xrightarrow{\alpha} \langle S_1'; S_2, s'\rangle}$	where $\alpha \in \{c?v, c!v\}$

Table 8.2 *Rules defining the capability semantics*

The rules defining $\rightarrow$ are given in Table 8.2. We now present the content of the most important rules.

The axiom [INPUT$_{\text{C-SSS}}$] should be read as follows: A process which is ready to receive a value will accept an *arbitrary* value. The output axiom [OUTPUT$_{\text{C-SSS}}$] states that a process which is ready to emit a *specific* value can do so. The value is found by evaluating the arithmetic expression a.

Problem 8.3 Show that, if $\langle S, s\rangle \xrightarrow{c!v} \langle S, s'\rangle$, then we have $s = s'$. In other words, the state does not change because a capability is offered.

Rules defining rendezvous

We can now describe the global semantics; here, we view the system of parallel components as a 'solution' whose 'molecules' may interact.

Our transition system for programs is $(\Gamma_g, T_g, \Rightarrow_g)$ and is meant to capture how communications happen. Our communications are either elements of **Proc** × **States** – start configurations – or 'solution configurations' of the form $\{|S_1, \ldots, S_n|\}$, where each 'molecule' S_i in the 'solution' is a process.

More precisely, let $\mathcal{M}(\textbf{Stm})$ denote the set of all *multisets*[3] of statements. Consequently, we have that $\Gamma_g = (\textbf{Proc} \times \textbf{States}) \cup \mathcal{M}(\textbf{Stm})$ and $T_g = \{\emptyset\} \times \textbf{States}$. The transition relation $\Rightarrow_g$ is defined by the transition rules in Table 8.3. Note that in the rule [COMM$_{\text{G-SSS}}$] we do not require that the parallel component $\langle S_i, s\rangle$ has index i smaller than j, only that they are different; communication is possible between any two components in either direction, if they possess the right capabilities.

---

[3] A *multiset* is a collection where elements may appear more than once. An example is $\{|1, 1, 2, 3, 5, 2|\}$ – which is different from the multiset $\{|1, 2, 3, 5|\}$.

[START$_{\text{G-SSS}}$] $\langle \mathbf{par}(S_1, \ldots, S_n), s \rangle \Rightarrow_g (\{\!\!| S_1, \ldots, S_n |\!\!\}, s)$

[LOCAL-1$_{\text{G-SSS}}$] $\dfrac{\langle S_i, s \rangle \Rightarrow_l \langle S_i', s' \rangle}{(\{\!\!| \cdots, S_i, \cdots |\!\!\}, s) \Rightarrow_g (\{\!\!| \cdots S_i', \cdots |\!\!\}, s')}$

[LOCAL-2$_{\text{G-SSS}}$] $\dfrac{\langle S_i, s \rangle \Rightarrow_l s'}{(\{\!\!| \cdots S_i \cdots |\!\!\}, s) \Rightarrow_g (\{\!\!| \cdots |\!\!\}, s')}$

[COMM$_{\text{G-SSS}}$] $\dfrac{\langle S_i, s \rangle \xrightarrow{c?v} \langle S_i', s' \rangle \quad \langle S_j, s \rangle \xrightarrow{c!v} \langle S_j', s \rangle}{(\{\!\!| \cdots, S_i, \cdots, S_j, \cdots |\!\!\}, s) \Rightarrow_g (\{\!\!| \cdots, S_i', \cdots, S_j', \cdots |\!\!\}, s')}$

Table 8.3 *Synchronous communication: transition rules for the global level*

Problem 8.4   Let the statements S_1, S_2 and S_3 be given by

$$
\begin{aligned}
S_1: \quad & x_1 := 1; \\
& c?x_2; \\
& \text{if } x_1 = x_2 \text{ then } \quad x_1 := x_1 + 1; \\
& \qquad\qquad\qquad\qquad\;\; a!x_1 \\
& \qquad\qquad\;\; \text{else} \quad x_2 := x_2 + 1; \\
& \qquad\qquad\qquad\;\; b!x_2
\end{aligned}
$$

$$
\begin{aligned}
S_2: \quad & z_1 = 5; \\
& z_2 := 1; \\
& c!z_2
\end{aligned}
$$

$$
\begin{aligned}
S_3: \quad & r := 7; \\
& c!r + 2; \\
& a?r
\end{aligned}
$$

Find all computation steps from $\mathbf{par}(S_1, S_2, S_3)$ starting in state s where $sx_1 = sx_2 = sr = sz_1 = sz_2 = 0$.

As we can see from the semantics in this section and the ones that follow, parallel programs are in general *nondeterministic*, so, even in a setting where programs are known to terminate, there are complications: for a given initial state and a given statement, more than one final state may be possible.

8.4 Other communication models

The literature describes several other models of communicating processes; this section is devoted to a presentation of some of these.

8.4.1 Asynchronous Cab

In a rendezvous the participating processes must *synchronize* when they communicate. However, one can imagine a different kind of communication, namely *asynchronous* concurrency, where processes still communicate via channels but emit values to a *medium* where messages may reside indefinitely before they are received.

Let us say that a medium is an element of the set **Media** and that this set is an abstract datatype which has the following operations:

- put : $\mathbb{Z} \times$ **Channels** $\times$ **Media** $\to$ **Media**
- get : **Channels** $\times$ **Media** $\to \mathbb{Z}$
- remove : **Channels** $\times$ **Media** $\to$ **Media**
- isempty : **Channels** $\times$ **Media** $\to \{tt, ff\}$.

We should think of a medium as a collection of 'waiting rooms', one for each channel (or as a single waiting room, in which each value is labelled by a channel). An output places a value in a waiting room; an input retrieves a value from a waiting room. The intended workings of the operations are now as follows:

- $\mathsf{put}(v, c, m)$ places a value v on channel c in the medium m
- $\mathsf{get}(c, m)$ reads a value from the medium m on channel c
- $\mathsf{remove}(c, m)$ removes a value from the medium m and puts it on channel c
- $\mathsf{isempty}(c, m)$ returns tt if and only if the medium m contains no values on channel c.

Often a medium is implemented as a queue and in this case the above operations are then simply the corresponding operations on queues.

In our semantics, the connection between the local and the global level is now affected, since our understanding of communication capabilities becomes different.

Asynchronous communication capabilities

In what follows, we shall assume that our medium has unlimited capacity, i.e. that it can contain arbitrarily many values.

[INPUT$_\text{L-SSS}$] $\langle c?x, s, \mathsf{m} \rangle \xrightarrow{c?v} \langle \mathsf{skip}, s[x \mapsto v], \mathsf{remove}(c, \mathsf{m}) \rangle$

               if $\mathsf{isempty}(c, \mathsf{m}) = f\!f$
               and $v = \mathsf{get}(c, \mathsf{m})$

[OUTPUT$_\text{L-SSS}$] $\langle c!a, s, \mathsf{m} \rangle \xrightarrow{c!v} \langle \mathsf{skip}, s, \mathsf{put}(v, c, \mathsf{m}) \rangle$

               where $s \vdash a \rightarrow_a v$

[COMP$_\text{L-SSS}$] $\dfrac{\langle S_1, s, \mathsf{m} \rangle \xrightarrow{\alpha} \langle S_1', s', \mathsf{m}' \rangle}{\langle S_1; S_2, s, \mathsf{m} \rangle \xrightarrow{\alpha} \langle S_1'; S_2, s', \mathsf{m}' \rangle}$

               where $\alpha \in \{c?v, c!v\}$

Table 8.4 *Asynchronous communication: communication capabilities*

Our transition system is $(\Gamma_c, \mathrm{T}, \rightarrow_c)$, where $\Gamma_c = \mathbf{Stm} \times \mathbf{States} \times \mathbf{Media}$ and transitions are of the forms

$$\langle S, s, \mathsf{m} \rangle \xrightarrow{c?v} \langle S', s', \mathsf{m}' \rangle$$

and

$$\langle S, s, \mathsf{m} \rangle \xrightarrow{c!v} \langle S', s', \mathsf{m}' \rangle.$$

The rules defining $\rightarrow_c$ are given in Table 8.4.

The global level

The only changes to the transition rules at the global level are caused by the fact that a medium is now involved. Let $\mathsf{m}_\emptyset$ denote the empty medium. See Table 8.5.

Problem 8.5 Find all transitions starting from $\mathbf{par}(S_1, S_2, S_3)$ as defined in Problem 8.4, now assuming asynchronous communication. First assume that the medium m is a queue. Then repeat the exercise, this time assuming that the medium is a stack.

Problem 8.6 Define an operational semantics for asynchronous communication where the capacity of the medium is *bounded*.

[start$_g$]	$\langle \texttt{par}(S_1, \ldots, S_n), s \rangle \Rightarrow_g (\{\!|S_1, \ldots, S_n|\!\}, s, \mathsf{m}_{\emptyset})$

$$[\text{LOCAL-1}_{\text{G-SSS}}] \qquad \frac{\langle S_i, s \rangle \Rightarrow_l \langle S_i', s' \rangle}{(\{\!|\cdots S_i, \cdots|\!\}, s, \mathsf{m}) \Rightarrow_g (\{\!|\cdots S_i', \cdots|\!\}, s', \mathsf{m})}$$

$$[\text{LOCAL-2}_{\text{G-SSS}}] \qquad \frac{\langle S_i, s \rangle \Rightarrow_l s'}{(\{\!|\cdots S_i \cdots|\!\}, s, \mathsf{m}) \Rightarrow_g (\{\!|\cdots \cdots \cdots|\!\}, s', \mathsf{m})}$$

$$[\text{COMM-1}_{\text{G-SSS}}] \qquad \frac{\langle S_i, s, \mathsf{m} \rangle \overset{c?v}{\rightarrow} \langle S_i', s', \mathsf{m}' \rangle}{(\{\!|\cdots S_i, \cdots|\!\}, s, \mathsf{m}) \Rightarrow_g (\{\!|\cdots S_i', \cdots|\!\}, s', \mathsf{m}')}$$

$$[\text{COMM-2}_{\text{G-SSS}}] \qquad \frac{\langle S_i, s, \mathsf{m} \rangle \overset{c!v}{\rightarrow} \langle S_i', s', \mathsf{m}' \rangle}{(\{\!|\cdots S_i, \cdots|\!\}, s, \mathsf{m}) \Rightarrow_g (\{\!|\cdots S_i', \cdots|\!\}, s', \mathsf{m}')}$$

Table 8.5 *Asynchronous communication: the global level*

8.4.2 Implicit parallelism

There is nothing sacred about the concurrency model in **Cab**. One could just as well imagine a slightly different language, **Pif**,[4] whose syntax is the following extension of **Bims**:

$$S ::= \ldots \mid \texttt{fork}(S_1)$$

The new statement $\texttt{fork}(S)$ denotes that a new parallel component S is created. This understanding of concurrency can be found in many programming languages, including C and the functional language Concurrent ML (Reppy, 1992), and is also similar to the notion of process forking used in Unix.

One can imagine both synchronous and asynchronous versions of communication in this setting. In both cases we need only modify the semantics of the global level. In both cases we replace the rule [START$_G$] by the rule

$$\{\!|\texttt{fork}(S_1); S_2, \ldots|\!\} \Rightarrow_g \{\!|S_2, S_1, \ldots|\!\}$$

In this rule the parallel component $\texttt{fork}(S_1); S_2$ turns into two parallel components, of which one continues executing the statement S_2 and the other continues by executing the newly forked statement S_1.

Problem 8.7   Find all transitions from $\texttt{fork}(S_1); (\texttt{fork}(S_2); S_3)$ and from

---

[4]   **Parallelism introduced by forking.**

$\texttt{fork}(S_1; (\texttt{fork}(S_2)); S_3)$, where S_1, S_2 and S_3 are again defined as in Problem 8.4,

8.5 Bisimulation equivalence

In Chapter 5 we introduced a notion of semantic equivalence in the setting of **Bims**. How should we define semantic equivalence in the setting of this chapter? We choose an approach different from the one taken in Definitions 2.16 and 5.6. These definitions have as a central assumption that only terminating computations are of interest; two statements are semantically equivalent if, in any initial state, they lead to the same final state.

However, parallel programs are often not supposed to terminate. Operating systems and control software are examples of *reactive systems*, that is, highly parallel systems that react with their environment and are not supposed to terminate.

Communication capabilities are essential to our revised definition of semantic equivalence. It seems reasonable to say that two programs exhibit the same behaviour if they *always* have the same communication capabilities – that is, whenever two equivalent programs have used the same communication capability, they remain equivalent.

Definition 8.8 Let $(\Gamma, A, \overset{a}{\rightarrow})$ be a labelled transition system. A *bisimulation* is a relation $R \subseteq \Gamma \times \Gamma$ which satisfies the following conditions.

If xRy then for all $a \in A$ we have the following.

1. If $x \overset{a}{\rightarrow} x'$ then there exists a y' such that $y \overset{a}{\rightarrow} y'$ where $x'Ry'$.
2. If $y \overset{a}{\rightarrow} y'$ then there exists an x' such that $x \overset{a}{\rightarrow} x'$ where $x'Ry'$.

If xRy for some bisimulation R over Γ, we say that x and y are *bisimilar* and write $x \sim y$.

This definition tells us that two programs are equivalent if we can find a 'well-behaved' relation that the successor configurations can remain within.

Problem 8.9 Show that $\sim$ is an equivalence relation. *Hint:* We need two axuiliary definitions here: if R is a binary relation over Γ, then its inverse R^1 is defined as $R^{-1} = \{(y, x) | xRy\}$. If R_1 and R_2 are binary relations over Γ, we define their composition by $R_1 \circ R_2$ where $R_1 \circ R_2 = \{(x, z) | \exists y : xRy, yRz\}$. Now it suffices (why?) to show the following.

- The identity relation is a bisimulation.
- If R is a bisimulation, then so is R^{-1}.
- If R_1 and R_2 are bisimulations, then so is $R_1 \circ R_2$.

The notion of bisimilarity was originally proposed by David Park in 1981 (Park, 1981), but it was through the work by Robin Milner (Milner, 1989) that the importance of the concept became clear. Bisimilarity has become important in the field known as *process calculus theory*; the mathematical theory of bisimilarity has been extensively studied and various notions of bisimilarity have been used in the verification of real-life concurrent systems.

Bisimilarity has also been applied in the setting of modal logic and to the study of the foundations of mathematics through its use in what is known as non-well-founded set theory (Aczel, 1988).

8.6 Channels as data – the π-calculus

In this section we give a short introduction to the π-calculus. This is a very different language for concurrency, where channel names are first-class values.

8.6.1 A process calculus of references

What if we could send not just simple values but also names of channels in a communication? The π-calculus was devised by Robin Milner, Joachim Parrow and David Walker (Milner *et al.*, 1992a,b) as a process calculus which will allow precisely that. The resulting calculus allows one to express and reason about the behaviour of concurrent systems whose communication pattern may change dynamically, i.e. processes whose interconnections can change as they interact. Here is a very simple example.

Alice has access to a resource R, which could be, say, a physical device or a program library. She can make use of R by communicating with it on the channel r. Suppose Alice would like to enable Bob to use the resource as well. She has a channel b which she uses for communication with Bob. Alice outputs the name r on this channel, and Bob can then use the channel to send a request (whose name is d) to R. Expressed as a transition, this would look as follows in the π-calculus:

$$\underbrace{\bar{b}r.A_1}_{\text{Alice}} \mid \underbrace{b(x).\bar{x}d.B_1}_{\text{Bob}} \mid R \xrightarrow{\tau} A_1 \mid \bar{r}d.B_1 \mid R.$$

Here, r is used in two different ways. First, r is seen as the name of a data object which is transferred between Alice and Bob. Next, r is seen as the name of the communication channel used in communication with R.

This notion of reference passing has many counterparts in the setting of communication – and not only when computers are involved. For instance, the topic of a phone conversation may be a phone number.

In fact, the notion of transfer of references is very general and versions of the π-calculus have been successfully used to describe phenomena as diverse as object-oriented programs (Sangiorgi, 1998; Walker, 1991), cryptographic protocols (Abadi and Gordon, 1999), biochemical processes (Regev *et al.*, 2001) and workflow processes in human organizations (Puhlmann and Weske, 2005).

8.6.2 Syntax

The π-calculus has two syntactic categories:

- the syntactic category of *processes* **Proc**, where $P \in$ **Proc** (sometimes we also use Q as a metavariable for processes)
- the syntactic category of *names*, where $n, x, c \in$ **Names**; we assume that **Names** is a countably infinite set[5]

The formation rules are

$$P ::= (\nu n)P_1 \mid P_1 \mid P_2 \mid \overline{x}y.P_1 \mid x(y).P_1$$
$$\mid \texttt{if } x_1 = x_2 \texttt{ then } P_1 \mid \texttt{if } x_1 \neq x_2 \texttt{ then } P_1 \mid !P_1 \mid \mathbf{0}$$

The intuitive interpretations of these constructs are as follows. The *restriction* construct (νn) declares a new name n whose scope is P_1. $P_1 \mid P_2$ is the *parallel composition* of processes P_1 and P_2. The process $\overline{x}y.P_1$ outputs a name y on the channel named x and continues as P_1, whereas the process $x(y).P_1$ inputs a name on the channel x and uses it to instantiate y in the P_1 that follows. We have two tests for equality of names. In $\texttt{if } x_1 = x_2 \texttt{ then } P_1$, if x_1 and x_2 are the same name, P_1 is executed, otherwise the process terminates. In $\texttt{if } x_1 \neq x_2 \texttt{ then } P_1$, P_1 is executed only if x_1 and x_2 are distinct names. Finally, the *replication* construct $!P_1$ denotes a process that can always start a new copy of the process P_1. The $\mathbf{0}$ process cannot do anything.

Note that in the π-calculus there are no variable assignments, no loops and no sequential composition. A process is able only to pass around names. Names, on the other hand, are now a very general notion; names can stand for either channels or variables. It turns out that this seemingly restrictive setting of name passing is in fact a very powerful one. To see this, remember that we need not physically transfer a resource (such as R in Section 8.6.1) to make others able to use it – transferring the 'key' to the resource suffices.

---

[5] A set M is *countably infinite* if it is infinite and there exists a bijection $f : M \to \mathbb{N}$ between M and the natural numbers.

This observation has been made precise and helped establish one of the first major results about the π-calculus, namely that one can use it to implement the λ-calculus by means of an encoding (Milner, 1992).

8.6.3 A tiny example

Here is a tiny π-calculus process P that contains three parallel components:

$$(\nu a)(\overline{x}a.\mathbf{0} \mid a(w).\overline{w}e.\mathbf{0}) \mid (\nu d)\, x(z).\overline{z}d.\mathbf{0}\,. \qquad (8.1)$$
$$\underbrace{\phantom{\overline{x}a.\mathbf{0}}}_{P_1} \quad \underbrace{\phantom{a(w).\overline{w}e.\mathbf{0}}}_{P_2} \qquad \underbrace{\phantom{x(z).\overline{z}d.\mathbf{0}}}_{P_3}$$

Notice how the restriction construct describes the scope of the names.

- All three components know the names x and e; these names are not under the scope of any restriction and are said to be *free* in P.
- The components P_1 and P_2 know the name a, and a is said to be *bound* in $P_1 \mid P_2$.
- The component P_3 knows d; d is bound in P_3.

The process P can perform a communication over the channel x; after this communication, P_1 is the empty process and should disappear. On the other hand, P_3 now knows the name a and, since z becomes instantiated to a, P_3 can send d on the channel a. In other words, *the scope of x is extended as the result of a communication*. The semantics of the π-calculus must be able to express this phenomenon, which is known as *scope extrusion*.

8.6.4 Free and bound names

We see that there are two binding constructs in the π-calculus, namely the input prefix $x(y).P$ and the restriction $(\nu x)P$. Both of these bind the name x within the continuation P.

Given this observation, we can then make the notions of free and bound names precise.

Definition 8.10 The set of free names of a process P is defined inductively by

$$fn((\nu x)P_1) = fn(P_1) \setminus \{x\}$$
$$fn(P_1 \mid P_2) = fn(P_1) \cup fn(P_2)$$
$$fn(\overline{x}y.P_1) = \{x, y\} \cup fn(P_1)$$
$$fn(x(y).P_1) = \{x\} \cup fn(P_1) \setminus \{y\}$$
$$fn(\text{if } x_1 = x_2 \text{ then } P_1) = \{x_1, x_2\} \cup fn(P_1)$$
$$fn(\text{if } x_1 \neq x_2 \text{ then } P_1) = \{x_1, x_2\} \cup fn(P_1),$$
$$fn(!P_1) = fn(P_1).$$
$$fn(\mathbf{0}) = \emptyset$$

Definition 8.11 The set of bound names of a process P is defined inductively by

$$bn((\nu x)P_1) = bn(P_1) \cup \{x\}$$
$$bn(P_1 \mid P_2) = bn(P_1) \cup bn(P_2)$$
$$bn(\overline{x}y.P_1) = bn(P_1)$$
$$bn(x(y).P_1) = \{y\} \cup bn(P_1)$$
$$bn(\text{if } x_1 = x_2 \text{ then } P_1) = bn(P_1)$$
$$bn(\text{if } x_1 \neq x_2 \text{ then } P_1) = bn(P_1)$$
$$bn(! \, P_1) = bn(P_1).$$
$$bn(\mathbf{0}) = \emptyset$$

A moment's thought 8.12 Use the definitions to check that e is free in P in (8.1) and that a is bound.

Note that a name can be both free and bound in the same process! Another example shows this:

$$\underbrace{x(y).(\overline{y}z.\mathbf{0} \mid b(w).\mathbf{0})}_{P_1} \mid \underbrace{(\nu b)\overline{x}b.\mathbf{0}}_{P_2}. \tag{8.2}$$

Here, the name b is free in P_1 and bound in P_2; clearly, these two name occurrences should be thought of as referring to different channels. We do *not* want the following to be the result of a communication on the x-channel:

$$(\overline{b}z.\mathbf{0} \mid b(w).\mathbf{0}), \tag{8.3}$$

since we could then have a communication over the b-channel.

A moment's thought 8.13 Why do the definitions of free and bound names tell us that b is both free and bound?

We need to deal with this phenomenon, which is known as *scope intrusion*. Our solution is to *rename* the bound occurrence of b to another, different name that will eliminate the confusion. Notice the similarity to the treatment of name clashes in the treatment of call-by-name in Section 7.5. If we rename the bound b to d, which does not occur anywhere in (8.2) and therefore is a *fresh name*, we get

$$\underbrace{x(y).(\overline{y}z.\mathbf{0} \mid b(w).\mathbf{0})}_{P_1} \mid \underbrace{(\nu d)\overline{x}d.\mathbf{0}}_{P_2}. \tag{8.4}$$

After a communication along the channel named x, the resulting process is

$$(\nu d)(\overline{d}z.\mathbf{0} \mid b(w).\mathbf{0}), \tag{8.5}$$

which cannot perform a communication. This systematic renaming of bound names is called *alpha-conversion*. We return to this in Chapter 12, where we introduce the same notion in our treatment of the λ-calculus (which is where the notion originally arose). If process P_1 can be obtained from process P_2 by a systematic renaming of some bound names (maybe none at all), we write $P_1 \equiv_\alpha P_2$.

8.6.5 Structural congruence

We introduce a notion of structural congruence in Table 8.6. This is not a behavioural equivalence; rather, as the name suggests, its purpose is to define which processes have 'the same structure'.

The first rule, [ALPHA$_{\text{STR}}$], describes that alpha-convertible processes must be thought of as having the same structure.

Taken together, axioms [PAR-COMMUTE$_{\text{STR}}$] and [PAR-ASSOC$_{\text{STR}}$] tell us that the order of parallel composition does not matter, and [PAR-ABSORB$_{\text{STR}}$] tells us that empty parallel components do not matter.

From the point of view of algebra, these three axioms tell us that the set of processes form a *commutative semigroup with absorption* under parallel composition, where $\equiv$ is used to identify terms. From the point of view of parallel programming, the three axioms tell us that a process can be regarded as a 'solution' of 'molecules' analogous to the way in which a parallel system is viewed in the Chemical Abstract Machine (Berry and Boudol, 1992).

The axioms [RES-ABSORB$_{\text{STR}}$] and [RES-COMMUTE$_{\text{STR}}$] tell us that restrictions over empty processes can be omitted and that the order of successive restrictions will not matter.

Two central axioms are [REPLICATE$_{\text{STR}}$] and [EXTEND$_{\text{STR}}$]. The replication rule [REPLICATE$_{\text{STR}}$] tells us that a replicated process $!P$ should be regarded

$[\text{ALPHA}_{\text{STR}}]$	$\dfrac{P_1 \equiv_\alpha P_2}{P_1 \equiv P_2}$
$[\text{PAR-COMMUTE}_{\text{STR}}]$	$P_1 \mid P_2 \equiv P_2 \mid P_1$
$[\text{PAR-ASSOC}_{\text{STR}}]$	$P_1 \mid (P_2 \mid P_3) \equiv (P_1 \mid P_2) \mid P_3$
$[\text{PAR-ABSORB}_{\text{STR}}]$	$P_1 \mid \mathbf{0} \equiv P_1$
$[\text{RES-ABSORB}_{\text{STR}}]$	$(\nu x)(\nu y)P \equiv (\nu y)(\nu x)P$
$[\text{RES-COMMUTE}_{\text{STR}}]$	$(\nu x)\mathbf{0} \equiv \mathbf{0}$
$[\text{RES-IF}_{\text{STR}}]$	$(\nu z)(\texttt{if } x = y \texttt{ then } P_1) \equiv \texttt{if } x = y \texttt{ then } (\nu z)P_1$
	if $z \neq x$ and $z \neq y$
$[\text{RES-IFNOT}_{\text{STR}}]$	$(\nu z)(\texttt{if } x \neq y \texttt{ then } P_1) \equiv \texttt{if } x \neq y \texttt{ then } (\nu z)P_1$
	if $z \neq x$ and $z \neq y$
$[\text{REPLICATE}_{\text{STR}}]$	$!P_1 \equiv P_1 \mid !P_1$
$[\text{EXTEND}_{\text{STR}}]$	$((\nu x)P_1) \mid P_2 \equiv (\nu x)(P_1 \mid P_2)$ if $x \notin \text{fn}(P_2)$
$[\text{REFLEX}_{\text{STR}}]$	$P_1 \equiv P_1$
$[\text{SYMM}_{\text{STR}}]$	$\dfrac{P_1 \equiv P_2}{P_2 \equiv P_1}$
$[\text{TRANS}_{\text{STR}}]$	$\dfrac{P_1 \equiv P_2 \quad P_2 \equiv P_3}{P_1 \equiv P_3}$
$[\text{MATCH-CONG}_{\text{STR}}]$	$\dfrac{P_1 \equiv P_1'}{\texttt{if } x = y \texttt{ then } P_1 \equiv \texttt{if } x = y \texttt{ then } P_1'}$
$[\text{MISMATCH-CONG}_{\text{STR}}]$	$\dfrac{P_1 \equiv P_1'}{\texttt{if } x \neq y \texttt{ then } P_1 \equiv \texttt{if } x \neq y \texttt{ then } P_1'}$
$[\text{PAR-CONG}_{\text{STR}}]$	$\dfrac{P_1 \equiv P_2}{P \mid P_1 \equiv P \mid P_2}$
$[\text{NEW-CONG}_{\text{STR}}]$	$\dfrac{P_1 \equiv P_2}{(\nu x)P_1 \equiv (\nu x)P_2}$
$[\text{REPLICATE-CONG}_{\text{STR}}]$	$\dfrac{P_1 \equiv P_2}{!P_1 \equiv !P_2}$

Table 8.6 *The structural congruence rules*

as the same as the process $P \mid !P$, where an occurrence of P exists as a separate parallel component. [EXTEND$_{\text{STR}}$] tells us that the scope of a bound name can be extended without causing any harm.

The rest of the rules define closure properties of $\equiv$. The rules [REFLEX$_{\text{STR}}$], [SYMM$_{\text{STR}}$] and [TRANS$_{\text{STR}}$] express that structural congruence is an *equivalence* relation (Definition 2.16), and, taken together, the remaining rules (from [PAR-CONG$_{\text{STR}}$] onwards) express that structural congruence is a *congruence relation* for parallel composition, restriction and replication, i.e. is preserved by these constructs of the π-calculus.

8.6.6 Semantics

We now have everything necessary to present a semantics of the π-calculus. In fact, we present two semantics, a reduction semantics, which is simple but cannot describe communication capabilities, and a labelled semantics as seen elsewhere in this chapter.

In both of our semantics, we write $P\{y/x\}$ for P, where all free occurrences of the name x have been substituted by the name y in such a way that no name clashes between free and bound occurrences of y occur.

Problem 8.14 Give an inductive definition of the substitution operation $P\{y/x\}$.

A reduction semantics

In the reduction semantics, configurations are just process terms from **Proc**. Transitions are of the form $P \rightarrow P'$, and we call such a transition a *reduction*.

The rules of Table 8.7 define the reduction relation. [COMM$_{\text{RED}}$] tells us that, in a communication on channel z, the output name y is received and the input name x instantiated to it. [PAR$_{\text{RED}}$] tells us that, if a parallel component can reduce, then so can the entire system. [RES$_{\text{RED}}$] tells us that reductions are allowed within the scope of a name. The rules [MATCH$_{\text{RED}}$] and [MISMATCH$_{\text{RED}}$] describe when a conditional process can proceed. Finally, [STR$_{\text{RED}}$] tells us that processes that have the same structure also have the same reductions. It is the use of [STR$_{\text{RED}}$] together with the axiom [EXTEND$_{\text{STR}}$] that will allow us to describe scope extrusion.

It is now easy to explain the behaviour of the process (8.1). First, since $a \notin \text{fn}((\nu d)x(z).\overline{z}d.\mathbf{0})$, we can use [EXTEND$_{\text{STR}}$] and then [SYMM$_{\text{STR}}$] and [PAR-CONG$_{\text{STR}}$] to get

$$(\nu a)(\overline{x}a.\mathbf{0} \mid a(w).\overline{w}e.\mathbf{0}) \mid (\nu d)x(z).\overline{z}d.\mathbf{0} \equiv$$
$$(\nu a)(\overline{x}a.\mathbf{0} \mid (\nu d)x(z).\overline{z}d.\mathbf{0} \mid a(w).\overline{w}e.\mathbf{0}).$$

[COMMRED]	$\bar{z}y.P_1 \mid z(x).P_2 \rightarrow P_1 \mid P_2\{y/x\}$

[PARRED]
$$\frac{P_1 \rightarrow P_1'}{P_1 \mid P \rightarrow P_1' \mid P}$$

[RESRED]
$$\frac{P_1 \rightarrow P_1'}{(\nu x)P_1 \rightarrow (\nu x)P_1'}$$

[STRRED]
$$\frac{P_1 \equiv Q_1 \quad Q_1 \rightarrow Q_1' \quad Q_1' \equiv P_1'}{P_1 \rightarrow P_1'}$$

[MATCHRED]   if $x = x$ then $P_1 \rightarrow P_1$

[MISMATCHRED]   if $x \neq y$ then $P_1 \rightarrow P_1$

Table 8.7 *Rules of the reduction semantics of the π-calculus*

We then use [EXTENDSTR] again to get

$$(\nu a)(\bar{x}a.\mathbf{0} \mid (\nu d)x(z).\bar{z}d.\mathbf{0} \mid a(w).\bar{w}e.\mathbf{0}) \equiv$$
$$(\nu a)(\nu d)(\bar{x}a.\mathbf{0} \mid x(z).\bar{z}d.\mathbf{0} \mid a(w).\bar{w}e.\mathbf{0}).$$

Note that we have now pushed the restrictions as far outwards as possible. By [COMMRED] we can then get that $\bar{x}a.\mathbf{0} \mid x(z).\bar{z}d.\mathbf{0} \rightarrow \mathbf{0} \mid (\bar{z}d.\mathbf{0})\{a/z\} \equiv \bar{a}d.\mathbf{0}$. But then, by [PARRED], we have

$$\bar{x}a.\mathbf{0} \mid x(z).\bar{z}d.\mathbf{0} \mid a(w).\bar{w}e.\mathbf{0} \rightarrow \bar{a}d.\mathbf{0} \mid a(w).\bar{w}e.\mathbf{0}$$

and we now apply [RESRED] twice to get

$$(\nu a)(\nu d)(\bar{x}a.\mathbf{0} \mid x(z).\bar{z}d.\mathbf{0} \mid a(w).\bar{w}e.\mathbf{0}) \rightarrow$$
$$(\nu a)(\nu d)(\bar{a}d.\mathbf{0} \mid a(w).\bar{w}e.\mathbf{0}).$$

Problem 8.15 Find the next reduction step using the definitions in Tables 8.6 and 8.7.

A labelled semantics

Our labelled semantics also has configurations that are process terms from **Proc**. The labels must now describe communication capabilities, so the set of labels is given by the formation rules

$$\alpha ::= \tau \mid \bar{a}x \mid a(x) \mid \bar{a}\nu x.$$

The three first cases are similar to ones that we have seen earlier in this chapter. The label τ denotes an *internal* action that arises from a communication. $\bar{a}x$ denotes an output action, and $a(x)$ denotes an input action. The fourth label, $\bar{a}\nu x$, is a so-called *bound output*, which describes that the name x is a bound name which is sent out of a scope.

We can define the bound and free names of a label as follows:

$$bn(\tau) = \emptyset$$
$$bn(\bar{a}x) = \emptyset$$
$$bn(a(x)) = \{x\}$$
$$bn(\bar{a}\nu x) = \{x\}$$

and

$$fn(\tau) = \emptyset$$
$$fn(\bar{a}x) = \{a, x\}$$
$$fn(a(x)) = \{a\}$$
$$fn(\bar{a}\nu x) = \{a\}$$

The rules defining the labelled transition relation are shown in Table 8.8. Some of the rules require some further explanation. The rule [STR$_{\text{LAB}}$] is similar in spirit to the corresponding rule of the reduction semantics; here, we use it to say that processes with the same structure have the same capabilities. The rule [PREFIX$_{\text{LAB}}$] tells us how labels arise.

In the rule [PAR$_{\text{LAB}}$], we see an interesting side condition, namely that $bn(\alpha) \cup fn(Q) = \emptyset$. This is necessary, since we could otherwise introduce name clashes. A simple example which shows this is

$$a(x).\bar{x}e.\mathbf{0} \mid x(z).\mathbf{0}.$$

We have that $a(x).\bar{x}e.\mathbf{0} \xrightarrow{a(x)} \bar{x}e.\mathbf{0}$. If we allowed the labelled transition

$$a(x).\bar{x}e.\mathbf{0} \mid x(z).\mathbf{0} \xrightarrow{a(x)} \bar{x}e.\mathbf{0} \mid x(z).\mathbf{0},$$

we would now be able to communicate on the name x – but the x in $a(x).\bar{x}e.\mathbf{0}$ is a bound name which must therefore be different from the free name x in $x(z).\mathbf{0}$.

In the rule [RES$_{\text{LAB}}$] we see that a restricted name x is local. Whenever we want to describe scope extrusion, the trick is to use this rule together with [COMM$_{\text{LAB}}$] and [STR$_{\text{LAB}}$]. Here is a small example. Consider a process

[STR$_{\text{LAB}}$]	$$\dfrac{P_1 \equiv Q_1 \quad Q_1 \xrightarrow{\alpha} Q_1' \quad Q_1' \equiv P_1'}{P_1 \xrightarrow{\alpha} P_1'}$$
[PREFIX$_{\text{LAB}}$]	$\alpha.P \xrightarrow{\alpha} P$
[MATCH$_{\text{LAB}}$]	$$\dfrac{P \xrightarrow{\alpha} P'}{\text{if } x = x \text{ then } P \xrightarrow{\alpha} P'}$$
[MISMATCH$_{\text{LAB}}$]	$$\dfrac{P \xrightarrow{\alpha} P'}{\text{if } x \neq y \text{ then } P \xrightarrow{\alpha} P'}$$
[PAR$_{\text{LAB}}$]	$$\dfrac{P \xrightarrow{\alpha} P'}{P \mid Q \xrightarrow{\alpha} P' \mid Q} \qquad \text{if } \text{bn}(\alpha) \cap \text{fn}(Q) = \emptyset$$
[COMM$_{\text{LAB}}$]	$$\dfrac{P \xrightarrow{a(x)} P' \quad Q \xrightarrow{\bar{a}u} Q'}{P \mid Q \xrightarrow{\tau} P'\{u/x\} \mid Q}$$
[RES$_{\text{LAB}}$]	$$\dfrac{P \xrightarrow{\alpha} P' \quad x \notin \alpha}{(\nu x)P \xrightarrow{\alpha} (\nu x)P'}$$

Table 8.8 *Rules of the labelled semantics of the π-calculus*

of the form

$$a(x).P \mid (\nu u)\bar{a}u.Q,$$

where P and Q are arbitrary processes and we assume that $u \notin \text{fn}(P)$. Here, we have by [COMM$_{\text{LAB}}$] that

$$a(x).P \mid \bar{a}u.Q \xrightarrow{\tau} P\{u/x\} \mid Q,$$

and by [RES$_{\text{LAB}}$] we see that

$$(\nu u)(a(x).P \mid \bar{a}u.Q) \xrightarrow{\tau} (\nu u)(P\{u/x\} \mid Q).$$

By [STR$_{\text{LAB}}$] we now get, since $(\nu u)(a(x).P \mid \bar{a}u.Q) \equiv a(x).P \mid (\nu u)(\bar{a}u.Q)$, that

$$a(x).P \mid (\nu u)(\bar{a}u.Q) \xrightarrow{\tau} (\nu u)(P\{u/x\} \mid Q),$$

where the scope of u has now been extended after the τ-transition.

Relating the two semantics

Earlier in our text we have seen examples of semantics that are equivalent. Here, we would expect the reduction semantics to describe the same communications as the τ-labelled transitions. Indeed, this is the case. One can prove the following theorem.

Theorem 8.16 *For any process P, we have that $P \rightarrow P'$ if and only if $P \xrightarrow{\tau} P'$.*

Problem 8.17 Prove this equivalence result. The proof involves proving the two implications separately and uses induction in the transition rules of the two semantics.

There is a wealth of research on the π-calculus, and this section is only able to scratch the surface. We refer the reader who would like to read more to two excellent books on the π-calculus: Milner's introduction to process calculi and in particular to the π-calculus (Milner, 1999); and Sangiorgi and Walker (2001) which provides an extensive account of the many aspects of the basic theory of the π-calculus, such as behavioural equivalences (including versions of bisimulation equivalence) and type systems.

9

Structured declarations

In this chapter we give a general treatment of structured declarations. This allows us to give an account of language constructs such as structs in C-like languages and objects in object-oriented languages.

In Section 9.2, we describe a big-step semantics of **Bur**.[1] Then, in Section 9.3, we consider **Coat**, a small object-oriented language with classes and dynamically generated objects.

9.1 Records

In this chapter, we will use the term *record* to stand for a structured declaration. We shall allow record declarations inside records. Moreover, records may contain both variables and procedures; this is in contrast to languages such as C and Pascal that allow only the declaration of variables in structured declarations. By allowing procedure declarations as part of a record, we can now view a record as an object. Variables then correspond to the local variables of an object and procedures correspond to object methods. Later, in Section 9.3, we extend this understanding so that we can speak of objects that are dynamically generated instances of classes.

In Figure 9.1 we see an example of a program that has nested record declarations. The program consists of a block which has a record r1 that contains the declaration of a variable x, a procedure p and a record r2. The record r2 contains the declaration of two variables, y and z. After the declarations have been performed, the procedure p found in r1 is called and a variable assignment is performed, modifying x, and another assignment modifies the variable y of r2 by adding the value of x in r1 and then adding 30.

---

[1] Bip using records.

```
begin
  record r1 =
              var x := 4;
              proc p is x := x +4;
              record r2 =
                            var y := 5;
                            var z := 3
              end;
  end;
  call r1.p;
  r1.r2.y := r1.r2.y + r1.x + 30
end
```

Figure 9.1 A program with nested record declarations

9.2 The language Bur

Bur is an extension of **Bip** with record declarations and constructs that allow us to refer to the components of records.

9.2.1 Abstract syntax of Bur

The syntactic categories of **Bur** are those of **Bip** as well as the following important additions:

- The category **DecR** of record declarations

- The category **Rnames** of record declarations

- The category **Gvar** of generalized variables

- The category **Gpnames** of generalized procedure names.

We let D_R range over **DecR** and let $r_1, r_2, \ldots$ range over **Rnames**. Further, we let X range over **Gvar**. Generalized variables $r_1.r_2 \ldots r_n.x$ are sequences of record names $r_1.r_2 \ldots r_n$ concluded by a variable name x. The generalized variable $r_1.r_2 \ldots r_n.x$ refers to the variable x found in record r_n occurring within record r_{n-1} occurring within record $r_{n-2} \ldots$ Likewise, we introduce generalized procedure names $r_1.r_2 \ldots r_n.p$ and let P range over **Gpnames**.

The formation rules of **Bur** are given below; note that generalized variables can occur in arithmetic expressions.

$$X ::= x \mid r.X$$
$$P ::= p \mid r.P$$
$$a ::= n \mid X \mid a_1 + a_2 \mid a_1 * a_2 \mid a_1 - a_2 \mid (a_1)$$
$$b ::= a_1 = a_2 \mid a_1 > a_2 \mid \neg b_1 \mid b_1 \wedge b_2$$
$$S ::= X := a \mid \text{skip} \mid S_1; S_2 \mid \text{if } b \text{ then } S_1 \text{ else } S_2$$
$$\mid \text{while } b \text{ do } S \mid \text{begin } D_V \; D_P \; D_R \; S \text{ end} \mid \text{call } P$$
$$D_V ::= \text{var } x := a; D_V \mid \epsilon$$
$$D_P ::= \text{proc } p \text{ is } S; D_P \mid \epsilon$$
$$D_R ::= \text{record } r = D_V \; D_P \; D_R \text{ end}; D_R \mid \epsilon$$

9.2.2 Environments

According to the environment-store model the value of a variable is stored in the location associated with the variable. As before, we therefore let

$$\textbf{EnvV} = \textbf{Var} \cup \{\text{next}\} \rightharpoonup \textbf{Loc}$$

and

$$\textbf{Sto} = \textbf{Loc} \rightharpoonup \mathbb{Z}.$$

Since we are now also able to declare records, we need to keep track of record bindings as well. For this we use a *record environment*. The set of record environments is called **EnvR**.

A record environment must, given a record name r, hold information about the variables, procedures and records bound within record r. Consequently, the appropriate definition of the set of record environments **EnvR** is

$$\textbf{EnvR} = \textbf{Rnames} \rightharpoonup \textbf{EnvV} \times \textbf{EnvP} \times \textbf{EnvR}.$$

Notice that this definition is recursive (as will be the case for the definition of **EnvP**).

We assume static scope rules, and for this reason every procedure name p must be able to retrieve the variables, procedures and records that were known when p was declared. Consequently, the appropriate definition of **EnvP** is

$$\textbf{EnvP} = \textbf{Pnames} \rightharpoonup \textbf{EnvV} \times \textbf{EnvP} \times \textbf{EnvR}.$$

$$[\text{GVAR-1}_{\text{BSS}}] \quad \frac{env'_R, env'_V \vdash X \to l}{env_R, env_V \vdash r.X \to l}$$

where $env_R\, r = (env'_V, env'_P, env'_R)$

$[\text{GVAR-1}_{\text{BSS}}] \quad env_R, env_V \vdash x \to l$

where $env_V\, x = l$

Table 9.1 *Transition rules for generalized variables*

9.2.3 Transition rules

We now describe the semantics of **Bur**. Notice that all transition rules are affected, since generalized variables can appear as constituents of elements from the syntactic categories **Aexp**, **Bexp**, **Stm**, **DecV** and **DecR** and since generalized procedure names can appear in statements.

Generalized variables

A generalized variable refers to a variable appearing within a record. Since the value of a variable is held in a location, the semantics of generalized variables must describe how this location is to be found. The transitions are therefore of the form

$$env_R, env_V \vdash X \to l.$$

Notice that the transitions are dependent on a variable environment as well as a record environment. The transition rules are given in Table 9.1.

Arithmetic expressions

We now redefine the semantics of arithmetic expressions such that we can capture the presence of generalized variables. The value of an arithmetic expression can now depend on the record environment.

A moment's thought 9.1 Why can the value of an arithmetic expression depend on the record environment?

Transitions are therefore of the form

$$env_R, env_V, sto \vdash a \to v.$$

The transition rules are given in Table 9.2.

$[\text{GVAR}_{\text{BSS}}]$ $$\dfrac{env_R, env_V \vdash X \to l}{env_R, env_V, sto \vdash X \to_a v}$$ where $sto\,l = v$

$[\text{PLUS}_{\text{BSS}}]$ $$\dfrac{env_R, env_V, sto \vdash a_1 \to_a v_1 \quad env_R, env_V, sto \vdash a_2 \to_a v_2}{env_R, env_V, sto \vdash a_1\texttt{+}a_2 \to_a v}$$

where $v = v_1 + v_2$

$[\text{MINUS}_{\text{BSS}}]$ $$\dfrac{env_R, env_V, sto \vdash a_1 \to_a v_1 \quad env_R, env_V, sto \vdash a_2 \to_a v_2}{env_R, env_V, sto \vdash a_1\texttt{-}a_2 \to_a v}$$

where $v = v_1 - v_2$

$[\text{MULT}_{\text{BSS}}]$ $$\dfrac{env_R, env_V, sto \vdash a_1 \to_a v_1 \quad env_R, env_V, sto \vdash a_2 \to_a v_2}{env_R, env_V, sto \vdash a_1\texttt{*}a_2 \to_a v}$$

where $v = v_1 \cdot v_2$

$[\text{PARENT}_{\text{BSS}}]$ $$\dfrac{env_R, env_V, sto \vdash a_1 \to_a v_1}{env_R, env_V, sto \vdash (a_1) \to_a v_1}$$

$[\text{NUM}_{\text{BSS}}]$ $\quad env_R, env_V, sto \vdash n \to_a v \qquad$ where $\quad \mathcal{N}[\![n]\!] = v$

Table 9.2 *Transition rules for arithmetic expressions*

Boolean expressions

Boolean expressions may compare arithmetic expressions, and, since these can now have occurrences of generalized variables, the semantics of Boolean expressions will also need to take this into account.

Problem 9.2 Define the big-step semantics of Boolean expressions.

Variable declarations

Variable declarations also depend on the record environment, since the variable in a declaration **var** $x := a$ must be initialized with the value of a.

The transitions here have the form

$$env_R \vdash \langle D_V, env_V \rangle \to_{DV} env_V'.$$

The transition rules are given in Table 9.3.

Procedure declarations

Since we assume static scope rules, every procedure p that gets declared must be associated with the variables, procedures and records that were known when p was declared. The rules are given in Table 9.4.

[VAR-DECL$_{BSS}$]	$$\frac{env_R \vdash \langle D_V, env_V', sto[l \mapsto v] \rangle \to_{DV} (env_V', sto')}{env_R \vdash \langle \text{var } x := a; D_V, env_V, sto \rangle \to_{DV} (env_V', sto')}$$

where $env_R, env_V, sto \vdash a \to_a v$
and $l = env_V$ next
and $env_V' = env_V[x \mapsto l][\text{next} \mapsto \text{new } l]$

[EMPTY-VAR-DECL$_{BSS}$] $env_R \vdash \langle \epsilon, env_V, sto \rangle \to_{DV} (env_V, sto)$

Table 9.3 *Transition rules for variable declarations*

[PROC$_{BSS}$]	$$\frac{env_V, env_R \vdash \langle D_P, env_P' \rangle \to_{DP} env_P'}{env_V, env_R \vdash \langle \text{ proc } p \text{ is } S; D_P, env_P \rangle \to_{DP} env_P'}$$

where $env_P' = env_P[p \mapsto (S, env_V, env_P, env_R)]$

[PROC-EMPTY$_{BSS}$] $env_V \vdash \langle \epsilon, env_P \rangle \to_{DP} env_P$

Table 9.4 *Transition rules for procedure declarations*

Generalized procedure names

A generalized procedure name refers to a procedure declared inside a record. For this reason, the semantics of generalized procedure names must tell us how to retrieve the body of a procedure and its associated bindings, when we are given a generalized procedure name.

Transitions are of the form

$$env_R, env_P \vdash P \to (S, env_V', env_P', env_R').$$

The rules are given in Table 9.5.

Record declarations

A record declaration will update the record environment and will also update the variable environment, in that the next-pointer will now point to a new location.

Transitions therefore have the form

$$\langle D_R, env_R, env_V \rangle \to_{DR} (env_R', env_V').$$

The transition rules are given in Table 9.6.

$$[\text{GPROC-1}_{\text{BSS}}] \quad \frac{env'_R, env'_P \vdash P \to (S, env''_V, env''_P, env''_R)}{env_R, env_P \vdash r.P \to (S, env''_V, env''_P, env''_R)}$$

where $env_R r = (env'_V, env'_P, env'_R)$

$$[\text{GPROC-2}_{\text{BSS}}] \quad env_R, env_P \vdash p \to (S, env''_V, env''_P, env''_R)$$

where $env_P p = (S, env''_V, env''_P, env''_R)$

Table 9.5 *Transition rules for generalized procedure names*

$$env_R \vdash \langle D_V, env_V \rangle \to env'_V$$

$$env_R, env'_V \vdash \langle D_P, env_P \rangle \to env'_P$$

$$[\text{RECORD}_{\text{BSS}}] \quad \langle D_R, env_R, env'_V \rangle \to_{DR} (env'_R, env''_V)$$

$$\frac{\langle D'_R, env_R[r \mapsto (env'_R, env''_V, env'_P)], env''_V \rangle \to_{DR} (env''_R, env'''_V)}{\langle \mathbf{record}\, r = D_V\, D_P\, D_R\, \mathbf{end}; D'_R, env_R, env_V \rangle \to_{DR} (env''_R, env'''_V)}$$

$$[\text{EMPTY}_{\text{BSS}}] \quad \langle \epsilon, env_R, env_V \rangle \to_{DR} (env_R, env_V)$$

Table 9.6 *Transition rules for record declarations*

Statements

In the semantics of statements, the most important change is that we can now modify the values of generalized variables.

As before, statements can modify the store, since a statement may change the value of a variable. Since statements can modify and inspect the values of variables (including those of variables found inside records) and invoke procedures (including procedures that are local to records), transitions in semantics of statements must depend on environments for variables, procedures and records.

Transitions therefore have the form

$$env_R, env_V, env_P \vdash \langle S, sto \rangle \to sto'.$$

The transition rules are given in Table 9.7.

[ASS$_{\text{BSS}}$] $env_R, env_V, env_P \vdash \langle X := a, sto \rangle \rightarrow sto[l \mapsto v]$

where $env_R, env_V, sto \vdash a \rightarrow_a v$
and $env_R, env_V \vdash X \rightarrow l$

[SKIP$_{\text{BSS}}$] $env_R, env_V, env_P \vdash \langle \textbf{skip}, sto \rangle \rightarrow sto$

[COMP$_{\text{BSS}}$]
$$\frac{env_R, env_V, env_P \vdash \langle S_1, sto \rangle \rightarrow sto'' \quad env_R, env_V, env_P \vdash \langle S_2, sto'' \rangle \rightarrow sto'}{env_R, env_V, env_P \vdash \langle S_1; S_2, sto \rangle \rightarrow sto'}$$

[IF-TRUE$_{\text{BSS}}$]
$$\frac{env_R, env_V, env_P \vdash \langle S_1, sto \rangle \rightarrow sto'}{env_R, env_V, env_P \vdash \langle \textbf{if } b \textbf{ then } S_1 \textbf{ else } S_2 \ sto \rangle \rightarrow sto'}$$

if $env_R, env_V, sto \vdash b \rightarrow_b tt$

[IF-FALSE$_{\text{BSS}}$]
$$\frac{env_R, env_V, env_P \vdash \langle S_2, sto \rangle \rightarrow sto'}{env_R, env_V, env_P \vdash \langle \textbf{if } b \textbf{ then } S_1 \textbf{ else } S_2 \ sto \rangle \rightarrow sto'}$$

if $env_R, env_V, sto \vdash b \rightarrow_b ff$

[WHILE-SAND$_{\text{BSS}}$]
$$\frac{env_R, env_V, env_P \vdash \langle S, sto \rangle \rightarrow sto'' \quad env_R, env_V, env_P \vdash \langle \textbf{while } b \textbf{ do } S, sto'' \rangle \rightarrow sto'}{env_R, env_V, env_P \vdash \langle \textbf{while } b \textbf{ do } S, sto \rangle \rightarrow sto'}$$

if $env_V, sto \vdash b \rightarrow_b tt$

[WHILE-FALSE$_{\text{BSS}}$] $env_V, env_P \vdash \langle \textbf{while } b \textbf{ do } S, sto \rangle \rightarrow sto$

if $env_V, sto \vdash b \rightarrow_b ff$

[BLOK$_{\text{BSS}}$]
$$\frac{\begin{array}{c} env_R \vdash \langle D_V, env_V, sto \rangle \rightarrow_{DV} (env'_V, sto'') \\ env'_V \vdash \langle D_R, env_R \rangle \rightarrow_{DR} (env'_R, env''_V) \\ env''_V \vdash \langle D_P, env_P \rangle \rightarrow_{DP} env'_P \\ env'_R, env''_V, env'_P \vdash \langle S, sto'' \rangle \rightarrow sto' \end{array}}{env_R, env_V, env_P \vdash \langle \textbf{begin } D_V \ D_P \ D_R \ S \textbf{ end}, sto \rangle \rightarrow sto'}$$

[CALL$_{\text{BSS}}$]
$$\frac{env'_R, env'_V, env'_P \vdash \langle S, sto \rangle \rightarrow sto'}{env_R, env_V, env_P \vdash \langle \textbf{call } P, sto \rangle \rightarrow sto'}$$

where $env_R, env_P \vdash P \rightarrow (S, env'_R, env'_V, env'_P)$

Table 9.7 *Transition rules for statements in* **Bur**

9.3 The class-based language Coat

So far we have just shown how structured declarations can be used to describe simple objects. However, almost all object-oriented programming languages have a notion of *class*. In this section we outline a big-step semantics of the language **Coat**,[2] which is a class-based language with objects.

9.3.1 Syntax

The **Coat** language is an extension of **Bims** and has several syntactic categories, many of which are familiar from the previous section:

$n \in$ **Num** – the category of numerals

$x \in$ **Var** – the category of variables

$X \in$ **EVar** – the category of extended variables

$a \in$ **Aexp** – the category of arithmetic expressions

$b \in$ **Bexp** – the category of Boolean expressions

$m \in$ **Mnames** – the category of method names

$M \in$ **EMnames** – the category of extended method names

$o \in$ **Onames** – the category of object names

$O \in$ **Oseq** – the category of object sequences

$OE \in$ **Oexp** – the category of object expressions

$c \in$ **Cnames** – the category of class names

$D_V \in$ **DecV** – the category of variable declarations

$D_M \in$ **DecM** – the category of method declarations

$D_O \in$ **DecO** – the category of object declarations

$D_C \in$ **DecC** – the category of class declarations

$S \in$ **Stm** – the category of statements

$S \in$ **Prog** – the category of programs

---

[2] Classes, objects and that's all.

The formation rules are as follows:

$$A ::= n \mid X \mid a_1 \mathtt{+} a_2 \mid a_1 \mathtt{*} a_2 \mid (a_1)$$
$$b ::= a_1 = a_2 \mid a_1 < a_2 \mid \neg b_1 \mid b_1 \wedge b_2 \mid (b_1)$$
$$S ::= X := a \mid \mathtt{skip} \mid S_1; S_2 \mid \mathtt{if}\ b\ \mathtt{then}\ S_1\ \mathtt{else}\ S_2$$
$$\mid \mathtt{while}\ b\ \mathtt{do}\ S \mid \mathtt{call}\ M \mid o := OE$$
$$O ::= \epsilon \mid O.o$$
$$OE ::= O \mid \mathtt{new}\ c.O$$
$$M ::= OE.m$$
$$X ::= OE.x$$
$$D_V ::= \mathtt{var}\ x := a; D_V \mid \epsilon$$
$$D_M ::= \mathtt{method}\ m\ \mathtt{is}\ S; D_M \mid \epsilon$$
$$D_O ::= \mathtt{object}\ o := O; D_O \mid \epsilon$$
$$D_C ::= \mathtt{class}\ c\ \mathtt{is}\ D_V D_M D_O\ \mathtt{end}; D_C \mid \epsilon$$
$$P ::= D_V\ D_C\ D_O\ S$$

The most notable new features of the syntax of **Coat** are the following.

- The introduction of *programs* P and *class declarations* D_C. A program P consists of a series of declarations followed by a statement S. The declarations are the following: first, a declaration of global variables D_V, next, a declaration of classes D_C (wherein the global variables may be mentioned), and finally a declaration of objects D_O. These objects must be created as instances of the classes by means of dynamical object creation.
- The introduction of *dynamically created objects* using **new** c. This creates a new instance of the class c.
- We introduce *object path expressions* OE; these describe a path of object names that describes the path to an object variable or method. Notice that the first object in the path can be dynamically created using the **new** construct. Otherwise, the object path is an object sequence, i.e. a sequence of known object names.

Example 9.3 Figure 9.2 shows an example of a **Coat** program.
In the example, we declare the following.

- Three global variables, x, y and w.
- A class **tiny** with an instance variable z and a method called **increase**. This method updates the value of the global variable y and adds it to the instance of z.
- An object **increaser**, which is an instance of the class **tiny**.

```
var x:= 3;
var y:= 2;
var w:= 45;

class tiny is
        var z is x+3;
        method increase is
                y:= x+y;
                z:= z+y
end;

object increaser:= new tiny;

w:= (new tiny).z
call tiny.increase;
w:= w + increaser.z
```

Figure 9.2 A **Coat** program example

The body of the program first assigns a new value to the global variable **w**. This is done by dynamically creating a new instance of the class **tiny** and then using the value of the **z**, found in this dynamically created object. In the second line of the program body, the method **increase** is called for the object **tiny**. Finally, **w** is again assigned a new value, this time by adding the value of the instance **z** in the **increaser** object.

Problem 9.4   What is the final value of **w**? And of **y**?

9.3.2 Environments and stores

In the semantics that follows, we extend the environment-store model so that object names are bound to locations. A location will then contain information about the bindings found within the object.

In the extended model, we follow the standard practice of keeping track of the bindings of variables, objects and methods by means of environments.

Variables are bound to locations, just as before, so therefore the set of *variable environments* is again given by

$$\mathbf{EnvV} = \mathbf{Var} \rightharpoonup \mathbf{Loc}.$$

As before, we assume a special next-pointer and a function new : **Loc** $\rightarrow$ **Loc** that returns a successor location. However, we cannot associate the next-pointer with a variable environment, since object declarations can also allocate new locations. Instead, we keep this information in the store (see below).

We assume static scope rules, so the *method environments* of the **Coat** semantics look very similar to the procedure environments that we have seen previously in this chapter. We have

$$\mathbf{EnvM} = \mathbf{Mnames} \rightharpoonup \mathbf{Stm} \times \mathbf{EnvV} \times \mathbf{EnvM} \times \mathbf{EnvO}.$$

A moment's thought 9.5   Why is **EnvM** defined in this way, when we have static scope rules?

Every object name refers to a location. This location contains information about the variable bindings of the object, the name of the class that the object is an instance of and the bindings of its local objects in the form of an *object environment*. We do not need to store information about the methods of an object, since these methods are common to all objects that are instances of a given class.

Finally, we need to keep track of the next free location. Since both variable declarations and object declarations can cause new locations to be used, it is now more natural to keep this information in the store component than in any of the environments. We can then write e.g. $l = sto$ next to signify that l is the next free location.

Summing up, we have the following definitions.

$$\mathbf{EnvO} = \mathbf{Onames} \rightharpoonup \mathbf{Loc},$$
$$\mathbf{Sto} = \mathbf{Loc} \cup \{\text{next}\} \rightharpoonup \mathbf{EnvV} \times \mathbf{Cnames} \times \mathbf{EnvO} \cup \mathbb{Z} \cup \mathbf{Loc}.$$

In the rest of this section, we often write $\mathsf{env}_{\mathsf{VMO}}$ instead of a long triple (env_V, env_M, env_O) and use superscripts and dashes accordingly so that e.g. $\mathsf{env}_{\mathsf{VMO}}'$ stands for (env_V', env_M', env_O'). If we are considering only e.g. the pair (env_V, env_O) we write $\mathsf{env}_{\mathsf{VO}}$.

We keep track of classes by using a *class library*. A class library lib is a function which belongs to the set **Lib** defined by

$$\mathbf{Lib} = \mathbf{Cnames} \rightharpoonup \mathbf{DecV} \times \mathbf{DecM} \times \mathbf{DecO}$$

In other words, we associate with each class name its declarations of variables, methods and local objects.

9.3.3 Transition systems and transition rules

In this section we give the highlights of the semantics of **Coat**. The reader is encouraged to fill in the remaining rules.

$$[\text{CLASS}_{\text{BSS}}] \quad \frac{\text{env}_{\text{VMO}} \vdash \langle D_C, \text{lib}'' \rangle \rightarrow \text{lib}'}{\text{env}_{\text{VMO}} \vdash \langle \text{class } c \text{ is } D_V \, D_M \, D_O \text{ end}; D_C, \text{lib} \rangle \rightarrow \text{lib}'}$$

$$\text{where } \text{lib}'' = \text{lib}[c \mapsto (D_V, env_M, D_O, \text{env}_{\text{VMO}})]$$

$$[\text{NONE}_{\text{BSS}}] \quad \text{env}_{\text{VMO}} \vdash \langle \epsilon, \text{lib} \rangle \rightarrow \text{lib}$$

Table 9.8 *The semantics of class declarations*

Class declarations update the class library. Because of this, the transitions describing class declarations are of the form

$$env_V, env_M \vdash \langle D_C, \text{lib} \rangle \rightarrow \text{lib}'$$

and our transition system for class declarations is

$$(\mathbf{DecC} \times \mathbf{Lib} \cup \mathbf{Lib}, \rightarrow, \mathbf{Lib}),$$

where the transition relation is defined by the rules in Table 9.8.

Variable declarations are a little more complex, since these may have side effects. A simple variable declaration var $x := a$ updates the variable environment and the store, but we will also need to know the object declarations in order to evaluate a, since a may contain occurrences of extended variables. A method environment is not needed for the declaration itself, but we may need to pass it along when a variable declaration happens as part of the instantiated dynamically created object. We will discover why in our treatment of object expressions.

Consequently, transitions are of the form

$$\text{env}_{\text{VMO}} \vdash \langle D_V, env_V, sto \rangle \rightarrow (env_V', sto')$$

and our transition system for variable declarations is

$$(\mathbf{DecV} \times \mathbf{EnvV} \times \mathbf{Sto} \cup \mathbf{EnvV} \times \mathbf{Sto}, \rightarrow, \mathbf{EnvV} \times \mathbf{Sto}).$$

The transition rules are given in Table 9.9.

Method declarations update a method environment. For this reason, the transitions describing method declarations are of the form

$$\text{env}_{\text{VO}} \vdash \langle D_M, env_M \rangle \rightarrow env_M'$$

[VAR$_{BSS}$]
$$\frac{env_{VMO}, \text{lib} \vdash a \to v \qquad env_{VMO} \vdash \langle D_V, env_V'', sto'' \rangle \to (env_V', sto')}{env_{VMO} \vdash \langle \text{var } x := a; D_V, env_V, sto \rangle \to (env_V', sto')}$$

where $env_V'' = env_V[x \mapsto l]$
and $sto'' = sto[l \mapsto v][\text{next} \mapsto \text{new } l]$

[NONE$_{BSS}$] $\quad env_{VMO} \vdash \langle \epsilon, env_V, sto \rangle \to (env_V, sto)$

Table 9.9 *The semantics of variable declarations*

[NONE$_{BSS}$] $\qquad env_{VO} \vdash \langle \epsilon, env_M \rangle \to env_M$

[METHOD$_{BSS}$]
$$\frac{env_{VO} \vdash \langle D_M, env_M'' \rangle \to env_M'}{env_{VO} \vdash \langle \text{method } m \text{ is } S; D_M, env_M \rangle \to env_M'}$$

where $env_M'' = env_M[m \mapsto (S, env_V, env_M, env_O)]$

Table 9.10 *The semantics of method declarations*

and our transition system for method declarations is

$$(\textbf{DecM} \times \textbf{EnvM} \cup \textbf{EnvM}, \to, \textbf{EnvM}).$$

The transition rules are given in Table 9.10.

Object declarations have a semantics that involves creation of new objects, and transitions must be relative to the class library. Moreover, new locations will be used to store the objects that have been declared. Transitions are therefore of the form

$$\text{lib} \vdash \langle D_O, env_O, sto \rangle \to env_O', sto'$$

and the transition system is

$$(\textbf{DecO} \times \textbf{EnvO} \times \textbf{Sto} \cup \textbf{EnvO} \times \textbf{Sto}, \to, \textbf{EnvO} \times \textbf{Sto}).$$

The transition rules are shown in Table 9.11. The important rule here is [OBJECT$_{BSS}$]. Whenever an object o is declared, we first need to look up the contents of an object of class c in the class library. Then these declarations are performed, and a new location is added to the environment. In this

$[\text{NONE}_{\text{BSS}}]$ $\quad$ $\mathsf{lib} \vdash \langle \epsilon, env_O \rangle \to env_O$

$[\text{OBJECT}_{\text{BSS}}]$
$$env_O^1 \vdash \langle D_V, env_V^1, sto \rangle \to (env_V'', sto'')$$
$$env_V'', env_O^1 \vdash \langle D_M, env_M^1 \rangle \to env_M''$$
$$\mathsf{lib} \vdash \langle D_O^1, env_O^1, sto'' \rangle \to \langle env_O'', sto^{(3)} \rangle$$
$$\frac{\mathsf{lib} \vdash \langle D_O, env_O[o \mapsto l], sto^{(4)} \rangle \to \langle env_O', sto' \rangle}{\mathsf{lib} \vdash \langle \mathbf{object}\ o := \mathbf{new}\ c; D_O, env_O, sto \rangle \to (env_O', sto')}$$

$\quad$ where $\mathsf{lib}\,c = (D_V, D_M, D_O^1, \mathsf{env_{VMO}}^1)$

$\quad$ and $l = sto^{(3)}\,\mathsf{next}$

$\quad$ and $sto^{(4)} = sto^{(3)}[l \mapsto \mathsf{env_{VMO}}''][\mathsf{next} \mapsto \mathbf{new}\ l]$

Table 9.11 *The semantics of object declarations*

location we place the environments that we obtained by performing the declarations of local variables, methods and objects.

Object sequences are crucial, since these are the paths that tell us where to find methods and instance variables. The result of evaluating an object sequence is a triple of environments that describe the bindings that hold in the subobject which is found at the end of the path.

$\quad$ Therefore, we see that transitions are of the form

$$\mathsf{env_{VMO}}, sto \vdash O \to \mathsf{env_{VMO}}'$$

and the transition system is

$$(\mathbf{Oexp} \cup \mathbf{EnvV} \times \mathbf{EnvM} \times \mathbf{EnvO}, \to, \mathbf{EnvV} \times \mathbf{EnvM} \times \mathbf{EnvO}).$$

The transition rules are given in Table 9.12.

Object expressions The value of an object expression is the environment triple $\mathsf{env_{VMO}}$ that holds at the end of the object expression path together with a modified store.

$\quad$ Therefore transitions are of the form

$$\mathsf{env_{VMO}}, \mathsf{lib} \vdash \langle OE, sto \rangle \to (\mathsf{env_{VMO}}', sto')$$

and our transition system is

$$(\mathbf{Oexp} \times \mathbf{Sto} \cup \mathbf{Sto}, \to, \mathbf{Sto}).$$

[NONE-SEQ$_{\text{BSS}}$]	env$_{\text{VMO}}$, $sto \vdash \epsilon \rightarrow$ env$_{\text{VMO}}$

$$[\text{SOME-SEQ}_{\text{BSS}}] \quad \frac{\text{env}_{\text{VMO}}, sto \vdash O \rightarrow \text{env}_{\text{VMO}}''}{\text{env}_{\text{VMO}}, sto \vdash O.o \rightarrow \text{env}_{\text{VMO}}'}$$

$$\begin{aligned}
\text{where} \quad & env_O'' o = l \\
\text{and} \quad & sto\ l = \text{env}_{\text{VMO}}'
\end{aligned}$$

Table 9.12 *The semantics of object sequences*

The semantics of object expressions is given in Table 9.13.

The evaluation of an object expression can modify the store, since the object expression can start with a dynamically created object that will typically need to use new locations. To see this, consider the rule [NEW$_{\text{BSS}}$]. Here, the first premise $env_O^1 \vdash \langle D_V, env_V^1, sto \rangle \rightarrow (env_V'', sto')$ describes that the local declarations of the class are performed. The local variables will need to be bound to fresh locations.

Note that, for an object expression **new** $c.O$, the rule [SEQ-EXP$_{\text{BSS}}$] and then the rule [NONE-SEQ$_{\text{BSS}}$] from Table 9.12 will eventually be invoked to return an environment triple. Since we want to return all three components in our evaluation of an object expression, the env_M component will have to be present as an assumption in the semantics of object sequences, even though a method environment does not appear to be necessary when the rules for sequences are seen in isolation.

Arithmetic expressions have a big-step semantics which is almost as before. Transitions are of the form

$$\text{env}_{\text{VMO}}, \text{lib}, sto \vdash a \rightarrow v,$$

so the transition system is

$$(\mathbf{Aexp}, \rightarrow, \mathbb{Z}).$$

The notable modification is the rule for extended variables; here we may dynamically create an object and return the value of one of its instance variables. Therefore the evaluation must be relative to the class library lib. Note that any store modifications that may result from evaluating an extended variable of this kind are discarded in the conclusion of [EVAR$_{\text{BSS}}$]. This rule can be seen in Table 9.14.

A moment's thought 9.6 Why are the store modifications discarded?

[SEQ-EXP$_{\text{BSS}}$] $$\frac{\mathsf{env}_{\text{VMO}}, sto \vdash O \rightarrow \mathsf{env}_{\text{VMO}}'}{\mathsf{env}_{\text{VMO}}, \mathsf{lib} \vdash \langle O, sto \rangle \rightarrow (\mathsf{env}_{\text{VMO}}', sto')}$$

[NEW-EXP$_{\text{BSS}}$]
$$env_O^1 \vdash \langle D_V, env_V^1, sto \rangle \rightarrow (env_V'', sto')$$
$$env_V'', env_O^1 \vdash \langle D_M, env_M^1 \rangle \rightarrow env_M''$$
$$\mathsf{lib} \vdash \langle D_O, env_O, sto \rangle \rightarrow \langle env_O'', sto'' \rangle$$
$$\mathsf{env}_{\text{VMO}}'', \mathsf{lib}, sto'' \vdash O \rightarrow \mathsf{env}_{\text{VMO}}'$$
$$\overline{\mathsf{env}_{\text{VMO}}, \mathsf{lib} \vdash \langle \mathbf{new}\ c.O, sto \rangle \rightarrow (\mathsf{env}_{\text{VMO}}', sto')}$$

$$\text{where } \mathsf{lib}\, c = (D_V, D_M, D_O, \mathsf{env}_{\text{VMO}}{}^1)$$
$$\text{and } sto'' = sto'[l \mapsto \mathsf{env}_{\text{VMO}}']$$

Table 9.13 *The semantics of object expressions*

[EVAR$_{\text{BSS}}$] $$\frac{\mathsf{env}_{\text{VMO}}, \mathsf{lib} \vdash \langle OE, sto \rangle \rightarrow (\mathsf{env}_{\text{VMO}}', sto')}{\mathsf{env}_{\text{VMO}}, \mathsf{lib} \vdash \langle OE.x, sto \rangle \rightarrow v}$$

$$\text{where } env_V'\, x = l \text{ and } sto'\, l = v$$

Table 9.14 *Evaluating extended variables (in the semantics of arithmetic expressions)*

Problem 9.7 Complete the definition of the semantics of **Aexp**.

Problem 9.8 Give the definition of the semantics of **Bexp**.

Statements modify the store. The execution of a statement may need to consult the bindings of all forms, so transitions are of the form

$$\mathsf{env}_{\text{VMO}}, \mathsf{lib} \vdash \langle S, sto \rangle \rightarrow sto'.$$

Here, there are three interesting transition rules, which are the ones shown in Table 9.15.

The rule [CALL-METHOD$_{\text{BSS}}$] describes the behaviour of a method call call m. Here we first need to retrieve the body of the method which is referred to by the object path expression M. We do this by evaluating the prefix OE and then looking up m in the method environment that we got from the evaluation of OE. Finally, we can execute the body of method m using the environments known at declaration time.

$$\text{[CALL-METHOD}_{\text{BSS}}] \quad \frac{\begin{array}{c} \text{env}_{\text{VMO}}, \text{lib} \vdash \langle OE, sto \rangle \to (\text{env}_{\text{VMO}}{}', sto'') \\ \text{env}_{\text{VMO}}{}'', \text{lib} \vdash \langle S, sto'' \rangle \to sto' \end{array}}{\text{env}_{\text{VMO}}, \text{lib} \vdash \langle \text{call } M, sto \rangle \to sto'}$$

where $M = OE.m$
and $env'_M\, m = (S, \text{env}_{\text{VMO}}{}'')$

$$\text{[VAR-ASSIGN}_{\text{BSS}}] \quad \frac{\begin{array}{c} \text{env}_{\text{VMO}}, \text{lib} \vdash \langle O, sto \rangle \to (\text{env}_{\text{VMO}}{}'', sto') \\ \text{env}_{\text{VMO}}, \text{lib} \vdash \langle a, sto' \rangle \to v \end{array}}{\text{env}_{\text{VMO}}, \text{lib} \vdash \langle X := a, sto \rangle \to sto'[l \mapsto v]}$$

where $X = O.x$
and $env''_V\, x = l$
and $sto'\, l = v$

$$\text{[OBJ-ASSIGN}_{\text{BSS}}] \quad \frac{\begin{array}{c} env^1_O[\text{next} \mapsto \text{new}l'][\vdash \langle D_V, env^1_V, sto \rangle \to (env''_V, sto'') \\ env''_V, env^1_O \vdash \langle D_M, env^1_M \rangle \to env''_M \\ \text{env}_{\text{VMO}}{}^1, \text{lib} \vdash \langle D_O, env_O, sto \rangle \to \langle env''_O, sto'' \rangle \end{array}}{\text{env}_{\text{VMO}}, \text{lib} \vdash \langle o := \text{new } c, sto \rangle \to sto'}$$

where $\text{lib}\, c = (D_V, D_M, D_O, \text{env}_{\text{VMO}}{}^1)$
and $sto' = sto''[l \mapsto \text{env}_{\text{VMO}}{}'']$
and $l = env_O\, o$

Table 9.15 Important transition rules for statements

A moment's thought 9.9 Many object-oriented languages allow an object to call any of its own methods. Why is this not possible in the semantics given here?

The rule [VAR-ASSIGN$_{\text{BSS}}$] requires us to first find the location referred to by the extended variable X. This is similar to what we have just described; the main difference is that the extended variable cannot start with a dynamically created object, since this would not make sense.

In the rule [OBJ-ASSIGN$_{\text{BSS}}$] we first look up the information about the class c, namely the initial environments env^1_V and env^1_O known when c was declared and the declarations D_V, D_M and D_O that must be made in any object instance. We then perform these declarations; note that the next-pointer must be updated to point to the next free location at the time of the assignment.

Finally, we look up the location l of the object named o and store the results of the declaration in this location.

Again, note that the store modification that may be the result of performing the declarations will *not* be discarded but carries over. This is the case, since a store modification will have to take place if a new object is generated and this new object contains local variables.

Problem 9.10   Find the remaining transition rules in the semantics of **Stm**.

Programs are easily described, given what we now have. Transitions are of the form

$$\text{env}_{\text{VMO}}, \text{lib} \vdash \langle P, sto \rangle \rightarrow sto'$$

and the transition system is

$$(\mathbf{Prog} \times \mathbf{Sto} \cup \mathbf{Sto}, \rightarrow, \mathbf{Sto}).$$

The transition rule [PROGRAM$_{\text{BSS}}$] defining the transition relation is given in Table 9.16.

$$[\text{PROGRAM}_{\text{BSS}}] \quad \frac{\begin{array}{l} env_O^0 \vdash \langle D_V, env_V^0, sto \rangle \rightarrow (env_V, sto^{(1)}) \\ env_V, env_M^0, env_O^0 \vdash \langle D_C, \text{lib}^0 \rangle \rightarrow \text{lib} \\ env_V, env_M^0, env_O^0, \text{lib} \vdash \langle D_O, sto^{(1)} \rangle \rightarrow (env_O, sto^{(2)}) \\ env_V, env_M^0, env_O \vdash \langle S, sto^{(2)} \rangle \rightarrow sto' \end{array}}{\text{env}_{\text{VMO}}, \text{lib} \vdash \langle D_V \; D_C \; D_O \; S, sto \rangle \rightarrow sto'}$$

Table 9.16 *Transition rule for programs*

The rule has four premises that describe the following.

1. First, we declare the global variables found in D_V using the empty variable environment as the initial environment.
2. Then, we declare the classes from the empty class library using the global variable bindings and empty method and object environments.
3. Then, we declare the global objects found in D_O using the global variable bindings and the newly found class library. The method environment must be empty, since there are no global methods.
4. Finally, we execute the statement S with the bindings that we now have.

Problem 9.11 Extend the syntax of **Coat** with the object expression self. The intended interpretation of a method call `call self` m occurring in the body of a method is that the method named m within the same object is invoked. Modify the semantics such that all methods within an object are able to call each other in this way.

10

Blocks and procedures (2)

In Chapter 6 we saw a big-step semantics of the language **Bip**, which extends **Bims** with blocks and procedures. In this chapter we present a small-step semantics of **Bip**. This semantics extends that of **Bims** given in Section 4.3, more precisely the small-step semantics of statements given in Table 4.4. Again, we shall consider how the various choices of scope rules can be captured.

10.1 Run-time stacks

As before, we shall assume the environment-store model introduced in Section 6.2. The set of variable environments is given by

$$\mathbf{EnvV} = \mathbf{Var} \cup \{\text{next}\} \rightharpoonup \mathbf{Loc}.$$

The set of stores is defined by

$$\mathbf{Sto} = \mathbf{Loc} \rightharpoonup \mathbb{Z}.$$

As in Chapter 6 the definion of procedure environments will depend on our choice of scope rules. We shall return to this later.

An important change is due to the fact that configurations in a small-step semantics represent intermediate stages in the execution of a statement.

Where transitions in the big-step semantics of Chapter 6 were of the form

$$env_V, env_P \vdash \langle S, sto \rangle \rightarrow sto'$$

and where a transition described the execution of an entire statement, we must now describe the individual execution steps. A single step may be a procedure call or the beginning of a block and may therefore involve new, temporary bindings. In other words, transitions should now have the form

$$\langle S, \text{bindings} \rangle \Rightarrow \langle S', \text{new bindings} \rangle.$$

This will then require us to keep track of the bindings that are currently in effect. We achieve this by introducing a notion of *run-time stack*. The run-time stack $envl$ is a list of pairs (env_V, env_P), i.e. $envl$ is an element of the set of run-time stacks **Envl**:

$$\mathbf{Envl} = (\mathbf{EnvV} \times \mathbf{EnvP})^*;$$

$(\mathbf{EnvV} \times \mathbf{EnvP})^*$ here denotes the set of all lists whose elements belong to the set $\mathbf{EnvV} \times \mathbf{EnvP}$.

The top element of a run-time stack is the pair (env_V, env_P) which is currently in effect. Whenever a new scope is entered, i.e. whenever we enter a block or call procedure, we push a new pair (env_V', env_P') on top of the run-time stack. Such a pair corresponds closely to the notion of *activation record* used in compiler construction. We indicate that the top of the run-time stack $envl$ is (env_V, env_P) by writing $envl = (env_V, env_P) : envl'$ for some $envl'$.

10.2 Declarations

The semantics of variable and procedure declarations will be that of the big-step semantics of Chapter 6. This is the sensible choice, since a declaration should be thought of as an indivisible action performed in a single step – when the declaration is executed, we allocate storage to all variables mentioned and note the address of the code of the procedure bodies.

Note that the transition relation is defined for simple variable environments, i.e. not for run-time stacks. This will suffice, since the semantics of declarations is invoked only whenever a block is entered and is then invoked only in order to create a new, updated environment to be placed on top of the run-time stack. In other words, we can simply reuse the definitions found in Section 6.4.

10.3 Statements

As always, in a small-step semantics a configuration is an instantaneous description of the program that contains information about the part of the program which remains to be executed as well as information on the bindings that are in effect.

10.3.1 Evaluation contexts

Since we are now considering run-time stacks, we need to indicate the *active part* of the program, i.e. the part of the program that uses the bindings which are on top of the run-time stack. If S is the active part, we denote this by encapsulating it as `active` S `end`. We call this an *evaluation context*.

Our abstract syntax will now include the syntactic category **EvCxt** of evaluation contexts, and we let C range over the set of evaluation contexts. The formation rules are now

$$C ::= \texttt{active } C \texttt{ end} \mid x := a \mid \texttt{skip} \mid C_1; C_2 \mid$$
$$\texttt{if } b \texttt{ then } C_1 \texttt{ else } C_2 \mid \texttt{while } b \texttt{ do } C \mid$$
$$\texttt{begin } D_V \ D_P \ C \texttt{ end} \mid \texttt{call } p$$
$$D_V ::= \texttt{var } x := a; D_V \mid \epsilon$$
$$D_P ::= \texttt{proc } p \texttt{ is } C; D_P \mid \epsilon$$

In our semantics of statements, the configurations are

- $\langle C, sto, envl \rangle$, which are intermediate configurations; C is a statement that may contain `active`-encapsulations
- $(sto, envl)$, which are terminal configurations.

Our transition system now becomes

$$((\mathbf{EvCxt} \times \mathbf{Sto}) \cup (\mathbf{Sto} \times \mathbf{Envl}), \Rightarrow, \mathbf{Sto} \times \mathbf{Envl})$$

and transitions are of the form

$$\langle C, sto, envl \rangle \Rightarrow (sto', envl');$$

$\Rightarrow$ is actually a transition relation relating configurations containing evaluation contexts. However, this also tells us of the behaviour of statements, since a statement is simply an evaluation context devoid of `active`-encapsulations.

10.3.2 Transition rules for statements

The transition rules for procedure calls depend on our choice of scope rules. All other rules defining $\Rightarrow$ are independent of our choice of scope rules and can be found in Table 10.1.

A moment's thought 10.1 Why are the rules for procedure calls the only transition rules in the semantics for statements that depend on the choice of scope rules?

[ASS$_{\text{SSS}}$]	$\langle x := a, sto, envl \rangle \Rightarrow (sto[l \mapsto v], envl)$ where $envl = (env_V, env_P) : envl'$ and $l = env_V\ x$ and $env_V, sto \vdash a \rightarrow_a v$
[SKIP$_{\text{SSS}}$]	$\langle \textbf{skip}, sto, envl \rangle \Rightarrow (sto, envl)$

[COMP-1$_{\text{SSS}}$]
$$\frac{\langle C_1, sto, envl \rangle \Rightarrow \langle C_1', sto', envl' \rangle}{\langle C_1; C_2, sto, envl \rangle \Rightarrow \langle C_1'; C_2, sto', envl' \rangle}$$

[COMP-2$_{\text{SSS}}$]
$$\frac{\langle C_1, sto, envl \rangle \Rightarrow (sto', envl')}{\langle C_1; C_2, sto, envl \rangle \Rightarrow \langle C_2, sto', envl' \rangle}$$

[IF-TRUE$_{\text{SSS}}$]	$\langle \textbf{if } b \textbf{ then } C_1 \textbf{ else } C_2\ sto, envl \rangle \Rightarrow \langle C_1, sto, envl \rangle$ if $env_V, sto \vdash b \rightarrow_b \textit{tt}$ where $envl = (env_V, env_P) : envl'$
[IF-FALSE$_{\text{SSS}}$]	$\langle \textbf{if } b \textbf{ then } C_1 \textbf{ else } C_2\ sto, envl \rangle \Rightarrow \langle C_2, sto, envl \rangle$ if $env_V, sto \vdash b \rightarrow_b \textit{ff}$ where $envl = (env_V, env_P) : envl'$
[WHILE$_{\text{SSS}}$]	$\langle \textbf{while } b \textbf{ do } C, sto, envl \rangle \Rightarrow$ $\quad\quad\quad \langle \textbf{if } b \textbf{ then } (C; \textbf{while } b \textbf{ do } C) \textbf{ else skip}, sto, envl \rangle$

[BLOCK-1$_{\text{SSS}}$]
$$\frac{\langle D_V, env_V, sto \rangle \rightarrow_D (sto', env_V')\quad env_V' \vdash \langle D_P, env_P \rangle \rightarrow_{DP} env_P'}{\langle \textbf{begin } D_V\ D_P\ C \textbf{ end}, sto, envl \rangle \Rightarrow \langle \textbf{active } C \textbf{ end}, sto', envl' \rangle}$$

where $\quad envl' = (env_V', env_P') : envl$
and $\quad\ envl = (env_V, env_P) : envl''$

[BLOCK-2$_{\text{SSS}}$]
$$\frac{\langle C, sto, envl \rangle \Rightarrow \langle C', sto', envl' \rangle}{\langle \textbf{active } C \textbf{ end}, sto, envl \rangle \Rightarrow \langle \textbf{active } C' \textbf{ end}, sto', envl' \rangle}$$

[BLOCK-3$_{\text{SSS}}$]
$$\frac{\langle C, sto, envl \rangle \Rightarrow (sto', (env_V, env_P) : envl')}{\langle \textbf{active } C \textbf{ end}, sto, envl \rangle \Rightarrow (sto', envl')}$$

Table 10.1 *Transition rules for statements other than procedure calls*

The rules that come from the **Bims** small-step semantics are only slightly modified from those of Table 4.4. The modification amounts to the change that the evaluation of Boolean and arithmetic expressions must now be made relative to the variable environment found *on top of the run-time stack* (cf. the side condition of these rules).

Transition rules for blocks

There are three rules that together describe the behaviour of a block. The rule [BLOCK-1$_{SSS}$] describes what happens when a block is entered: we declare variables and procedures, place the updated environments on top of the run-time stack and place the body of the block in an `active`-encapsulation. The two other rules for blocks describe the behaviour of an evaluation context. [BLOCK-2$_{SSS}$] expresses that an evaluation context performs a step by performing a step of its content, and [BLOCK-3$_{SSS}$] describes what will happen when the execution of a block ends. Since the block has now terminated, the topmost environment-pair must be removed from the run-time stack.

Procedure calls

The semantics of procedure calls depends on our choice of scope rules, that is, on which variable and procedure bindings we assume during the execution of a procedure body. We here limit ourselves to the two most common choices:

- Static scope rules for variables and procedures
- Dynamic scope rules for variables and procedures

In the case of *static scope rules for variables and procedures*, the procedure environment must hold information about the variable and procedure bindings known at the time of declaration for each procedure. This then means that our set of procedure environments is given by (6.5):

$$\mathbf{EnvP} = \mathbf{Pnames} \rightharpoonup \mathbf{Stm} \times \mathbf{EnvV} \times \mathbf{EnvP}.$$

When we call a procedure p, the run-time stack must be updated with the bindings that were in effect when p was declared.

Whenever a procedure is called, the body of the procedure and the associated declaration-time environments must be retrieved. This is done by a lookup in the procedure environment which is found at the top of the run-time stack. We place the declaration-time environments on top of the run-time stack and encapsulate the procedure body.

As always, there are two rules for procedure calls – one allowing for recursive calls and another which does not allow for recursive calls. If we *call a procedure that allows for recursive calls*, we must also add a binding which makes the procedure aware of its own presence (cf. Section 7.3).

The transition rules are given in Table 10.2.

[CALL$_{SSS}$] $\langle$call $p, sto, envl \rangle \Rightarrow \langle$active C end$, sto, (env'_V, env'_P) : envl \rangle$

where $env_P\ p = (C, env'_V, env'_P)$
and $envl = (env_V, env_P) : envl'$

[CALL-REC$_{SSS}$] $\langle$call $p, sto, envl \rangle \Rightarrow$
    $\langle$active C end$, sto, (env'_V, env'_P [p \mapsto (C, env'_V, env'_P)]) : envl \rangle$

where $env_P\ p = (C, env'_V, env'_P)$
and $envl = (env_V, env_P) : envl'$

Table 10.2 *Transition rules for procedure calls assuming static scope rules*

In the case of *dynamic scope rules for variables and procedures* the procedure environments need only contain information about the body of each procedure. The set of procedure environments is therefore again given by (6.2):

$$\mathbf{EnvP} = \mathbf{Pnames} \rightharpoonup \mathbf{Stm}.$$

Here, the run-time stack *does not* need to be updated when a procedure is called, since no new bindings are introduced. We do not even need to place the procedure body inside an evaluation context. The transition rule is given in Table 10.3.

A moment's thought 10.2   Why is it not necessary to place the body of the procedure inside an evaluation context, if we assume dynamic scope rules?

Moreover, when we assume dynamic scope rules for variables and procedures, there is no need for a special rule that allows recursive calls. Because of our choice of scope rules. any call of p within the body of p is seen as a recursive call of p itself.

A moment's thought 10.3   Why is this the case?

Problem 10.4   Give transition rules that capture the 'mixed' scope rules found in Chapter 6.

A moment's thought 10.5   Which theorem would you expect to hold for the small-step semantics presented in this chapter and the big-step semantics of Chapter 6?

[CALL$_{\text{SSS}}$] $\langle \text{call } p, sto, envl \rangle \Rightarrow \langle C \ sto, envl \rangle$

where $env_P \ p = C$

Table 10.3 *Transition rule for procedure calls assuming dynamic scope rules*

11

Concurrent object-oriented languages

In this chapter we shall consider a tiny object-oriented language, **Cola**,[1] inspired by Emerald (Hutchinson *et al.*, 1987) In **Cola** , objects are executed concurrently and an object o_1 can communicate with another object o_2 by calling a method found in o_2. This is known as a *remote procedure call*.

Our semantics is a small-step semantics combining ideas from Chapters 8 and 10.

11.1 The language Cola

We make the following simplifying assumptions about **Cola**:

- Objects are 'orphans' – there is no notion of class
- Objects do not contain subobjects
- Methods have no parameters
- Methods do not contain local methods.

Moreover, we shall assume static scope rules for objects, so that any method in an object o knows only of the variables and methods found within o.

11.1.1 Abstract syntax

The abstract syntax of **Cola** extends that of **Bims**. We have the following syntactic categories and associated metavariables:

$D_O \in \textbf{DecO}$ – Object declarations
$D_M \in \textbf{DecM}$ – Method declarations
$D_V \in \textbf{DecV}$ – Variable declarations

---

[1] Concurrent object-oriented language.

$o \in \mathbf{Onames}$ – Object names
$m \in \mathbf{Mnames}$ – Method names
$x \in \mathbf{Var}$ – Variables
$S \in \mathbf{Stm}$ – Statements
$a \in \mathbf{Aexp}$ – Arithmetic expressions
$b \in \mathbf{Bexp}$ – Boolean expressions

and the formation rules are

$$D_O ::= \texttt{object } o \texttt{ is } D_M; S \texttt{ end}; D_O \mid \epsilon$$
$$D_V ::= \texttt{var } x := a; D_V \mid \epsilon$$
$$D_M ::= \texttt{method } m \texttt{ is } D_V; S; D_M \mid \epsilon$$
$$S ::= x := a \mid \texttt{skip} \mid S_1; S_2 \mid \texttt{if } b \texttt{ then } S_1 \texttt{ else } S_2 \mid$$
$$\texttt{while } b \texttt{ do } S \mid \texttt{begin } D_V \; S \texttt{ end} \mid o?m \mid o!m \mid$$
$$\texttt{active } S \texttt{ end} \mid \texttt{serve } o \; S \texttt{ end} \mid \texttt{wait } o \texttt{ end}$$

The two new statements are $o?m$ and $o!m$; as can be seen from the chosen notation, these statements are related to the communication primitives described in Chapter 8. The statement $o?m$ is a *remote procedure call*, i.e. a request for calling the method m found in object o. The statement $o!m$ permits another object o to call method m in object o. (We shall explain these statements in more detail later.)

In our semantics, we need to have three evaluation contexts – $\texttt{active } S \texttt{ end}$ appears when a local block is executed, $\texttt{serve } o \; S \texttt{ end}$ appears when a method called by object o is executed, and $\texttt{wait } o \texttt{ end}$ appears when we wait for the object o to complete its execution of a method whose service we have requested. The latter two evaluation contexts always appear together, as we shall see later.

11.1.2 Rendezvous with Cola

As the formation rules of the abstract syntax indicate, a **Cola** program consists of a sequence of object declarations. Each object contains a sequence of method declarations and a body, which is a statement. The execution of the program consists of the concurrent execution of the objects that have been declared.

The execution of an object amounts to executing its body. The body may contain requests for methods found in other objects.

Let us consider the situation where object o_1 requests the use of method m found in object o_2. As we have seen, we express this by the statement

$o_2?m$. The method m can be executed only once this is allowed by o_2, i.e. when the statement $o_1!m$ is executed. When both objects are ready, the remote procedure call can proceed. This is the **Cola** version of a *rendezvous* (see Chapter 8). The body of m is executed and upon completion – and only then – o_1 and o_2 complete the rendezvous and continue.

11.2 A small-step semantics of concurrent behaviour

As in Chapter 8, we describe concurrent behaviour as *interleaving*, i.e. the parallel components take turns performing individual computation steps. Conceptually, we can think of the parallel components as sharing access to a single processor.

Again, our semantics is nondeterministic in that it does not describe how to schedule this access; a description of the scheduling is left to the actual implementation.

11.2.1 Environments

Like the small-step semantics for **Bip** in Chapter 10, the semantics of **Cola** will utilize the notion of run-time stacks in order to describe the bindings that are in effect at any given point during execution. Again, we shall use the environment-store model introduced in Chapter 6.

Moreover, we shall need to introduce *method environments* in order to describe method bindings. Method environments are very similar to the procedure environments of Chapter 6; the set of method environments is given by

$$\mathbf{EnvM} = \mathbf{Mnames} \rightharpoonup \mathbf{Stm} \times \mathbf{EnvV}.$$

Since we do not allow method declarations within methods, a run-time stack is simply a list of variable environments, i.e. a run-time stack *envl* is an element of

$$\mathbf{Envl} = \mathbf{EnvV}^*.$$

The top element is the variable environment which is currently in effect. We write $envl = env_V : envl'$ to denote that the run-time stack *envl* has env_V as its top element.

11.3 Transition systems

In the operational semantics of **Cola** we need three transition systems to describe the behaviour of objects.

- A local transition system $(\Gamma_l, \Rightarrow_l, T_l)$ describing local behaviour
- A labelled transition system $(\Gamma_c, \{ \overset{a}{\Longrightarrow} \mid a \in A \}, T_c)$ describing the communication capabilities of an object. The label set A is defined as

$$A = \textbf{Onames} \times \textbf{Onames} \times \textbf{Mnames} \times \{?, !\}$$

- A global transition system $(\Gamma_g, \Rightarrow_g, T_g)$ describing global behaviour. This is done by referring to transitions from the other two transition systems.

Moreover, we need to describe the semantics of declarations.

11.3.1 Declarations

Since a statement may contain local declarations, we also need to give an account of the semantics of declarations. As in the semantics of **Bip** we give a big-step semantics of variable declarations, and again it suffices to consider how a single variable environment gets modified by a declaration. We leave the details of the semantics as an exercise for the reader.

Problem 11.1   Define the transition rules for variable declarations.

11.3.2 The local transition system

The local transition system describes the behaviour of a single object. It is of the form $(\Gamma_l, \Rightarrow_l)$.

An intermediate configuration is an instantaneous description of an object, i.e. the statements yet to be executed by the object, its store and its run-time stack. A terminal configuration describes the result of executing the object, i.e. a run-time stack and a store. Consequently

$$\Gamma_l = (\textbf{Stm} \times \textbf{Sto} \times \textbf{Envl}) \cup (\textbf{Sto} \times \textbf{Envl}).$$

The transition rules defining $\Rightarrow_l$ are essentially those of the small-step of **Bims**. See Table 11.1.

11.3.3 The labelled transition system

We describe the communication between objects using the labelled transition system $(\Gamma_c, A_c, \{ \overset{a}{\Longrightarrow} \mid a \in A_c \})$. Its set of configurations Γ_c is simply the set of pairs of statements and object names,

$$\Gamma_c = (\textbf{Stm} \cup \{\epsilon\}) \times \textbf{Onames}.$$

[ASS$_{\text{LOCAL-SSS}}$]	$\langle x := a, sto, envl \rangle \Rightarrow_l (sto[l \mapsto v], envl)$ where $envl = env_V : envl'$, $l = env_V\ x$ and $env_V, sto \vdash a \rightarrow_a v$
[SKIP$_{\text{LOCAL-SSS}}$]	$\langle \textbf{skip}, sto, envl \rangle \Rightarrow_l (sto, envl)$
[COMP-1$_{\text{LOCAL-SSS}}$]	$\dfrac{\langle S_1, sto, envl \rangle \Rightarrow_l \langle S_1', sto', envl' \rangle}{\langle S_1; S_2, sto, envl \rangle \Rightarrow_l \langle S_1'; S_2, sto', envl' \rangle}$
[COMP-2$_{\text{LOCAL-SSS}}$]	$\dfrac{\langle S_1, sto, envl \rangle \Rightarrow_l (sto', envl')}{\langle S_1; S_2, sto, envl \rangle \Rightarrow_l \langle S_2, sto', envl' \rangle}$
[IF-TRUE$_{\text{LOCAL-SSS}}$]	$\langle \textbf{if } b \textbf{ then } S_1 \textbf{ else } S_2\ sto, envl \rangle \Rightarrow_l \langle S_1, sto, envl \rangle$ if $env_V, sto \vdash b \rightarrow_b tt$ where $envl = env_V : envl'$
[IF-FALSE$_{\text{LOKAL-SSS}}$]	$\langle \textbf{if } b \textbf{ then } S_1 \textbf{ else } S_2\ sto, envl \rangle \Rightarrow_l \langle S_2, sto, envl \rangle$ if $env_V, sto \vdash b \rightarrow_b ff$ where $envl = env_V : envl'$
[WHILE$_{\text{LOCAL-SSS}}$]	$\langle \textbf{while } b \textbf{ do } S, sto, envl \rangle \Rightarrow_l$ $\quad \langle \textbf{if } b \textbf{ then } (S; \textbf{while } b \textbf{ do } S) \textbf{ else skip}, sto, envl \rangle$
[BLOCK-1$_{\text{LOCAL-SSS}}$]	$\dfrac{\langle D_V, env_V, sto \rangle \rightarrow_D (sto', env_V') }{\langle \textbf{begin } D_V; S \textbf{ end}, sto, envl \rangle \Rightarrow_l \langle \textbf{active } S \textbf{ end}, sto', envl' \rangle}$ where $envl' = env_V' : envl$ and $envl = env_V : envl''$
[BLOCK-2$_{\text{LOCAL-SSS}}$]	$\dfrac{\langle S, sto, envl \rangle \Rightarrow_l \langle S', sto', envl' \rangle}{\langle \textbf{active } S \textbf{ end}, sto, envl \rangle \Rightarrow_l \langle \textbf{active } S' \textbf{ end}, sto', envl' \rangle}$
[BLOCK-3$_{\text{LOCAL-SSS}}$]	$\dfrac{\langle S, sto, envl \rangle \Rightarrow_l (sto', env_V : envl')}{\langle \textbf{active } S \textbf{ end}, sto, envl \rangle \Rightarrow_l (sto', envl')}$

Table 11.1 *Transition rules for the local transition system*

The labels on transitions describe communication capabilities: who wants to communicate, which method is involved, and to which object the method belongs and whether we are dealing with a request or a permission.

$$[\text{CALL}_C] \qquad \langle o_1?m, o_2 \rangle \xrightarrow{o_2, o_1, m, ?} \langle \epsilon, o_2 \rangle$$

$$[\text{ACCEPT}_C] \qquad \langle o_1!m, o_2 \rangle \xrightarrow{o_1, o_2, m, !} \langle \epsilon, o_2 \rangle$$

$$[\text{COMP}_C] \qquad \frac{\langle S_1, o_1 \rangle \xrightarrow{o_2, o_1, m, d} \langle S_1', o_1 \rangle}{\langle S_1; S_2, o_1 \rangle \xrightarrow{o_2, o_1, m, d} \langle S_1'; S_2, o_1 \rangle} \qquad \text{where } d \in \{?, !\}$$

Table 11.2 *Transition rules of the labelled transition systems*

Consequently, a label is a triple (o_1, o_2, d), where o_1 and o_2 are object names and $d \in \{?, !\}$ is a direction,

$$A_c = \textbf{Onames} \times \textbf{Onames} \times \textbf{Mnames} \times \{?, !\}.$$

The transition

$$< S, o_1 > \xrightarrow{o_1, o_2, m, ?} < S', o_1 >$$

should be read as follows. Object o_1 requests use of the method m found in object o_2. The transition

$$< S, o_1 > \xrightarrow{o_1, o_2, m, !} < S', o_1 >$$

should be read as follows: Object o_1 is allowed to use the method m found in object o_2.

Most of the rules defining the labelled transition relation can be found in Table 11.2.

Problem 11.2 The only rule missing from Table 11.2 is the rule for evaluation contexts. Define it. For which evaluation contexts do we need a rule?

Problem 11.3 Why are there no rules for e.g. if- and while-statements in Table 11.2 ?

11.3.4 *The global transition system*

The global transition system is of the form $(\Gamma_g, \Rightarrow)$. The set Γ_g contains three kinds of configurations:

- The initial configurations are object declarations

[START$_G$] $D_O \Rightarrow_g (\mathcal{S}(D_O), sto_\emptyset)$

where

$\mathcal{S}(\epsilon) = \emptyset$
$\mathcal{S}(\text{object } o \text{ is } D_M; S \text{ end}; D_O) =$
$\qquad \{|\langle S, envl_\emptyset, upd_M(D_M, env_M^\emptyset), o\rangle|\} \cup \mathcal{S}(D_O)$

Table 11.3 *Transition rules for the global level (1) – initialization*

- Intermediate configurations are instantaneous descriptions comprised of a set of configurations corresponding to the parallel components and a store, shared by all objects.
- The terminal configurations are stores, because the result of running a program will be a modified store.

Thus[2]

$$\Gamma_g = \mathbf{DecO} \cup (\mathcal{P}(\mathbf{Stm} \times \mathbf{Envl} \times \mathbf{EnvM} \times \mathbf{Onames}) \times \mathbf{Sto})$$

Notice that the intermediate configurations contain a subconfiguration for each object present, but that these subconfigurations are *not* the configurations found in Γ_l for they do not contain an element of **Sto**, since the store is now treated as a global component.

The transition rules fall into three categories.

Table 11.3 describes how the 'solution' containing parallel objects is created. Here, we use an auxiliary function $\mathcal{S}$ that creates the solution by traversing the list of object declarations.

$env_M^\emptyset$ denotes the empty method environment, $envl_\emptyset$ denotes the empty run-time stack and $sto_\emptyset$ denotes the empty store.

Problem 11.4 (Important) upd_M in Table 11.3 is an auxiliary function for updating method environments. Find its domain and range and give a formal definition of it; you will need to define a similar function that extracts a variable environment from the variable declaration local to a method.

The other rules describe the behaviour of a program following initialization. First we need to describe that an object acting on its own will cause a change to the 'solution' (expressed in [LOCAL1$_G$]). This is where interleaving

---

[2] Remember that, if M is a set, then $\mathcal{P}(M)$ denotes the *power set* of M, cf. Section 2.4.3

$$[\text{LOCAL1}_\text{G}] \quad \frac{\langle S_1, envl_1, sto\rangle \Rightarrow_g \langle S_1', envl_1', sto'\rangle}{(\{|\langle S_1, envl_1, env_M^l, o_1\rangle, \cdots|\}, sto) \Rightarrow_g}$$
$$(\{|\langle S_1', envl_1', env_M^l, o_1\rangle, \cdots|\}, sto')$$

$$[\text{LOCAL2}_\text{G}] \quad \frac{\langle S_1, envl, sto\rangle \Rightarrow_g \langle envl, sto'\rangle}{(\{|\langle S_1, envl_1, env_M^l, o_1\rangle \cdots|\}, sto) \Rightarrow_g (\{|\cdots|\}, sto')}$$

Table 11.4 *Transition rules for the global level (2) – the connection between global and local behaviour*

shows up in our semantics in the form of *nondeterminism*; if more than one object is able to proceed, any one of them will be able to do so.

We also need a rule which expresses that terminated objects disappear; this is the rule [LOCAL2$_\text{G}$].

The remaining rules describe how remote procedure calls affect the 'solution'; they are to be found in Tables 11.4 and 11.5.

Taken together, the rules describe that a rendezvous is possible if two objects agree on it. This is captured using the labelled transitions.

A rendezvous starts when the calling object waits for the method to become available; this is the content of [BONJOUR$_\text{GLOBAL-SSS}$]. The calling object is encapsulated and the object containing method m starts executing the body of m inside an evaluation context.

Notice how this resembles the rule [CALL$_\text{SSS}$] for procedure calls in Table 10.1 in Chapter 10. Also note that the evaluation contexts carry the name of the other object involved in the rendezvous so that we can determine when the rendezvous is supposed to finish.

[MAINTENANT$_\text{GLOBAL-SSS}$] describes the behaviour of an evaluation context. Finally, the rule [AU REVOIR$_\text{GLOBAL-SSS}$] expresses that the run-time stack has its top element removed and that the encapsulation of the evaluation context disappears as soon as the method call is over. It is in this rule that we see the importance of evaluation contexts containing the names of both objects involved in the remote call.

Problem 11.5 We can introduce a simple notion of class into **Cola** and thereby get the language **Ble++** (similar to **Coat** of Chapter 9). Let us introduce two new syntactic categories:

[BONJOURGLOBAL-SSS]

$$\frac{\langle S_1, o_1 \rangle \xrightarrow{o1,o2.m.?} \langle S_1', o_1 \rangle \quad \langle S_2, o_2 \rangle \xrightarrow{o2,o1,m.!} \langle S_2', o_2 \rangle}{(\{|\langle S_1, envl_1, envl_M^1, o_1 \rangle, \langle S_2, envl_2, envl_M^2, o_2 \rangle|\}, sto) \Rightarrow_g}$$
$$(\{|\langle S_1', envl_1, envl_M^1, o_1 \rangle, \langle \text{serve } o_1 \; S \text{ end}; S_2', envl_2', envl_M^2, o_2 \rangle \cdots |\}, sto)$$

where $envl_M^1 \, m = (S_1, env_v)$
and $envl_2' = env_v : envl_2$

[MAINTENANTGLOBAL-SSS]

$$\frac{\langle S_1, envl_1, sto \rangle \Rightarrow \langle S_1', envl_1', sto' \rangle}{(\{|\langle \text{serve } o_2 \; S_1 \text{ end}; S, envl_1, envl_M^1, o_1 \rangle, \cdots |\}, sto) \Rightarrow_g}$$
$$(\{|\langle \text{serve } o_2 \; S_1' \text{ end}; S, envl_1', envl_M^1, o_1 \rangle, \cdots |\}, sto')$$

[AU REVOIRGLOBAL-SSS]

$$\frac{\langle S_1, envl, sto \rangle \Rightarrow_g \langle envl, sto' \rangle}{(\{|\langle \text{serve } o_2 \; S_1 \text{ end}; S, envl_1, envl_M^1, o_1 \rangle, \langle \text{wait } o_1 \; S_2, envl_2, envl_M^2, o_2 \rangle \cdots |\}, sto) \Rightarrow_g}$$
$$(\{|\langle S, envl_1', envl_M^1, o_1 \rangle, \langle S_2, envl_2, envl_M^2, o_2 \rangle \cdots |\}, sto')$$

where $envl_1 = envl_1'$

Table 11.5 *Transition rules for the global level (3) – rendezvous*

$P \in \textbf{Prog}$ – Programs
$D_C \in \textbf{DecC}$ – Class declarations

and we now get

$$P ::= D_V \; D_C \; D_O \; S$$
$$D_C ::= \texttt{class } c \texttt{ is } D_M; S \texttt{ end}; D_C \mid \epsilon$$
$$D_O ::= o : c; D_O \mid \epsilon$$

– the rest is as before. A program now consists of a sequence of declarations of global variables, followed by a sequence of class declarations, a sequence of declarations of instances of these classes and a final statement. Define a small-step operational semantics of **Ble++** by augmenting the semantics of **Cola**. *Hint:* A 'molecule' should now contain not a method environment but the name of the class that the object molecule is an instance of. The definitions of methods are now retrieved from a class library (which should of course also be defined).

Problem 11.6 Extend the syntax of **Cola** with local declarations such that an object can contain subobjects and such that a method can contain submethods. Modify the semantics of **Cola** to capture this. *Hint:* A 'molecule' must now contain information about its 'parent molecule', and this must also be reflected in the labelled transition system for communication capabilities.

Problem 11.7 Extend methods in **Cola** with parameter passing. *Hint:* The rules for rendezvous and the definition of the set of method environments must be modified. (Is there anything else that needs to be modified?)

12

Functional programming languages

This chapter gives a short introduction to functional programming languages and their structural operational semantics.

In the first sections we take a look at the characteristic features of programming languages of this kind (Section 12.1) and how they arose (Section 12.2). Then, in Section 12.3, we provide a short introduction to the theoretical foundations of functional programming languages, the λ-calculus.

Finally, in Section 12.4 we introduce the language **Flan**, which is a subset of ML, and show how to give it a big-step and a small-step semantics.

12.1 What is a functional programming language?

In languages such as C, Java, Pascal and **Bims** variable assignment is a central language construct. A program in any of these languages is essentially a highly structured sequence of variable assignments that change the contents of the store. Languages with this central characteristic are known as *imperative* languages. It is not particularly surprising that the environment-store model is well suited for the semantics of imperative languages.

However, there are programming languages that take a very different approach. A *functional programming language* is an expression-based language – a functional program is essentially a collection of declarations of functions, as opposed to a sequence of statements. A function f is a function in the sense of ordinary mathematics – given an argument x, the value of the application $f(x)$ depends only on the value of x.

The body of a function is an expression, which can be built from function applications, variables and constant values. A function itself can be a value, and the argument and result value of a function can themselves be functions.

A *pure* functional language has only these features, i.e. does not have assignments. Haskell (Peyton Jones, 2003) is a prominent example of this class of functional languages. *Impure* functional languages add imperative features such as assignment and imperative input/output statements to the language syntax . Well-known impure functional languages include members of the ML family – Standard ML (NJ-SML, 2002; Paulson, 1996; Hansen and Rischel, 1999) and OCaml (Hickey, 2007) – and the many dialects of Lisp. However, in impure functional languages it is often possible to keep the use of imperative features to a minimum or avoid them altogether.

As a first example, let us have a look at two different implementations of the Euclidean algorithm for finding the greatest common divisor of two natural numbers.

First, consider the Standard ML implementation. In normal mathematical parlance, the function *gcd* would usually be defined as

$$gcd(m, n) = \begin{cases} n & \text{if } m = 0 \\ gcd(n \bmod m, m) & \text{otherwise.} \end{cases}$$

A program for computing *gcd* may look as follows in Standard ML:

```
fun gcd (m,n) = if m = 0 then n else gcd (n mod m,m)
```

Note the close resemblance to the original definition. In the imperative language Pascal (Jensen and Wirth, 1975), one might write the following implementation:

```
function gcd(m,n: integer): integer
   var prevm : integer
begin
    while m <> 0 do
            begin prevm := m; m:= n mod m;
                  n := prevm
            end;
       gcd := n
end
```

This small example shows an important difference in programming style: Functional programs rely on *recursion* where imperative programs use *iteration*.

Pure functional languages are *referentially transparent* – within a given scope, all occurrences of an expression have the same meaning. This is not the case in imperative programming languages. Consider as an example the tiny program fragment

```
x := 1;
```

```
x  := x+1;
y  := x;
```

Here the variable x does not have a unique meaning, and this is because of the presence of assignments. Note that this is not how we think of variables in mathematics; consider as an example the quadratic equation $x^2 - 4x + 3 = 0$. No-one would proceed to solve this equation as follows: 'First, x is 5 and then 7, since $5^2 - 4 \cdot 7 + 3 = 0$'. We always assume that x stands for the same number throughout the equation.

12.2 Historical background

Functional programming first saw the light of day in the 1950s, when John McCarthy invented the Lisp programming language. Lisp was (and still is) a conceptually simple language: data are lists of atoms, and a program is a collection of function definitions, each of which is a list.

In the years that followed, a lot of attention was devoted to the study of functions as a model of computation and as a means of defining the semantics of programs; the latter led to *denotational semantics*, the subject of Chapter 14. In 1964, Peter Landin devised the SECD machine (Landin, 1964) as a mathematical decription of the evaluation of computable functions. In this way, the SECD machine anticipates structural operational semantics.

Two years later, Landin proposed the language ISWIM (If you See What I Mean) (Landin, 1966). ISWIM is an abstract programming language and was never implemented.

ISWIM, which has a functional core as well as imperative features, was a major source of inspiration for the language ML. ML stands for MetaLanguage, since ML was originally conceived as an auxiliary language for use with the theorem prover LCF (Logic for Computable Functions) (Gordon *et al.*, 1978). In 1977, the first implementation of the language ML saw the light of day.

In 1978, John Backus received the ACM Turing Award. In his Turing Lecture (Backus, 1978) he proposed a language called FP (Functional Programming) whose underlying idea is that of *higher-order functions*, that is, functions that take functions as arguments and can return functions as results.

Two major dividing lines in the functional language community are between impure/pure languages and between strict/lazy languages. Strict languages employ the call-by-value parameter mechanism, whereas lazy languages use lazy evaluation, a variation on the notion of call-by-name.

While ML is an impure, strict language, by the mid 1980s, there were more than a dozen pure, lazy functional programming languages. The best-known of these was Miranda. The Miranda interpreter, however, was a proprietary piece of software. In 1987, there was a strong consensus that a committee should be established to define an open standard for languages of this kind. The result was the language Haskell, whose first version was defined in 1990 (Hudak *et al.*, 2007).

Most recently, the language F# (Microsoft, 2009) has been developed by Microsoft. The language is a variant of ML, is largely compatible with OCaml and will be distributed as a fully supported language in the .NET framework and as part of the Visual Studio.

Today, there are two major strands of ML dialects, one based around Standard ML (Milner *et al.*, 1997) and another based around CAML (Hickey, 2007; INRIA, 1995–2005).

12.3 The λ-calculus

The λ-calculus provides the theoretical foundations of functional programming languages; it is a theory of *computable functions* devised in the 1930s by the logician Alonzo Church (1932; 1936; 1941), who introduced the λ-calculus as a language of computable functions in his work on the foundations of formal logic.

Let λ-**Exp** be the syntactic category of λ-expressions and let $e \in \lambda$-**Exp**. The abstract syntax of the λ-calculus is then given by the formation rules

$$e ::= x \mid \lambda x.e_1 \mid e_1 e_2.$$

The underlying intuition of the λ-calculus is that its expressions denote *control structures*. Moreover, the syntax makes it very simple to describe higher-order functions.

We let x range over an infinite set of *variables*.

Abstraction, $\lambda x.e_1$, denotes a function with argument x and body e_1. Think of x as a formal parameter and e_1 as a procedure body. As an example, $\lambda x.x$ can be thought of as the identity function. Note that the syntax for abstraction allows the body of the abstraction to be any λ-expression – so the body of an abstraction can itself be an abstraction. Consequently, the return value of a function can be a function.

Also note that functions in the λ-calculus are *anonymous*; a function does not have to be declared prior to its use.

Application, $e_1 e_2$, denotes that the function e_1 is applied to the argument e_2. Note that this syntax allows a λ-expression to have any λ-expression as argument, so functions can have functions as arguments. Applications associate to the left, so $e_1e_2e_3$ denotes $(e_1e_2)e_3$.

We often put parentheses in expressions in order to indicate other choices of precedence of applications, and we also omit repeated λs, so e.g. $\lambda x.\lambda y.x$ becomes $\lambda xy.x$.

An important notion is that of *free* and *bound* variables.

Definition 12.1 The set of *free variables* in a λ-expression is defined by the function $FV : \lambda\text{-}\mathbf{Exp} \to \mathcal{P}(\mathbf{Var})$ defined by

$$FV(x) = \{x\}$$
$$FV(e_1e_2) = FV(e_1) \cup FV(e_2)$$
$$FV(\lambda x.e_1) = FV(e_1) \setminus \{x\}$$

Similarly, we can define the set of *bound variables* in a λ-expression by the function $BV : \lambda\text{-}\mathbf{Exp} \to \mathcal{P}(\mathbf{Var})$ defined by

$$BV(x) = \emptyset$$
$$BV(e_1e_2) = BV(e_1) \cup BV(e_2)$$
$$BV(\lambda x.e_1) = BV(e_1) \cup \{x\}$$

Problem 12.2 Find the free and bound variables in

1. $\lambda x.xxxy$
2. $\lambda xyz.zx(yz)$
3. $\lambda xy.z$

A moment's thought 12.3 Are there any scope rules in the λ-calculus?

A moment's thought 12.4 Can a variable be both free and bound in the same expression?

The operational semantics of the λ-calculus is given by the transition system $(\lambda\text{-}\mathbf{Exp}, \to, \lambda\text{-}\mathbf{Exp})$ and is a small-step semantics. There is only one rule, β-reduction. This rule describes how an application e_1e_2 is to be evaluated, when e_1 is an abstraction: the argument (the actual parameter) e_2 is substituted for each occurrence of the formal parameter found in the body of e_1.

$$[\textsc{beta}] \qquad (\lambda x.e_1)e_2 \to e_1[x \mapsto e_2].$$

A moment's thought 12.5 Which parameter mechanism is this?

The definition of substitution is somewhat involved, since we must avoid capturing free variables. Compare this with the involved definition of substitution in the setting of call-by-name in Section 7.5.

Definition 12.6 $e_1[x \mapsto e_2]$, substitution of e_2 for all free occurrences of the variable x in e_1 is defined inductively in the structure of e_1 by

$$(e'e'')[x \mapsto e_2] = e'[x \mapsto e_2]e''[x \mapsto e_2]$$

$$y[x \mapsto e_2] = \begin{cases} y & \text{if } y \neq x \\ e_2 & \text{if } y = x \end{cases}$$

$$(\lambda y.e')[x \mapsto e_2] = \begin{cases} \lambda y.e' & \text{if } y = x \\ \lambda y.(e'[x \mapsto e_2]) & \text{if } y \neq x \text{ and } y \notin FV(e_2) \\ \lambda z.((e'[y \mapsto z])[x \mapsto e_2]) & \text{if } y \neq x \text{ and } y \in FV(e_2) \end{cases}$$

where z is a fresh variable, i.e. $z \neq x$, $z \notin FV(e_2)$ and $z \notin FV(\lambda y.e')$.

Problem 12.7 Perform the following substitutions:

1. $(\lambda x.xx)[x \mapsto xx]$
2. $(\lambda zy.x)[z \mapsto y]$
3. $(\lambda x.x)(\lambda y.yx)[x \mapsto xy]$
4. $((\lambda y.xy)z)[x \mapsto \lambda x.xy]$

We often want to rename bound variables; in the definition of substitution this is essential, since we need to prevent name clashes. This notion of renaming of bound variables is also known as alpha-conversion (compare with Section 7.5.4, page 109) and is defined by the rule

$$[\text{ALPHA}] \qquad \lambda x.e \to \lambda y.e[x \mapsto y] \quad y \notin FV(e).$$

Problem 12.8 Reduce $(\lambda yz.zy)p(\lambda x.x)$ by using the [ALPHA] and [BETA] rules. Next, try reducing $(\lambda x.xx)(\lambda x.xx)$.

12.3.1 The applied λ-calculus

An early, important result by Church (1936) is that the λ-calculus is a universal model of computation. Informally, this means that any algorithm can be expressed in it, i.e. the λ-calculus is Turing-complete.[1] On the other hand, it gets very tedious to express algorithms in this very simple language. As a consequence, it is common practice to extend the abstract syntax with data values (integers, for instance) and basic functions (integer arithmetic, for instance). The resulting language is called the *applied λ-calculus*.

Let $c \in \lambda\text{-}\mathbf{Con}$, where $\lambda\text{-}\mathbf{Con}$ is a set of *constants*. Then the formation rules are

$$e ::= x \mid \lambda x.e_1 \mid e_1 e_2 \mid c.$$

---

[1] See also the footnote on p. 29.

A functional programming language is in its essence simply an applied λ-calculus.

We must now describe the behaviour of constants. We can *either* do this by adding a number of rules that describe the intended behaviour of constants such as

$$[\text{PLUS}_{\text{CONST}}] \qquad \text{Plus } n_1 \, n_2 \rightarrow \mathcal{N}[\![n_1]\!] + \mathcal{N}[\![n_2]\!]$$

or introduce a function *apply* which for each constant c returns the result of applying c to its arguments.

The rule $[\text{PLUS}_{\text{CONST}}]$ corresponds to letting

$$apply(\text{Plus}, n_1, n_2) = \mathcal{N}[\![n_1]\!] + \mathcal{N}[\![n_2]\!].$$

In what follows, we shall use this, the latter approach.

12.4 Flan – a simple functional language

We now present **Flan**,[2] a strict, pure functional programming language which is a subset of ML.

12.4.1 Abstract syntax

Let **Fexp** denote the syntactic category of **Flan** programs (or expressions, if you want), let **Fcon** denote the syntactic category of **Flan** constants and let **Var** denote the set of variables.

Let $e \in$ **Fexp**, $c \in$ **Fcon** and $x, f \in$ **Var**. The formation rules are then

$$e ::= x \mid c \mid (e_1, e_2) \mid e_1 e_2 \mid \text{if } e_0 \text{ then } e_1 \text{ else } e_2 \mid$$
$$\text{fn } x.e \mid \text{let } x = e_1 \text{ in } e_2 \mid \text{letrec } x = e_1 \text{ in } e_2$$
$$c ::= n \mid \text{True} \mid \text{False} \mid \text{Plus} \mid \text{Times} \mid \text{Minus} \mid \text{Equal} \mid \text{Not} \mid \text{IsZero}$$

fn $x.e$ denotes a function with parameter x and body e. Function application is denoted by juxtaposition of expressions, so all functions have exactly one argument. The similarity to the λ-calculus is very deliberate – **Flan** is simply an applied λ-calculus extended with *local declarations*, conditionals and pairs.

Local declarations can be recursive or non-recursive. If letrec $x = e_1$ in e_2 has an occurrence of x in e_1, we treat this as a recursive call of x. But this is not the case, if x occurs in e_1 in the declaration let $x = e_1$ in e_2 – here, the x found in e_1 must be declared elsewhere for this to make sense.

---

[2] Functional language.

Example 12.9 The factorial function $n! = n \cdot (n-1) \cdots 1$ can be implemented in **Flan** as

```
fn y. letrec fac = fn x.
                   if IsZero(x) then 1
                   else Times x (fac (Minus x 1))
           in
              fac y
```

Example 12.10 The **Flan** function

```
fn f. fn x. let twice = fn g.
                        g (g x)
            in
               twice f
```

defines a function that takes a function f as argument and returns a function which applies f twice to its argument.

12.4.2 A big-step semantics of Flan

In our big-step semantics transitions are of the form $env \vdash e \rightarrow v$, where $env \in \textbf{Env}$. This must be read as follows: expression e evaluates to the value v, given the bindings in our environment env. In our environment we keep the bindings that are currently known. So here

$$\textbf{Env} = \textbf{Var} \rightharpoonup \textbf{Values}$$

The set of values, **Values**, is comprised of the following:

- All constants in **Fcon** are values, so $\textbf{Fcon} \subseteq \textbf{Values}$
- All *closures* $\langle x, e, env \rangle$ are values
- All *recursive closures* $\langle f, x, e, env \rangle$ are values.

In other words, we have

$$\textbf{Values} = \textbf{Fcon} \cup \textbf{Var} \times \textbf{Fexp} \times \textbf{Env} \cup \textbf{Var} \times \textbf{Var} \times \textbf{Fexp} \times \textbf{Fexp} \times \textbf{Env}.$$

As this definition shows, the set of environments is again recursively defined. Notice the resemblance to the definition of **EnvP** in Section 6.6.3.

In the transition rules that follow, the environment comes into play when we evaluate variables in [VAR$_{\text{FUN-BSS}}$] (we look up the value in the environment), when we reach a local declaration in [LET$_{\text{FUN-BSS}}$] (we add information about the local variable and its value to the environment) and when we

[VAR$_{\text{FUN-BSS}}$]	$env \vdash x \rightarrow v$ where $env\,x = v$
[CONST$_{\text{FUN-BSS}}$]	$env \vdash c \rightarrow c$
[PAIR$_{\text{FUN}}$]	$\dfrac{env \vdash e_1 \rightarrow v_1 \quad env \vdash e_2 \rightarrow v_2}{env \vdash (e_1, e_2) \rightarrow (v_1, v_2)}$
[APP-1$_{\text{FUN-BSS}}$]	$\dfrac{env \vdash e_1 \rightarrow \langle x, e, env' \rangle \quad env \vdash e_2 \rightarrow v \quad env'[x \mapsto v] \vdash e \rightarrow v'}{env \vdash e_1 e_2 \rightarrow v'}$
[APP-2$_{\text{FUN-BSS}}$]	$\dfrac{env \vdash e_1 \rightarrow c \quad env \vdash e_2 \rightarrow v'}{env \vdash e_1 e_2 \rightarrow v'}$ where $apply(c, v) = v'$
[IF-1$_{\text{FUN-BSS}}$]	$\dfrac{env \vdash e_0 \rightarrow \textbf{True} \quad env \vdash e_1 \rightarrow v}{env \vdash \textbf{if } e_0 \textbf{ then } e_1 \textbf{ else } e_2 \ \rightarrow v}$
[IF-2$_{\text{FUN-BSS}}$]	$\dfrac{env \vdash e_0 \rightarrow \textbf{False} \quad env \vdash e_2 \rightarrow v}{env \vdash \textbf{if } e_0 \textbf{ then } e_1 \textbf{ else } e_2 \ \rightarrow v}$
[FN$_{\text{FUN-BSS}}$]	$env \vdash \textbf{fn } x.e \rightarrow \langle x, e, env \rangle$
[LET$_{\text{FUN-BSS}}$]	$\dfrac{env \vdash e_1 \rightarrow v \quad env[x \mapsto v] \vdash e_2 \rightarrow v'}{env \vdash \textbf{let } x = e_1 \textbf{ in } e_2 \rightarrow v'}$
[LETREC$_{\text{FUN-BSS}}$]	$\dfrac{env \vdash e_1 \rightarrow \langle x, e, env' \rangle \quad env[f \mapsto [f, x, e, env']] \vdash e_2 \rightarrow v_2}{env \vdash \textbf{letrec } f = e_1 \textbf{ in } e_2 \rightarrow v_2}$
[APP-3$_{\text{FUN-BSS}}$]	$\dfrac{\begin{array}{l} env \vdash e_1 \rightarrow [f, x, e, env'] \\ env \vdash e_2 \rightarrow v \\ env'[x \mapsto v, f \mapsto \langle f, x, e, env' \rangle] \vdash e \rightarrow v' \end{array}}{env \vdash e_1 e_2 \rightarrow v'}$

Table 12.1 *Big-step semantics for* **Flan**

reach a recursive local declaration [LETREC$_{\text{FUN-BSS}}$] (where we also need to add information about the name of the recursive function).

Our transition system is (**Fexp** $\cup$ **Values**, $\rightarrow$, **Values**). The rules for $\rightarrow$ can be found in Table 12.1.

Problem 12.11 Write the *gcd*-program in **Flan** and find $gcd(3, 2)$ by building a derivation tree for a suitable big-step transition.

Problem 12.12 The semantics of Table 12.1 is a call-by-value semantics. Change the semantics so that it becomes a *call-by-name* semantics and

[PAIR-1$_\text{FUN-SSS}$]	$$\frac{e_1 \Rightarrow e_1'}{(e_1, e_2) \Rightarrow (e_1', e_2)}$$
[PAIR-2$_\text{FUN-SSS}$]	$$\frac{e_2 \Rightarrow e_2'}{(e_1, e_2) \Rightarrow (e_1, e_2')}$$
[LET-1$_\text{FUN-SSS}$]	$$\frac{e_1 \Rightarrow e_1'}{\texttt{let } x = e_1 \texttt{ in } e_2 \Rightarrow \texttt{let } x = e_1' \texttt{ in } e_2}$$
[LET-2$_\text{FUN-SSS}$]	$\texttt{let } x = v \texttt{ in } e_2 \Rightarrow e_2[x \mapsto v]$
[APP-1$_\text{FUN-SSS}$]	$$\frac{e_2 \Rightarrow e_2'}{e_1 e_2 \Rightarrow e_1 e_2'}$$
[APP-2$_\text{FUN-SSS}$]	$$\frac{e_1 \Rightarrow e_1'}{e_1 v \Rightarrow e_1' v}$$
[APP-3$_\text{FUN-SSS}$]	$(\texttt{fn } x.e)v \Rightarrow e[x \mapsto v]$
[APP-4$_\text{FUN-SSS}$]	$c\, v \Rightarrow apply(c, v)$

Table 12.2 *Some of the small-step semantics of **Flan***

show by an appropriate program example that the two semantics are *not* equivalent.

Problem 12.13   Implement the big-step semantics of **Flan** in SML.

12.4.3 A small-step semantics of Flan

It is of course also possible to give a small-step semantics of **Flan**. Here the transition system is (**Fexp** ∪ **Values**, ⇒, **Values**), where ⇒ is defined by the rules in Table 12.2 – and rules for conditionals and recursive local declarations, not presented here. In the semantics we use substitutions instead of environments; we leave the definition of substitution as an exercise for the reader.

Note how the small-step semantics is reminiscent of the reduction rules of the applied λ-calculus. Also note that our semantics is a call-by-value semantics, since the argument of an application must be a value (and applied to an abstraction) for the application itself to reduce.

Problem 12.14   Give an inductive definition of substitution in **Flan**. *Hint:* The definition is similar in spirit to that of substitution in the λ-calculus.

Problem 12.15 Add the missing rules to Table 12.2!

A moment's thought 12.16 How can we modify the semantics of Table 12.2 to a *call-by-name* semantics for **Flan**?

12.5 Further reading

The functional programming languages provide a good example of the interplay between programming language semantics and programming language design and implementation.

An important topic of programming language semantics is that of *types* and many of the central insights here arise from the study of functional programming languages. In Chapter 13 we describe a type system for **Flan**.

In the 1990s, researchers attempted to integrate notions of parallel programming into functional programming. Two prominent examples are Concurrent ML (Reppy, 1992) and Facile (Giacalone *et al.*, 1989). Both are based on Standard ML, using its implementation and type system. Moreover, both have synchronous, channel-based communication similar to that used in Chapter 8 as the means for interprocess communication.

PART IV
RELATED TOPICS

13

Typed programming languages

In this chapter we take a look at types. We give a type system for the imperative language **Bump** introduced in Chapter 7 and another type system for the functional language **Flan** from Chapter 12. We show that both type systems are sound under the operational semantics that we have. By this we mean that a well-typed program will never exhibit the run-time errors that the type system is intended to prevent.

This chapter is intended only as a short introduction; for a very thorough treatment of type systems for programming languages, Pierce's excellent book (Pierce, 2002) is highly recommended.

13.1 Type systems

Most programming languages today incorporate a type system of some kind that defines a way of classifying syntactic entities. Some languages such as C have very simple type systems, while others, notably functional languages such as the languages of the ML family (Milner *et al.*, 1997; INRIA, 1995–2005) and Haskell (Peyton Jones, 2003), have very strong type systems.

13.1.1 *Why are type systems useful?*

A first, very important reason for introducing a notion of type is that certain run-time errors can then be avoided by a simple compile-time analysis. Consider as a simple example the expression

```
7+(2=3).
```

Intuitively, this should not make sense. 7 is a numeral, that will evaluate to the integer 7, whereas (2=3) is a Boolean expression, that will evaluate to a truth value. If an interpreter of **Bims** tried to evaluate the above expression, it would cause a run-time error.

If we therefore give each expression a type, which is either the integer type Int or the type of truth values Bool, and require that in a sum expression $a_1 + a_2$ both subexpressions must have type Int, we can immediately rule out ill-fated examples such as the above. The use of types has become important in the setting of program analysis for computer and network security.

Another reason for introducing a notion of type is that the classification of data at compile-time will aid in better memory allocation and better effeciency. For instance, floating-point numbers, booleans, integers and strings have different memory requirements.

A third reason for introducing types is that of readability. It is often easier to read a large program if its variables are labelled according to their type and if its procedures/methods/functions are labelled according to the types of their parameters and return value.

13.1.2 The components of a type system

The notion of a type system originates in logic. Originally, the idea was introduced by Bertrand Russell and Alfred North Whitehead in *Principia Mathematica* (Russell and Whitehead, 1910) in order to deal with paradoxes in the foundations of set theory. A later development that became particularly important to programming language theory was Church's type system for the λ-calculus (Church, 1940).

Our presentation in this chapter will reveal that the mode of defining a type system is in many ways similar to that of defining a structural operational semantics. In particular, in both cases, the definition is syntax-directed and contains a collection of rules.

The definition of a type system must contain the following.

- A definition of the syntactic category of *types*.
- For the elements of each syntactic category in the programming language, a definition of the form of *type judgments*.
- For the elements of each syntactic category, a set of *type rules* that define the valid type judgments.

13.1.3 Type checking and type inference

Traditionally, type systems have been used to classify programs by means of *type checking*: given an assignment of types to data entities in program P, check that P is *well-typed*, i.e. does not contain type errors. Implementations of typed programming languages incorporate a type checker as an early part of the process of parsing and translation. For this reason, a natural requirement of a type system is that type checking is an *effective* notion, which means that there exists an algorithm which can determine whether a program P is well-typed.

Following the pioneering work by Milner (Milner, 1978), the notion of *type inference* has become increasingly important. Type inference can be seen as the inverse problem to type checking: given a program P, can we construct a type assignment that will make P well-typed? Implementations of many functional languages, including the ML family (Milner *et al.*, 1997; INRIA, 1995–2005; Hickey, 2007) and Haskell (Peyton Jones, 2003), incorporate type inference as a central aspect.

13.2 Typed Bump

In this section we describe a type system for **Bump**. At the end of the section, we describe a result that links our semantics to properties of the type system.

13.2.1 Abstract syntax

In order to better illustrate what happens, we here replace the syntactic categories **Aexp** and **Bexp** by the syntactic category of expressions **Exp** ranged over by e. Moreover, we require that variable declarations include type information.

In the following, T will range over the syntactic category **Types** of types. We define the elements of **Types** in Section 13.2.3.

$$e ::= e_1 = e_2 \mid e_1 < e_2 \mid \neg e_1 \mid e_1 \wedge e_2 \mid (e_1)$$
$$\mid n \mid x \mid e_1 \texttt{+} e_2 \mid e_1 \texttt{*} e_2 \mid e_1 \texttt{-} e_2 \mid (e_1)$$
$$D_V ::= T \texttt{ var } x := e; D_V \mid \varepsilon$$
$$S ::= x := e \mid \texttt{skip} \mid S_1; S_2 \mid \texttt{if } e \texttt{ then } S_1 \texttt{ else } S_2$$
$$\mid \texttt{while } e \texttt{ do } S \mid \texttt{begin } D_V \, D_P \, S \texttt{ end} \mid \texttt{call } p(e)$$
$$D_V ::= T \texttt{ var } x := e; D_V \mid \epsilon$$
$$D_P ::= \texttt{proc } p(T \, x) \texttt{ is } S; D_P \mid \epsilon$$

[plus-bump$_{bss}$]	$$\dfrac{env_V, sto \vdash e_1 \rightarrow_e v_1 \quad env_V, sto \vdash e_2 \rightarrow_e v_2}{env_V, sto \vdash e_1 + e_2 \rightarrow_e v}$$
	where $v = v_1 + v_2$
[minus-bump$_{bss}$]	$$\dfrac{env_V, sto \vdash e_1 \rightarrow_e v_1 \quad env_V, sto \vdash e_2 \rightarrow_e v_2}{env_V, sto \vdash e_1 - e_2 \rightarrow_e v}$$
	where $v = v_1 - v_2$
[mult-bump$_{bss}$]	$$\dfrac{env_V, sto \vdash e_1 \rightarrow_e v_1 \quad env_V, sto \vdash e_2 \rightarrow_e v_2}{env_V, sto \vdash e_1 * e_2 \rightarrow_e v}$$
	where $v = v_1 \cdot v_2$
[parent-bump$_{bss}$]	$$\dfrac{env_V, sto \vdash e_1 \rightarrow_e v_1}{env_V, sto \vdash (e_1) \rightarrow_e v_1}$$
[num-bump$_{bss}$]	$env_V, sto \vdash n \rightarrow_e v$ if $\mathcal{N}[\![n]\!] = v$
[var-bump$_{bss}$]	$env_V, sto \vdash x \rightarrow_e v$ if $env_V \, x = l$ and $sto \, l = v$

Table 13.1 *Big-step operational semantics of* **Exp** *(arithmetic part)*

13.2.2 Semantics

The semantics of Bump is revised slightly, since we now have a single syntactic category of expressions and since we can now have Boolean-valued variables.

For expressions, we define the transition system

$$(\textbf{Exp} \cup \mathbb{Z} \cup \{\textit{tt}, \textit{ff}\}, \rightarrow, \mathbb{Z} \cup \{\textit{tt}, \textit{ff}\}),$$

where the transition relation is defined by the rules in Table 13.1 and additional rules for the Boolean operations. The latter rules are not presented here but are straightforward.

13.2.3 Types in Bump

The syntactic category of types is called **Types** and is ranged over by T. A subset of this category is the set of *base types*, ranged over by the metavariable B. The type rules that we present in the following will guarantee that the type of an expression will always be a base type.

The type of a declaration or a statement will simply be ok; we say that the declaration or statement is *well-typed*.

[ASS-BUMP$_{\text{BSS}}$]
$$env_V, env_P \vdash \langle x := e, sto \rangle \rightarrow_e sto[l \mapsto v]$$
$$\text{where } env_V, sto \vdash e \rightarrow_e v \text{ and } env_V\, x = l$$

[SKIP-BUMP$_{\text{BSS}}$]
$$env_V, env_P \vdash \langle \textbf{skip}, sto \rangle \rightarrow_e sto$$

[COMP-BUMP$_{\text{BSS}}$]
$$\frac{env_V, env_P \vdash \langle S_1, sto \rangle \rightarrow_e sto'' \qquad env_V, env_P \vdash \langle S_2, sto'' \rangle \rightarrow_e sto'}{env_V, env_P \vdash \langle S_1; S_2, sto \rangle \rightarrow_e sto'}$$

[IF-TRUE-BUMP$_{\text{BSS}}$]
$$\frac{env_V, env_P \vdash \langle S_1, sto \rangle \rightarrow_e sto'}{env_V, env_P \vdash \langle \textbf{if } e \textbf{ then } S_1 \textbf{ else } S_2, sto \rangle \rightarrow_e sto'}$$

if $env_V, sto \vdash e \rightarrow_e tt$

[IF-FALSE-BUMP$_{\text{BSS}}$]
$$\frac{env_V, env_P \vdash \langle S_2, sto \rangle \rightarrow_e sto'}{env_V, env_P \vdash \langle \textbf{if } e \textbf{ then } S_1 \textbf{ else } S_2, sto \rangle \rightarrow_e sto'}$$

if $env_V, sto \vdash e \rightarrow_e ff$

[WHILE-TRUE-BUMP$_{\text{BSS}}$]
$$\frac{env_V, env_P \vdash \langle S, sto \rangle \rightarrow_e sto'' \qquad env_V, env_P \vdash \langle \textbf{while } e \textbf{ do } S, sto'' \rangle \rightarrow_e sto'}{env_V, env_P \vdash \langle \textbf{while } e \textbf{ do } S, sto \rangle \rightarrow_e sto'}$$

if $env_V, sto \vdash e \rightarrow_e tt$

[WHILE-FALSE-BUMP$_{\text{BSS}}$]
$$env_V, env_P \vdash \langle \textbf{while } e \textbf{ do } S, sto \rangle \rightarrow_e sto'$$
if $env_V, sto \vdash e \rightarrow_e ff$

[BLOCK-BUMP$_{\text{BSS}}$]
$$\frac{\langle D_V, env_V, sto \rangle \rightarrow_{DV} (env_V', sto'') \qquad env_V' \vdash \langle D_P, env_P \rangle \rightarrow_{DP} env_P' \qquad env_V', env_P' \vdash \langle S, sto'' \rangle \rightarrow_e sto'}{env_V, env_P \vdash \langle \textbf{begin } D_V\ D_P\ S \textbf{ end}, sto \rangle \rightarrow_e sto'}$$

Table 13.2 *Big-step transition rules for Bump statements (except procedure calls)*

The type of a procedure is the *composite type* $x : B \rightarrow$ ok, which is to be read as follows: if we know that the type of the formal parameter is B, then the body of the procedure will be well-typed.

Summing up, the formation rules for types are

$$B ::= \text{Int} \mid \text{Bool}$$
$$T ::= B \mid x : B \rightarrow \text{ok}.$$

13.2.4 Type environments

In an operational semantics for a language with variables, we must keep track of the values of the variables. This is done by making the semantics relative to a state for **Bims**, or, in the case of later extensions, by a variable environment and a store.

In the type system that we now present, we use a similar notion: a *type environment* keeps track of the types of variables and procedure names.

Definition 13.1 (Type environment)   A type environment is a partial function $E : \textbf{Var} \cup \textbf{Pnames} \rightharpoonup \textbf{Types}$.

Definition 13.2 (Update of type environments)   We write $E[x \mapsto T]$ for the type environment E' defined by

$$E'(y) = \begin{cases} E(y) & \text{if } y \neq x \\ T & \text{if } y = x. \end{cases}$$

13.2.5 Assigning types

We now describe the heart of the type system, namely the rules that define how types are assigned to syntactic entities. We need to describe how this assignment is done for each syntactic category.

Type rules for expressions

The type judgment $E \vdash e : T$ is to be read as e has type T, given the type bindings of type environment E.

We define the type judgment by the rules in Table 13.3. An essential type rule is [VAR$_{\text{EXP}}$], since this is the rule that invokes the type environment to find the type of x.

Type rules for declarations

In the type rules for non-empty declarations, we define the auxiliary functions $E(D_V, E)$ and $E(D_P, E)$ that return the updated type environments generated by a declaration D_V or D_P when starting with type environment E. The function is defined as follows:

$[\text{SUBS}_{\text{EXP}}]$ $\dfrac{E \vdash e_1 : \text{Int} \quad E \vdash e_2 : \text{Int}}{E \vdash e_1 - e_2 : \text{Int}}$ $\qquad$ $[\text{NUM}_{\text{EXP}}]$ $\quad E \vdash n : \text{Int}$

$[\text{ADD}_{\text{EXP}}]$ $\dfrac{E \vdash e_1 : \text{Int} \quad E \vdash e_2 : \text{Int}}{E \vdash e_1 + e_2 : \text{Int}}$ $\qquad$ $[\text{VAR}_{\text{EXP}}]$ $\quad \dfrac{E(x) = T}{E \vdash x : T}$

$[\text{MULT}_{\text{EXP}}]$ $\dfrac{E \vdash e_1 : \text{Int} \quad E \vdash e_2 : \text{Int}}{E \vdash e_1 * e_2 : \text{Int}}$ $\qquad$ $[\text{PAREN}_{\text{EXP}}]$ $\quad \dfrac{E \vdash e_1 : T}{E \vdash (e_1) : T}$

$[\text{EQUAL}_{\text{EXP}}]$ $\dfrac{E \vdash e_1 : T \quad E \vdash e_2 : T}{E \vdash e_1 = e_2 : \text{Bool}}$

$[\text{AND}_{\text{EXP}}]$ $\dfrac{E \vdash e_1 : \text{Bool} \quad E \vdash e_2 : \text{Bool}}{E \vdash e_1 \wedge e_2 : \text{Bool}}$ $\qquad$ $[\text{NEG}_{\text{EXP}}]$ $\quad \dfrac{E \vdash e_1 : \text{Bool}}{E \vdash \neg e_1 : \text{Bool}}$

Table 13.3 *Type rules for **Bump** expressions*

$[\text{EMPTY}_{\text{DEC}}]$ $\quad E \vdash \varepsilon : \text{ok}$

$[\text{VAR}_{\text{DEC}}]$ $\quad \dfrac{E[x \mapsto T] \vdash D_V : \text{ok} \quad E \vdash a : T}{E \vdash \textbf{var } T\ x := a; D_V : \text{ok}}$

$[\text{PROC}_{\text{DEC}}]$ $\quad \dfrac{E[p \mapsto (x : T \rightarrow \text{ok})] \vdash D_P : \text{ok}}{E \vdash \textbf{proc } p(T\ x) \textbf{ is } S; D_P : \text{ok}}$

Table 13.4 *Type rules for variable and procedure declarations in **Bump***

$$E(\varepsilon, E) = E$$
$$E(\textbf{var } T\ x; D_V, E) = E(D_V, E[x \mapsto T])$$
$$E(\textbf{proc } p(T\ x) \textbf{ is } S; D_P, E) = E(D_P, E[p \mapsto (x : T) \rightarrow \text{ok})]).$$

Note that we add a type assumption about the variable or procedure that is being declared when the remaining declarations are examined.

Type rules for statements

The type rules are shown in Table 13.5. In the rule $[\text{BLOCK}_{\text{STM}}]$ we need to type the block body in a type environment where we have added type assumptions from the local declarations.

$[\text{SKIP}_{\text{STM}}]$	$E \vdash \text{skip} : \text{ok}$

$[\text{ASS}_{\text{STM}}]$
$$\frac{E \vdash x : T \quad E \vdash a : T}{E \vdash x := a : \text{ok}}$$

$[\text{IF}_{\text{STM}}]$
$$\frac{E \vdash e : \text{Bool} \quad E \vdash S_1 : \text{ok} \quad E \vdash S_2 : \text{ok}}{E \vdash \text{if } e \text{ then } S_1 \text{ else; } S_2 : \text{ok}}$$

$[\text{WHILE}_{\text{STM}}]$
$$\frac{E \vdash e : \text{Bool} \quad E \vdash S : \text{ok}}{E \vdash \text{while } e \text{ do } S : \text{ok}}$$

$[\text{COMP}_{\text{STM}}]$
$$\frac{E \vdash S_1 : \text{ok} \quad E \vdash S_2 : \text{ok}}{E \vdash S_1; S_2 : \text{ok}}$$

$[\text{BLOCK}_{\text{STM}}]$
$$\frac{E \vdash D_V : \text{ok} \quad E_1 \vdash D_P : \text{ok} \quad E_2 \vdash S : \text{ok}}{E \vdash \text{begin } D_V \ D_P \ S \text{ end} : \text{ok}}$$

where $E_1 = E(D_V, E)$
and $E_2 = E(D_P, E_1)$

$[\text{CALL}_{\text{STM}}]$
$$\frac{E \vdash p : (x : T \rightarrow \text{ok}) \quad E \vdash e : T}{E \vdash \text{call } p(e) : \text{ok}}$$

Table 13.5 *Type rules for* **Bump** *statements*

13.2.6 Safety properties

Every type system is supposed to be *safe*. By this we mean that, if a term is well-typed, then certain properties of the term are guaranteed to hold. In our case, we would expect, among other things, that, if $E \vdash e : T$, then e will evaluate to a value from the set that the type T denotes. Moreover, we would expect, for instance, that, in a while loop $\text{while } b \text{ do } S$, b will evaluate to a truth value.

To reflect this, we must make precise what types denote. Base types are supposed to denote sets. The type Int denotes the set $\mathbb{Z}$, and the type Bool denotes the set $\{tt, ff\}$ of truth values. Let $\mathbf{set}(T)$ denote the set corresponding to type T.

We also need to make precise that the bindings of a type environment E correspond to the value bindings found in an environment–store pair. For instance, if x has type Int, then the location of x should contain an integer value.

Definition 13.3 (Agreement for variables)   A pair (env_V, sto) agrees with type environment E if it is the case that for any variable x, if $E(x) = T$, then $env_V x = l$ and $sto \, l = v$ where $v \in \mathbf{set}(T)$.

Theorem 13.4 (Safety for expressions) *Suppose (env_V, sto) agrees with type environment E and that $E \vdash e : T$. Then $env_V, sto \vdash e \to v$ and $v \in \mathbf{set}(T)$.*

Proof This is a result that states a property for all terms that are well-typed. We therefore prove this theorem by induction on the depth of the derivation tree for $E \vdash e : T$.

$n = 0$: Here, there are two cases to consider.

- If $E \vdash e : T$ was concluded using [VAR$_\mathrm{EXP}$], then $e = x$ for some variable x, and since E agrees with (env_V, sto) we have that $sto(env_V) = v$ for some $v \in \mathbf{set}(T)$. The desired property is now seen to hold immediately.
- If $E \vdash e : \mathsf{Int}$, we have that e is some numeral n, and $env_V, sto \vdash n \to_e v$ where $\mathcal{N}[\![n]\!] = v$. Since $\mathcal{N} : \mathbf{Aexp} \to \mathbb{Z}$, we have $v \in \mathbb{Z}$. Since $\mathbb{Z} = \mathbf{set}(\mathsf{Int})$, the property therefore holds in this case.

Assume for all $j \leq n$, prove for $n + 1$: Suppose the derivation tree for $E \vdash e : T$ has height $n + 1$, then one of the rules not covered by the base case above must have been used. We must then consider each rule in turn. All of the cases are similar, so we give the proof only for one of them here.

Suppose [ADD$_\mathrm{EXP}$] was the last rule used. The derivation tree for $E \vdash e_1 : \mathsf{Int}$ has height $j_1 \leq n$ and the derivation tree for $E \vdash e_2 : \mathsf{Int}$ has height $j_2 \leq n$. By virtue of our induction hypothesis we have $env_V, sto \vdash e_1 \to_e v_1$ with $v_1 \in \mathbb{Z}$ and $env_V, sto \vdash e_2 \to_e v_2$ with $v_2 \in \mathbb{Z}$. From the transition rule [PLUS-BUMP$_\mathrm{BSS}$] we have that $env_V, sto \vdash e_1 + e_2 \to_e v_1 + v_2$ and clearly $v_1 + v_2 \in \mathbb{Z}$ and $\mathbb{Z} = \mathbf{set}(\mathsf{Int})$, as we needed to prove.

$\square$

Theorem 13.5 (Safety for variable declarations) *Suppose (env_V, sto) agrees with type environment E and that $E \vdash D_V : \mathsf{ok}$. Then*

- $\langle D_V, sto, env_V \rangle \to (env_V', sto')$ *where (env_V', sto') agrees with E*
- $\vdash_E \langle D_V, sto, env_V \rangle \not\to$ wrong.

Proof This is a result that states a property for all variable declarations that are well-typed. We therefore prove this theorem by induction on the

---

[DECLERROR] $\vdash_E \langle x := e; D_V, sto, env_V \rangle \rightarrow$ wrong

> if $E(x) = T$ but $env_V, sto \vdash_E e \rightarrow v$ where $v \notin \mathbf{set}(T)$
> or $\vdash_E \langle D_V, env_V, sto \rangle \rightarrow$ wrong

---

Table 13.6 *The error predicate for variable declarations*

depth of the derivation tree for $E \vdash D_V$: ok. To show that a configuration does not lead to wrong, we show that the conditions in the definition of the error predicate do not apply.

$n = 0$: Here, the only case is that of [EMPTY$_{\text{DEC}}$]. Since $\langle \varepsilon, sto, env_V \rangle \rightarrow env_V$ and the error predicate is not defined for empty declarations, the result is immediate.

Assume for $j \leq n$, show for $n + 1$: If the derivation tree has height $n+1$, then the last rule must be [VAR$_{\text{DEC}}$]. By Theorem 13.4 we have that $env_V, sto \vdash a \rightarrow_e v$ where $v \in \mathbf{set}(T)$. We now see that $E[x \mapsto T]$ agrees with $(env_V[x \vdash l, \text{next} \mapsto new\ l], sto[l \mapsto v])$, and we can therefore apply the induction hypothesis. The induction hypothesis states that when $\langle D_V, sto[l \mapsto v], env_V[x \vdash l, \text{next} \mapsto new\ l] \rangle (env'_V, sto')$ we have that $E[x \mapsto T]$ agrees with (env'_V, sto'). Then, clearly it is also the case that E agrees with (env'_V, sto'). Moreover, by virtue of our induction hypothesis we have that $\vdash_E \langle D_V, sto, env_V \rangle \not\rightarrow$ wrong, so the conditions of the error predicate do not apply. This completes the proof.

□

Definition 13.6 (Agreement for procedure names)   A procedure environment env_P agrees with type environment E if it is the case that, for any procedure name p, if $E(p) = x : T \rightarrow$ ok, then $env_V p = (x, S, env'_V, env'_P)$ and $E, x : T \vdash S$: ok.

Theorem 13.7 (Safety for procedure declarations)   *Let env_V be a variable environment. Suppose there exists a sto such that (env_V, sto) agrees with type environment E and that $E \vdash D_P$: ok. Then $env_V \vdash \langle D_P, env_P \rangle \rightarrow env'_P$ where env'_P agrees with E.*

Proof   This is left as an exercise for the reader.   □

Problem 13.8   Prove Theorem 13.7.

[ASSERROR]	$env_V, env_P \vdash_E \langle x := e, sto \rangle \rightarrow$ wrong if $E(x) = T$ but $env_V, sto \vdash_E e \rightarrow v$ where $v \notin \mathbf{set}(T)$
[COMPERROR]	$env_V, env_P \vdash_E \langle S_1; S_2, sto \rangle \rightarrow$ wrong if $env_V, env_P \vdash_E \langle S_1, sto \rangle \rightarrow$ wrong or $env_V, env_P \vdash \langle S_1, sto \rangle \rightarrow sto'$ but $env_V, env_P \vdash_E \langle S_2, sto' \rangle \rightarrow$ wrong
[IFERROR]	$env_V, env_P \vdash_E \langle \text{if } e \text{ then } S_1 \text{ else } S_2, sto \rangle \rightarrow$ wrong if $env_V, sto \vdash_E e \rightarrow v$ with $v \notin \{tt, ff\}$ or $env_V, sto \vdash_E e \rightarrow tt$ but $env_V, env_P \vdash_E \langle S_1, sto \rangle \rightarrow$ wrong or $env_V, sto \vdash_E e \rightarrow ff$ but $env_V, env_P \vdash_E \langle S_2, sto' \rangle \rightarrow$ wrong
[WHILEERROR]	$env_V, env_P \vdash_E \langle \text{while } e \text{ do } S, sto \rangle \rightarrow$ wrong if $env_V, sto \vdash_E e \rightarrow v$ with $v \notin \{tt, ff\}$ or $env_V, sto \vdash e \rightarrow tt$ but $env_V, env_P \vdash_E \langle S, sto \rangle \rightarrow$ wrong or $env_V, sto \vdash e \rightarrow tt$ and $env_V, env_P \vdash_E \langle S, sto \rangle \rightarrow sto'$ but $env_V, env_P \vdash_E \langle \text{while } e \text{ do } S, sto' \rangle \rightarrow$ wrong
[BLOCKERROR]	$env_V, env_P \vdash_E \langle \mathbf{begin} \ D_V \ D_P \ S \ \mathbf{end}, sto \rangle \rightarrow$ wrong if $env_V, env_P \vdash_E \langle S, sto \rangle \rightarrow$ wrong or $\vdash_E \langle D_V, sto, env_V \rangle \rightarrow$ wrong
[CALLERROR]	$env_V, env_P \vdash_E \langle \mathtt{call} \ p(e), sto \rangle \rightarrow$ wrong if $E(p) = T \rightarrow$ ok but $env_V, sto \vdash_E e \rightarrow v$ where $v \notin \mathbf{set}(T)$

Table 13.7 *The error predicate for statements*

The main theorem for our type system states that a well-typed statement will not result in errors of certain kinds. To be precise about what an error is in our setting, we define an error predicate in Table 13.7. The idea is that a statement S results in an error if it assigns a value of the wrong type to a variable or if an expression occurring in S is not well-typed.

Since statements contain variable declarations where variables are initialized, we also need to define an error predicate on variable declarations. The definition, which can be found in Table 13.6, makes use of conditions that are similar to those for assignments.

Theorem 13.9 (Safety for statements)   *Suppose* (env_V, sto) *and* env_P
agree with type environment E *and that* $E \vdash S : \mathsf{ok}$. *Then, if* $env_V, env_P \vdash$
$\langle S, sto \rangle \rightarrow sto'$, E *agrees with* (env_V, sto') *and* $env_V, env_P \vdash \langle S, sto \rangle \not\rightarrow$
wrong.

Proof   In this theorem we state a property of all transitions, so here the
proof proceeds by induction on the height of the derivation tree of the transition $env_V, env_P \vdash \langle S, sto \rangle \rightarrow sto'$.

$n = 0$: Here, there are two cases to consider.

- If [SKIP-BUMP$_{\mathrm{BSS}}$] was used, the conclusion is immediate, since
  $env_V, env_P \vdash \langle \mathtt{skip}, sto \rangle \rightarrow sto$ and the error predicate is not
  defined for $\mathtt{skip}$.
- If [ASS-BUMP$_{\mathrm{BSS}}$] was used, we have that S is $x := e$ and that
  $E \vdash e : T$ where $E(x) = T$. But by Theorem 13.4 we have that
  $env_V, sto \vdash e \rightarrow v$ with $v \in \mathbf{set}(T)$, so the error predicate does not
  apply. Moreover, it then also follows that the pair $(env_V, sto[l \mapsto v])$ agrees with E.

Assume for $j \leq n$, **show for** $n + 1$: We describe only two of the cases below, namely the ones where the previous theorems about the type
system are invoked. The remaining cases are all similar or simpler
and the reader may want to complete these as an exercise.

- Consider the rule [WHILE-TRUE-BUMP$_{\mathrm{BSS}}$]. Here the premises tell
  us that $env_V, env_P \vdash \langle S, sto \rangle \rightarrow sto''$ for some sto'' and that
  $env_V, env_P \vdash \langle \mathtt{while}\ e\ \mathtt{do}\ S, sto'' \rangle \rightarrow sto'$. Since $E \vdash \mathtt{while}\ e\ \mathtt{do}\ S :$
  ok, we have that $E \vdash S : \mathsf{ok}$, so by virtue of our induction
  hypothesis we have that $env_V, env_P \vdash_E \langle S, sto \rangle \not\rightarrow$ wrong and
  $env_V, env_P \vdash_E \langle \mathtt{while}\ e\ \mathtt{do}\ S, sto'' \rangle \not\rightarrow$ wrong. Consequently, none
  of the conditions of the error predicate will hold in this case, so
  we conclude that $env_V, env_P \vdash_E \langle \mathtt{while}\ e\ \mathtt{do}\ S, sto \rangle \not\rightarrow$ wrong.
  Moreover, by virtue of our induction hypothesis we have that E
  agrees with (env_V, sto'') and with (env_V, sto'); the latter is what
  remained to be shown.
- Consider the rule [BLOCK-BUMP$_{\mathrm{BSS}}$]. In this case the premises
  tell us the following: that $\langle D_V, env_V, sto \rangle \rightarrow_{DV} (env_V', sto'')$, that
  $env_V' \vdash \langle D_P, env_P \rangle \rightarrow env_P'$ and that $env_V', env_P' \vdash \langle S, sto'' \rangle \rightarrow$
  sto'. The type rule that was used to conclude that the block is well-
  typed, can only have been [BLOCK$_{\mathrm{STM}}$]. The induction hypothesis
  then tells us that the pair (env_V', sto'') agrees with E_1, that env_P'
  agrees with E_2 and that (env_V', sto') agrees with E_2. Since env_V'

extends env_V and E_2 extends E with bindings for at least the variables in $\mathrm{dom}(env'_V) \setminus \mathrm{dom}(env_V)$, we get that E agrees with (env_V, sto').

To show that the error predicate does not hold, first note that by Theorem 13.5 we have that E agrees with (env'_V, sto'') and by Theorem 13.6 that E agrees with env'_P. We can then use the induction hypothesis to conclude that $env'_V, env'_P \vdash_E \langle S, sto'' \not\to$ wrong. Consequently, the conditions of the error predicate do not apply.

$\square$

13.2.7 The limitations of the type system

Our type system captures a certain class of run-time errors but there is a price to pay. Some statements that can be executed without problems will be rejected by the type system.

We say that a statement S is *safe* w.r.t. type environment E, (env_V, env_P) and sto if $env_V, env_P \vdash_E \langle S, sto \rangle \not\to$ wrong.

It is easy to find examples of statements that are not well-typed w.r.t. E but are safe wrt. E and any choice of (env_V, env_P) and sto that agree with E. A simple example is the statement S given by

```
begin
    var x := 42
    if 0=1
    then
        x := true
    else
        x := 44
end
```

It is easy to see that $E \not\vdash S : \mathsf{ok}$. The class of statements of this nature, i.e. ones that are safe, but not well-typed, constitutes what is called the *slack* of the type system. See Figure 13.1.

It should not be too much of a disappointment that the type system has slack. Even the small language **Bump** is Turing-complete (see page 29), and, because of this, it is easy to show that it is decidable whether a statement is well-typed while it is undecidable whether a statement is safe. This property – that type checking is tractable while safety checking is not – should hold if the type system is reasonable and the programming language under consideration is Turing-complete.

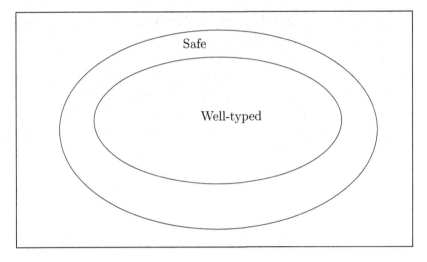

Figure 13.1 A type system is an overapproximation of safety

A moment's thought 13.10   How can we check whether a **Bump** statement is well-typed in some type environment E?

13.3 Typed Flan

We now describe a type system for the functional language **Flan**. We here use a *small-step semantics* of the language.

13.3.1 Syntax

Let **Fexp** denote the syntactic category of **Flan** programs (or expressions, if you want), let **Fcon** denote the syntactic category of **Flan** constants and let **Var** denote the set of variables.

Let $e \in$ **Fexp**, $c \in$ **Fcon** and $x, f \in$ **Var**. First, we consider a version of **Flan** where local declarations are nonrecursive. The formation rules are then

$$e ::= x \mid c \mid (e_1, e_2) \mid e_1 e_2 \mid \textsf{if } e_0 \textsf{ then } e_1 \textsf{ else } e_2 \mid$$
$$\textsf{fn } x.e \mid \textsf{let } x = e_1 \textsf{ in } e_2 \mid \textsf{letrec } x = e_1 \textsf{ in } e_2$$
$$c ::= n \mid \textsf{Plus} \mid \textsf{Times} \mid \textsf{Minus} \mid \textsf{Equal} \mid \textsf{IsZero}$$
$$\mid \textsf{True} \mid \textsf{False} \mid \textsf{Not} \mid \textsf{First} \mid \textsf{Second}$$

13.3.2 The type system

The set of types **Types** is this time given by the following formation rules:

$$T ::= \mathsf{Int} \mid \mathsf{Bool} \mid T_1 \rightarrow T_2 \mid T_1 \times T_2.$$

The central idea is that an expression has the *function type* $T_1 \rightarrow T_2$ if it represents a function that takes an argument of type T_1 and returns a value of type T_2. Moreover, an expression has the *pair type* $T_1 \times T_2$ if it represents a pair whose first coordinate has type T_1 and whose second coordinate has type T_2.

We also assume the existence of a *signature* σ that assigns types to the constants. For instance, we shall assume that $\sigma(\texttt{Plus}) = \mathsf{Int} \times \mathsf{Int} \rightarrow \mathsf{Int}$ and that $\sigma(\texttt{True}) = \mathsf{Bool}$.

Type judgments are of the form

$$E \vdash e : T,$$

where E is a *type environment*, that is, E is a partial function $E : \mathbf{Var} \rightharpoonup \mathbf{Types}$ assigning types to variables. If E is the empty type environment, we simply write $\vdash e : T$.

The type rules are given in Table 13.8. We here explain the most interesting rules. The rule [VAR$_{\text{FUN}}$] is a particularly important rule, since this is the rule that shows the rôle played by the type environment: to find the type of a variable, look it up in the type environment. In the application rule [APP$_{\text{FUN}}$] we require that expression e_1 represents a function, that is, has type $T_1 \rightarrow T_2$; and that e_2 is a valid argument, that is, has type T_1. In the abstraction rule [ABS$_{\text{FUN}}$] we express that a function $\texttt{fn } x.e$ is well-typed and has function type $T_1 \rightarrow T_2$ if it is the case that the body e is well-typed with result type T_2 whenever the argument is known to have type T_1.

The rule for non-recursive let-definitions [LET$_{\text{FUN}}$] states that we must be able to type the locally defined x with some type T_1 and then be able to type the body e_2 under the assumption that x has type T_1. The type rule for recursive let-definitions will be presented in Section 13.3.5.

13.3.3 Semantics

As noted before, **Flan** includes a slightly sugared version of the simply typed applied λ-calculus. We now present a small-step semantics of **Flan**.

In our semantics, values are functions and constants.

Definition 13.11 A *value v* is any expression given by the following

$$[\text{VAR}_{\text{FUN}}] \qquad \frac{E(x) = T}{E \vdash x : T}$$

$$[\text{PAIR}_{\text{FUN}}] \qquad \frac{E \vdash e_1 : T_1 \quad E \vdash e_2 : T_2}{E \vdash (e_1, e_2) : T_1 \times T_2}$$

$$[\text{APP}_{\text{FUN}}] \qquad \frac{E \vdash e_1 : T_1 \to T_2 \quad E \vdash e_2 : T_1}{E \vdash e_1 e_2 : T_2}$$

$$[\text{ABS}_{\text{FUN}}] \qquad \frac{E[x \mapsto T_1] \vdash e : T_2}{E \vdash \mathbf{fn}\ x.e : T_1 \to T_2}$$

$$[\text{IF}_{\text{FUN}}] \qquad \frac{E \vdash e_0 : \mathsf{Bool} \quad E \vdash e_1 : T \quad E \vdash e_2 : T}{E \vdash \mathbf{if}\ e_0\ \mathbf{then}\ e_1\ \mathbf{else}\ e_2 : T}$$

$$[\text{LET}_{\text{FUN}}] \qquad \frac{E \vdash e_1 : T_1 \quad E, x : T_1 \vdash e_2 : T_2}{E \vdash \mathbf{let}\ x = e_1\ \mathbf{in}\ e_2}$$

$$[\text{CONST}_{\text{FUN}}] \qquad E \vdash c : T \text{ if } \sigma(c) = T$$

Table 13.8 *Type rules for **Flan***

formation rules:

$$v ::= c \mid \mathbf{fn}\ x.e \mid x$$

The transition rules are presented in Table 13.9. In some of the rules, we need to perform substitutions. In order to define substitution, we need to be sure that we do not incorrectly capture variables. The situation is the same as in Section 7.5, where we had to avoid name clashes.

As an example of this subtlety, consider the expression $e = \mathbf{fn}\ y.\mathsf{Minus}\ y\ x$ and the value $v = \mathsf{Plus}\ y\ y$. What is $e[x \mapsto v]$? If we naïvely replaced all occurrences of x by $\mathsf{Plus}\ y\ y$ in the body of the function e, we would get $\mathbf{fn}\ y.\mathsf{Minus}\ y\ (\mathsf{Plus}\ y\ y)$ which is clearly not what we want.

The problem is caused by the confusion between the two ys and just as in the λ-calculus, the solution is to apply alpha-conversion to rename the bound occurrence of y found in e (cf. Section 12.3, page 176). First, let us define the notions of free and bound variables (cf. Section 12.3).

Definition 13.12 (Free variables)   The set of free variables of an expression

[PAIR1$_{\text{FUN-SSS}}$]	$$\frac{e_1 \Rightarrow e_1'}{(e_1, e_2) \Rightarrow (e_1', e_2)}$$
[PAIR2$_{\text{FUN-SSS}}$]	$$\frac{e_2 \Rightarrow e_2'}{(e_1, e_2) \Rightarrow (e_1, e_2')}$$
[LET1$_{\text{FUN-SSS}}$]	$$\frac{e_1 \Rightarrow e_1'}{\text{let } x = e_1 \text{ in } e_2 \Rightarrow \text{ let } x = e_1' \text{ in } e_2}$$
[LET2$_{\text{FUN-SSS}}$]	$\text{let } x = v \text{ in } e_2 \Rightarrow e_2[x \mapsto v]$
[LETREC1$_{\text{FUN-SSS}}$]	$$\frac{e_1 \Rightarrow e_1'}{\text{letrec } f = e_1 \text{ in } e \Rightarrow \text{letrec } f = e_1' \text{ in } e}$$
[LETREC2$_{\text{FUN-SSS}}$]	$\text{letrec } f = v \text{ in } e \Rightarrow e[f \mapsto (\text{letrec } f = v \text{ in } v)]$
[IF1$_{\text{FUN-SSS}}$]	$$\frac{e \Rightarrow e'}{\text{if } e \text{ then } e_1 \text{ else } e_2 \Rightarrow \text{if } e' \text{ then } e_1 \text{ else } e_2}$$
[IF2$_{\text{FUN-SSS}}$]	$\text{if } \textit{tt} \text{ then } e_1 \text{ else } e_2 \Rightarrow e_1$
[IF3$_{\text{FUN-SSS}}$]	$\text{if } \textit{ff} \text{ then } e_1 \text{ else } e_2 \Rightarrow e_2$
[APP1$_{\text{FUN-SSS}}$]	$$\frac{e_2 \Rightarrow e_2'}{e_1 e_2 \Rightarrow e_1 e_2'}$$
[APP2$_{\text{FUN-SSS}}$]	$$\frac{e_1 \Rightarrow e_1'}{e_1 v \Rightarrow e_1' v}$$
[APP3$_{\text{FUN-SSS}}$]	$(\textbf{fn } x.e)v \Rightarrow e[x \mapsto v]$
[APP4$_{\text{FUN-SSS}}$]	$c(e) \Rightarrow apply(c, e)$ if $apply(c, e)$ is defined

Table 13.9 *The small-step semantics of* **Flan**

is defined by

$$\text{fv}(x) = \{x\}$$
$$\text{fv}(c) = \emptyset$$
$$\text{fv}((e_1, e_2)) = \text{fv}(e_1) \cup \text{fv}(e_2)$$
$$\text{fv}(\text{if } e_0 \text{ then } e_1 \text{ else } e_2) = \text{fv}(e_0) \cup \text{fv}(e_1) \cup \text{fv}(e_2)$$
$$\text{fv}((\textbf{fn } x.e) = \text{fv}(e) \setminus \{x\}$$
$$\text{fv}(\text{let } y = e_1 \text{ in } e_2) = \text{fv}(e_1) \cup \text{fv}(e_2) \setminus \{y\}$$
$$\text{fv}(\text{letrec } y = e_1 \text{ in } e_2) = \text{fv}(e_1) \cup \text{fv}(e_2) \setminus \{y\}$$

Definition 13.13 (Bound variables)   The set of bound variables of an expression is defined by

$$bv(x) = \emptyset$$
$$bv(c) = \emptyset$$
$$bv((e_1, e_2)) = bv(e_1) \cup bv(e_2)$$
$$bv(\text{if } e_0 \text{ then } e_1 \text{ else } e_2) = bv(e_0) \cup bv(e_1) \cup bv(e_2)$$
$$bv((\text{fn } x.e) = bv(e) \cup \{x\}$$
$$bv(\text{let } y = e_1 \text{ in } e_2) = bv(e_1) \cup bv(e_2) \cup \{y\}$$
$$bv(\text{letrec } y = e_1 \text{ in } e_2) = bv(e_1) \cup bv(e_2) \cup \{y\}$$

Definition 13.14   An expression e is *closed* if $fv(e) = \emptyset$.

We can now deal with the problem of name clashes in a systematic fashion.

Definition 13.15 (Confusion-free expressions)   A **Flan** expression e is *confusion-free* if the sets of free and bound variables are disjoint, i.e. if $fv(e) \cap bv(e) = \emptyset$.

Every **Flan** expression can easily be rewritten as a confusion-free expression by alpha-conversion (see Section 12.3) of the bound names such that they are all distinct and distinct from the free names. It is therefore safe to assume in the following that **Flan** expressions are confusion-free.

Definition 13.16 (Substitution)   The substitution of free variable x by value v in an expression e is defined as follows (where z denotes a fresh variable):

$$y[x \mapsto v] = y$$
$$x[x \mapsto v] = v$$
$$(e_1, e_2)[x \mapsto v] = (e_1[x \mapsto v], e_2[x \mapsto v])$$
$$(\text{if } e_0 \text{ then } e_1 \text{ else } e_2)[x \mapsto v] = \text{if } e_0[x \mapsto v] \text{ then } e_1[x \mapsto v] \text{ else } e_2[x \mapsto v]$$
$$(\text{fn } y.e)[x \mapsto v] = (\text{fn } y.e[y \mapsto z]) \quad \text{if } y \in bv(v) \text{ and } z \text{ fresh}$$
$$(\text{fn } y.e)[x \mapsto v] = (\text{fn } y.e[y \mapsto z]) \quad \text{if } y \notin bv(v)$$
$$(\text{let } y = e_1 \text{ in } e_2)[x \mapsto v] = \text{let } y = e_1[x \mapsto v] \text{ in } e_2[x \mapsto v]$$
$$(\text{letrec } y = e_1 \text{ in } e_2)[x \mapsto v] = \text{letrec } y = e_1[x \mapsto v] \text{ in } e_2[x \mapsto v]$$

13.3.4 Properties of the type system

We can now analyse the type system for **Flan**. The first two sections deal only with **Flan⁻**, the sublanguage without recursive declarations. We consider `letrec`-declarations in Section 13.3.5.

Subject reduction

Our first result is a preservation result commonly known as the *subject reduction property*; it states that a well-typed expression e will remain well-typed after a small-step transition.

The proof of this result proceeds by an induction on the derivation tree for the type judgment $E \vdash e : T$. A complication is that we can perform substitutions as the result of a function application. Therefore we first need to show that whenever we substitute a variable x by a value v (where x does not occur free) of the same type within a well-typed expression e, the resulting expression $e[x \mapsto v]$ remains well-typed.

This is the content of the following important lemma.

Lemma 13.17 (Substitution lemma) *Suppose that e is a **Flan⁻** expression, that $E[x \mapsto T_1] \vdash e : T$ and that for value v where $x \notin \mathrm{fv}(v)$ we have $E \vdash v : T_1$. Then $E \vdash e[x \mapsto v]$, where $x \notin \mathrm{dom}(E)$.*

Proof The proof proceeds by induction on the structure of the derivation tree of the type judgment $E \vdash e : T$. Many of the cases are similar, so we consider only two here and leave the remaining ones as an exercise.

[var$_{\mathbf{fun}}$]: Here, $e = x$. Since $x[x \mapsto v] = v$ and we have $E \vdash v : T_1$, this case follows immediately.

[abs$_{\mathbf{fun}}$]: Here, $e = \mathbf{fn}\ y.e_1$. Since we are considering only confusion-free expressions, we know that $y \neq x$ and $e[x \mapsto v] = \mathbf{fn}\ y.e_1[x \mapsto v]$. By virtue of our induction hypothesis, we have that $E[y \mapsto T_1] \vdash e_1[x \mapsto v]$, where $x \notin \mathrm{dom}(E)$. By using [ABS$_{\mathrm{FUN}}$], we get that $E \vdash (\mathbf{fn}\ y.e_1)[x \mapsto v]$.

$\square$

Problem 13.18 Prove the remaining cases of the substitution lemma.

We can now prove the following theorem.

Theorem 13.19 (Subject reduction) *Suppose e is a **Flan⁻** expression and that $E \vdash e : T$ and $e \Rightarrow e'$. Then also $E \vdash e' : T$.*

Proof We proceed by induction on the derivation tree for $e \Rightarrow e'$. We do not include all cases below, since all of them are simple. The remaining ones are left to the reader as an exercise.

pair1: Assume that $E \vdash (e_1, e_2) : T$. By application of the type rule [PAIR$_{\text{FUN}}$] we conclude that $T = T_1 \times T_2$ and that $E \vdash e_1 : T_1$. By virtue of our induction hypothesis we have that $E \vdash e_1' : T_1$ and by an application of the type rule [PAIR$_{\text{FUN}}$] with premises $E \vdash e_1' : T_1$ and $E \vdash e_2 : T_2$, we get that $E \vdash (e_1', e_2) : T$ as desired.

app3 Assume that $E \vdash (\mathbf{fn}\ x.e)v : T$. By application of the type rules [ABS$_{\text{FUN}}$] and [APP$_{\text{FUN}}$] we conclude that $T = T_2$, that $E, x : T_1 \vdash e : T_2$ and that $E \vdash v : T_1$. From Lemma 13.17 we now get that $E \vdash e[x \mapsto v] : T_2$.

$\square$

Problem 13.20 Complete the proof of Theorem 13.19.

Termination

The safety property that we shall show for **Flan**$^-$ deals with termination.

Even without `letrec` we are able to express infinite behaviour. However, this leads to some complications. Consider the expression e_∞ given by

$$e_\infty = (\mathbf{fn}\ x.x\ x)(\mathbf{fn}\ x.x\ x).$$

Clearly, e_∞ is not a value and it is also easy to see from the small-step semantics that

$$e_\infty \Rightarrow e_\infty.$$

This then means that there is an infinite transition sequence

$$e_\infty \Rightarrow e_\infty \Rightarrow e_\infty \Rightarrow e_\infty \cdots.$$

Can e_∞ be well-typed? The answer is no. We are now going to establish a theorem which has the consequence that e_∞ cannot be well-typed!

Our theorem states that any well-typed program in the fragment **Flan**$^-$ will terminate.

Definition 13.21 (Termination) We write $e \downarrow$ if there exists a value such that $e \Rightarrow^* v$.

Theorem 13.22 *Let $e \in$ **Flan**$^-$ and assume e is closed. If $E \vdash e : T$ for some type T, then $e \downarrow$.*

To prove this theorem, we consider a slightly modified version of **Flan**$^-$.

The basic observation is that if-then-else expressions and let-declarations are both syntactic sugar that can be eliminated.

We can get rid of the construct if e_0 then e_1 else e_2 by introducing a new constant Cond, where the intended behaviour of $Cond(e_0, e_1, e_2)$ is defined by the rules

$$apply(\text{Cond}, (t\!t, (e_1, e_2))) = e_1,$$
$$apply(\text{Cond}, (f\!f, (e_1, e_2))) = e_2.$$

The type of Cond is $(\text{Bool} \times T \times T) \to T$ for any T. In fact, we should think of Cond as a family of constants, one for each type.[1]

Moreover, we can eliminate all local declarations let $x = e_1$ in e_2 by instead writing $(\text{fn } x.e_1)e_2$.

If we let $T(e)$ denote the version of expression e obtained by making the above transformation, one can show that this transformation preserves termination and typability.

Lemma 13.23 *For any* **Flan**$^-$ *expression e we have*

- $T(e) \Rightarrow^* v$ *iff* $e \Rightarrow^* v$
- $E \vdash T(e) : T$ *iff* $E \vdash e : T$.

Problem 13.24 Prove the above lemma.

So from now on we consider a version of **Flan**$^-$ without if-then-else or let-declarations and show that, in this simpler language, well-typed expressions always terminate.

How do we prove Theorem 13.22? It would of course be preferable if we could perform a proof by induction on the structure of e. However, it is not obvious how this should be done. The reason is that a reduction step may make the structure of the resulting expression more involved by duplicating expressions.

Problem 13.25 Try to prove Theorem 13.22 by induction on the structure of e. What happens?

Instead, we introduce a type-indexed reducibility predicate $\text{Red}_T(e)$ which we define by

- $\text{Red}_T(c)$ for any constant c
- For any other expression e
    - $\text{Red}_{\text{Int}}(e)$ iff $e \downarrow$
    - $\text{Red}_{\text{Bool}}(e)$ iff $e \downarrow$

---

[1] This amounts to saying that Cond is polymorphic.

- $\mathsf{Red}_{T_1 \to T_2}(e)$ iff $e \downarrow$ and, whenever $\mathsf{Red}_{T_1}(e_1)$, we have $\mathsf{Red}_{T_2}(e\ e_1)$
- $\mathsf{Red}_{T_1 \times T_2}(e)$ iff $e \downarrow$ and $\mathsf{Red}_{T_1}(\mathbf{First}\ e)$ and $\mathsf{Red}_{T_2}(\mathbf{Second}\ e)$.

This technique is an example of the method of *logical relations* that was originally introduced by Tait (Tait, 1967, 1975) in order to show termination in the simply typed λ-calculus. A logical relation is a type-indexed family of sets, and the family of $\mathsf{Red}_T(e)$-sets is just that.

The idea in the proof that follows is to show that if an expression e is well-typed, then it is reducible. Note that the converse does *not* hold!

A moment's thought 13.26 Find an example of a reducible expression that is not well-typed.

To show that well-typed expressions are reducible, we must first show two results. First, we must show that a reducible expression terminates. Second, we must show that reducibility is preserved by transitions in the small-step semantics.

The first of these results is immediate from our definition of the predicate.

Lemma 13.27 *If* $\mathsf{Red}_T(e)$ *then* $e \downarrow$.

Next, we come to the preservation result. This is stated as follows.

Lemma 13.28 *If* $\vdash e : T$ *and* $e \Rightarrow e'$, *then we have that* $\mathsf{Red}_T(e)$ *iff* $\mathsf{Red}_T(e')$.

Proof If e is a constant, the result is immediate. For any other expression, we proceed by induction on the structure of the type T.

$T = \mathsf{Int}$: Here, there is nothing to prove, as $\mathsf{Red}_{\mathsf{Int}}(e)$ for any expression e.

$T = \mathsf{Bool}$: Similarly, there is nothing to prove in this case.

$T = T_1 \to T_2$: We assume that the lemma holds for T_1 and for T_2 and prove each implication separately. First, suppose that $\mathsf{Red}_{T_1 \to T_2}(e)$ and let e_1 be an arbitrary expression such that $\mathsf{Red}_{T_1}(e_1)$. By definition this means that $\mathsf{Red}_{T_2}(e\ e_1)$. The small-step semantics tells us that $e\ e_1 \Rightarrow e'\ e_1$, and from the induction hypothesis we now get that $\mathsf{Red}_{T_2}(e'\ e_1)$. Because e_1 was arbitrary, we conclude that $\mathsf{Red}_{T_1 \to T_2}(e')$. This proves one implication.

The reverse implication is similar. Assume that $\mathsf{Red}_{T_1 \to T_2}(e')$ and let e_1 be an arbitrary expression such that $\mathsf{Red}_{T_1}(e_1)$. By definition this means that $\mathsf{Red}_{T_2}(e'\ e_1)$. The small-step semantics again tells us that $e\ e_1 \Rightarrow e'\ e_1$, and from the induction hypothesis we now get that $\mathsf{Red}_{T_2}(e\ e_1)$. Because e_1 was arbitrary, we conclude that $\mathsf{Red}_{T_1 \to T_2}(e)$, and we are done.

$T = T_1 \times T_2$: As before, we assume that the lemma holds for T_1 and for T_2 and prove the two implications separately. Suppose first that $\mathsf{Red}_{T_1 \times T_2}(e)$. This by definition means that we have $\mathsf{Red}_{T_1}(\texttt{First } e)$ and $\mathsf{Red}_{T_2}(\texttt{Second } e)$. We know that $e \Rightarrow e'$ implies that $\texttt{First } e \Rightarrow \texttt{First } e'$ and $\texttt{Second } e \Rightarrow \texttt{Second } e'$.

By application of the type rule [CONST$_{\text{FUN}}$] we know that $\vdash \texttt{First } e : T_1$ and that $\vdash \texttt{Second } e : T_2$. By virtue of our induction hypothesis we have that $\mathsf{Red}_{T_1}(\texttt{First } e')$ and that $\mathsf{Red}_{T_2}(\texttt{Second } e')$. But that then implies that $\mathsf{Red}_{T_1 \times T_2}(e')$.

The reverse implication is entirely similar and therefore omitted here.

□

The termination result follows directly from the following result, which states that the reducibility predicate is closed under substitution: if an expression e is well-typed and reducible and we replace all its free variables by reducible, well-typed expressions, the resulting expression will also be reducible.

Theorem 13.29 *Suppose $v_1, \ldots, v_k$ are closed values, that $\vdash v_i : T_i$ and $\mathsf{Red}_{T_i}(v_i)$ for $1 \le i \le k$. Let e be an expression where $\mathrm{fv}(e) = \{x_1, \ldots, x_k\}$ and suppose $[x_1 \mapsto T_1, \ldots, x_k : T_k] \vdash e : T$. Then we have that $\mathsf{Red}_T(e[x_1 \mapsto v_1, \cdots, x_k \mapsto v_k])$.*

Proof Since this is a theorem about all well-typed expressions, the proof is an induction on n, the depth of the derivation tree for $[x_1 \mapsto T_1, \ldots, x_k \mapsto T_k] \vdash e : T$.

$n = 0$: Here, we consider the two axioms.

[**var$_{\text{fun}}$**]: This case is immediate, since $e = x$ and $e[x \mapsto v] = v$ and since we already assume $\mathsf{Red}_T(v)$.

[**cons$_{\text{fun}}$**]: This case is also immediate, since $\mathsf{Red}_T(c)$ for any constant c and since $\mathrm{fv}(v) = \emptyset$.

Assume for n, prove for $n + 1$: Here, there are three rules to deal with.

[**abs$_{\text{fun}}$**]: Here we have that $e = \texttt{fn } x.e'$ with $[x_1 \mapsto T_1, \ldots, x_k \mapsto T_k] \vdash e : U_1 \to U_2$ and we also know that $[x_1 \mapsto T_1, \ldots, x_k \mapsto T_k, x \mapsto U_1] \vdash e' : U_2$.

We must now show that $\mathsf{Red}_{U_1 \to U_2}(e)$. To do this, we must show that for any e_1 for which $\mathsf{Red}_{U_1}(e_1)$ we have that $\mathsf{Red}_{U_2}(e\ e_1)$.

So let e_1 be an arbitrary expression where $\mathsf{Red}_{U_1}(e_1)$. By

Lemma 13.27 we know that there is a value v such that $e_1 \Rightarrow^* v$.

Now let $v_1, \ldots, v_k$ be values where $\vdash v_i : T_i$ and $\mathsf{Red}_{T_i}(v_i)$ for $1 \leq i \leq k$. By virtue of our induction hypothesis, $\mathsf{Red}_{U_2}(e'[x_1 \mapsto v_1, \cdots, x_k \mapsto v_k, x \mapsto v])$.

From the small-step semantics we see that

$$(\mathbf{fn}\ x.e'[x_1 \mapsto v_1, \cdots, x_k \mapsto v_k])e_1 \Rightarrow^*$$
$$e'[x_1 \mapsto v_1, \cdots, x_k \mapsto v_k, x \mapsto v]$$

and Lemma 13.28 gives us that

$$\mathsf{Red}_{U_2}((\mathbf{fn}\ x.e'[x_1 \mapsto v_1, \cdots, x_k \mapsto v_k])e_1)$$

Since e_1 was arbitrary, the case follows.

[**app$_{\mathbf{fun}}$**]: In this case we have that $e = e_1\ e_2$. We have that $[x_1 \mapsto T_1, \ldots, x_k \mapsto T_k] \vdash e_1 : U_1 \rightarrow U_2$ and $[x_1 \mapsto T_1, \ldots, x_k \mapsto T_k] \vdash e_2 : U_1$. We must show that $\mathsf{Red}_{U_2}(e[x_1 \mapsto v_1, \ldots, x_k \mapsto v_k])$.

To improve the readability of the rest of the proof of this case, let us abbreviate the substitution $[x_1 \mapsto v_1, \ldots, x_k \mapsto v_k]$ by σ in the following.

By virtue of our induction hypothesis, we now have that $\mathsf{Red}_{U_1 \rightarrow U_2}(e_1\sigma)$ and $\mathsf{Red}_{U_1}(e_2)$. But, by virtue of the definition of $\mathsf{Red}_{U_1 \rightarrow U_2}(e_1\sigma)$, we have that for all e' where $\mathsf{Red}_{U_1}(e')$ it is the case that $\mathsf{Red}_{U_2}(e_1\sigma\ e')$, so in particular it must hold that $\mathsf{Red}_{U_2}(e_1\sigma\ e_2\sigma)$. Then, since $(e_1\sigma\ e_2\sigma) = (e_1\ e_2)\sigma$, we get $\mathsf{Red}_{U_2}((e_1\ e_2)\sigma)$, which is what we wanted to show.

[**pair$_{\mathbf{fun}}$**]: Here $e = (e_1, e_2)$ with $[x_1 \mapsto T_1, \ldots, x_k \mapsto T_k] \vdash e : U_1 \times U_2$ and we also know that $[x_1 \mapsto T_1, \ldots, x_k \mapsto T_k] \vdash e_1 : U_1$ and that $[x_1 \mapsto T_1, \ldots, x_k \mapsto T_k] \vdash e_2 : U_2$.

Again, let us abbreviate the substitution $[x_1 \mapsto v_1, \ldots, x_k \mapsto v_k]$ by σ in the following.

Now we must show that $\mathsf{Red}_{U_1 \times U_2}(e\sigma)$. We know that $e\sigma = (e_1\sigma, e_2\sigma)$. By virtue of our induction hypothesis we have $\mathsf{Red}_{U_1}(e_1\sigma)$ and $\mathsf{Red}_{U_2}(e_2\sigma)$. From the small-step semantics we conclude that $\mathbf{First}\ (e_1\sigma, e_2\sigma) \Rightarrow e_1\sigma$, so we get from Lemma 13.28 that $\mathsf{Red}_{U_1}(\mathbf{First}\ (e_1\sigma, e_2\sigma))$. In the same fashion we can conclude that $\mathsf{Red}_{U_2}(\mathbf{Second}\ (e_1\sigma, e_2\sigma))$. From these and the definition of the reducibility predicate we now get that $\mathsf{Red}_{U_1 \times U_2}(e\sigma)$.

[LETRECFUN]	$\dfrac{E, x : T_1 \vdash e_1 : T_1 \quad E, x : T_1 \vdash e_2 : T_2}{E \vdash \texttt{letrec } x = e_1 \texttt{ in } e_2}$

Table 13.10 *The type rule for* letrec

$\square$

13.3.5 Well-typed recursion

If we want to be able to deal with potentially infinite behaviour within our type system, we need to introduce the letrec-construct and give it a suitable type rule. The rule is found in Table 13.10.

In the case of a recursive let-definition x may occur in e_1, and these occurrences of x must be recursive calls of e_1. So in [LETRECFUN] we further require that e_1 must have type T_1 under the assumption that x also has type e_1.

13.4 Type polymorphism and type inference

The type systems that we have described in this chapter are fairly weak; many reasonable programs remain untypable. A lot of research has been devoted to developing and understanding more powerful type systems and techniques for implementing them. In this short, final section we briefly outline two of these developments. The interested reader is again referred to Pierce (2002) for more details.

In the setting of functional programs, the notion of *type polymorphism* is central. Consider the identity function

```
fn x.x
```

in **Flan**. What is its type? Clearly, the identity function can take an argument of any type T and return an argument of type T. So we can say that the identity function has type $T \to T$ for all types T. A type of this kind is called a *polymorphic type*, and this is tantamount to introducing *type variables* (ranged over by α) and the notion of a universal quantifier into our language of types. Then the type of the identity function can be written $\forall \alpha. \alpha \to \alpha$.

Another development is that of *type inference*, the study of how to automatically find the types of all entities in a given program.

In a seminal paper Robin Milner relates these two notions; he describes a type inference algorithm for a functional programming language with polymorphic types (Milner, 1978). This work forms a cornerstone of the subsequent work on polymorphically typed functional programming languages such as the languages from the ML family and Haskell.

More recently, there has been work on extending Milner's ideas to other kinds of programming languages, involving traditional imperative languages.

14

An introduction to denotational semantics

This chapter gives a short introduction to the general principles of denotational semantics. We do this by giving a denotational semantics of **Bims**. It turns out that the semantics of while-loops poses a problem, as the obvious semantics is not compositional. However, at the end of the chapter we find a way to circumvent this problem of non-compositionality.

14.1 Background

Denotational semantics is a child of the 1960s and is based on the groundbreaking insights of Christopher Strachey and Dana Scott (Strachey, 1966, 1967; Scott and Strachey, 1971). Since then, a lot of work has gone into providing denotational semantics for existing programming languages such as Algol 60, Pascal, Smalltalk and Lisp.

Denotational semantics has also turned out to be a particularly useful tool in the design and implementation of languages such as Ada, CHILL and Lucid (Schmidt, 1986).

Denotational semantics can also be useful in *static program analysis*, which is the study of the correctness properties on the basis of analyses of the program text (as opposed to analyses of the behaviour of the program).

Simple examples of static analysis involve methods for code optimization. Here are two examples.

Consider the so-called *constant-folding problem*: when is it possible to replace an expression involving variables by a constant? For instance, a solution to the constant-folding problem will allow us to conclude that the variable y in the statement

```
x := 7; y := x + x + 26
```

always has the value 40.

Or consider *sign analysis*. In the above example we see that y will always have a positive integer as its value. This kind of information can be used to optimize the code generated during compilation. Consider the **Bims** fragment

```
x := 7; y:= x + x + 26; while y < 0 do...
```

Here, we will not need to generate code for the body of the while-loop.

The idea of static program analysis is to define a *non-standard semantics* that captures the property that we want to analyse – e.g. that of the sign of integer variables. This kind of non-standard semantics is a denotational semantics, where the meaning of an expression is its sign and the meaning of a program is either of the values *safe* or *not safe*. If we had wanted to, we could have given a structural operational semantics; the idea of static program analysis is not specific to denotational semantics.

A good introduction to the use and usefulness of denotational semantics in static program analysis is the book by Nielson and Nielson (2007).

Another advantage of denotational semantics is that it describes programs as computable functions; this makes it very easy to implement the definitions of a denotational semantics in a functional programming language. The pioneering system SIS (Mosses, 1975) developed by Mosses in 1975 made use of this observation.

For the same reason, it is fairly easy to describe the denotational semantics of a functional programming language.

Denotational semantics has its disadvantages, too. In particular, it is difficult to provide a simple account of nondeterminism and concurrency using this kind of semantics; this difficulty was one of the motivations behind the development of structural operational semantics.

14.2 λ-Notation

In this and the next chapter we shall devote a lot of attention to functions. For this reason it is important to establish a convenient notation for functions. Our choice of notation, λ-notation, is directly inspired by the λ-calculus (see Chapter 12). A function with argument x and body e is written as the *abstraction* $\lambda x.e$. A function f is said to have type $A \rightarrow B$ if the domain of f is the set A and the range of f is the set B.

Example 14.1 $\lambda z.3 + z$ denotes a function whose type is $\mathbb{Z} \rightarrow \mathbb{Z}$. This function adds 3 to its argument. $\lambda x.x \cdot x$ denotes a function of type $\mathbb{Z} \rightarrow \mathbb{Z}$ that squares its argument.

The body of a λ-expression always extends as far to the right as possible, i.e. $\lambda x.x + 1$ is $\lambda x.(x + 1)$ and not $(\lambda x.x) + 1$.

The λ-notation is therefore just another notation for functions. One of its advantages is that we do not need to name functions. Another, even more important advantage, which is inherited from the λ-calculus, is that we can now express higher-order functions, i.e. functions that take functions as arguments and/or return a function.

Example 14.2 $\lambda x.\lambda y.x + y$ denotes the function which takes an argument x and returns the function which takes an argument and adds x to it. Consequently, $\lambda x.\lambda y.x + y$ has the type $\mathbb{Z} \to (\mathbb{Z} \to \mathbb{Z})$.

Problem 14.3   For each of the following λ-expressions, describe its intended meaning and find its type:

1. $\lambda x.x - 2$
2. $\lambda x.\neg x$
3. $\lambda f.\lambda x.f(f(x + 3)) + 1$
4. $\lambda s.\lambda(x, v).s[x \mapsto v]$

As in the λ-calculus, we write the application of a λ-expression to an argument as the juxtaposition of the two.

Example 14.4   For example,

$$(\lambda x.x + 45)9 = 54, \tag{14.1}$$
$$(\lambda x.\lambda y.x + y)3 = \lambda y.3 + y. \tag{14.2}$$

Sometimes it is convenient to use *conditional expressions*, and here we use a simple *if. . . then . . . else . . .* notation. So

$$\lambda x.if\, x > 0\ then\ 1\ else - 1$$

denotes the function whose type is $\mathbb{Z} \to \{-1, 1\}$ and that returns 1 if the argument is positive and -1 otherwise.

If a function is not defined for all arguments (and therefore is a partial function), we indicate the missing cases by undef.

Example 14.5   The function whose type is $\mathbb{R} \rightharpoonup \mathbb{R}$,

$$\lambda x.if\, x \geq 0\ \ then\ \sqrt{x}\ \ else\ \underline{undef}$$

is the square-root function (which is a partial function when seen as a function over the reals).

14.3 Basic ideas

The central idea of denotational semantics is that a semantic definition defines a *semantic function* $\mathcal{SF}$ which to every element in the syntactic category **Syn** assigns a *denotation*, which is an element of a *semantic category*, **Sem**:

$$\mathcal{SF} : \mathbf{Syn} \to \mathbf{Sem}.$$

Consequently, there must a semantic function for each syntactic category in the language. $\mathcal{SF}$ must be specified by means of a syntax-directed and preferably also compositional definition.

We now make this idea concrete by presenting a denotational semantics of the arithmetic and Boolean expressions of **Bims**.

14.3.1 Denotational semantics of Aexp

Let us start by giving a denotational semantics of arithmetic expressions without variables, i.e. the elements of **Aexp** given by the formation rules

$$a ::= n \mid a_1 + a_2 \mid a_1 * a_2 \mid a_1 - a_2 \mid (a_1)$$

The denotation of an arithmetic expression is its value, which is an integer. This means that the semantic category is the set of integers, $\mathbb{Z}$. Our semantic function is called $\mathcal{A}^-$ and its type is

$$\mathcal{A}^- : \mathbf{Aexp} \to \mathbb{Z}.$$

We now define $\mathcal{A}^-$ by defining how the function acts on each construct of **Aexp**. Here, we again make use of the function $\mathcal{N} : \mathbf{Num} \to \mathbb{Z}$ whose value is the integer value of a given numeral.

$$\mathcal{A}^-[\![n]\!] = \mathcal{N}[\![n]\!]$$
$$\mathcal{A}^-[\![a_1 + a_2]\!] = \mathcal{A}^-[\![a_1]\!] + \mathcal{A}^-[\![a_2]\!]$$
$$\mathcal{A}^-[\![a_1 * a_2]\!] = \mathcal{A}^-[\![a_1]\!] \cdot \mathcal{A}^-[\![a_2]\!]$$
$$\mathcal{A}^-[\![a_1 - a_2]\!] = \mathcal{A}^-[\![a_1]\!] - \mathcal{A}^-[\![a_2]\!]$$
$$\mathcal{A}^-[\![(a)]\!] = \mathcal{A}^-[\![a]\!].$$

Example 14.6 Let us try to find $\mathcal{A}^-[\![(3+4)*(9-4)]\!]$. By directly applying the definition of $\mathcal{A}^-$ we get

$$
\begin{aligned}
\mathcal{A}^-[\![(3+4)*(9-4)]\!] &= \mathcal{A}^-[\![(3+4)]\!] \cdot \mathcal{A}^-[\![(9-4)]\!] \\
&= \mathcal{A}^-[\![3+4]\!] \cdot \mathcal{A}^-[\![9-4]\!] \\
&= (\mathcal{A}^-[\![3]\!] + \mathcal{A}^-[\![4]\!]) \cdot (\mathcal{A}^-[\![9]\!] - \mathcal{A}^-[\![4]\!]) \\
&= (3+4) \cdot (9-4) \\
&= 7 \cdot 5 \\
&= 35.
\end{aligned}
$$

Notice from the above example how important it is to have a *compositional* definition, i.e. a definition which satisfies that the denotation of a composite element can be determined by finding the denotations of its immediate constituents. This gives us a divide-and-conquer strategy for finding the denotation.

When variables are present, the value of an arithmetic expression will depend on the values of the variables, i.e. of a program state. So the denotation of an arithmetic expression is now a function from states to values:

$$
\mathcal{A} : \textbf{Aexp} \rightarrow (\textbf{States} \rightarrow \mathbb{Z})
$$

and our definition of $\mathcal{A}$ becomes

$$
\begin{aligned}
\mathcal{A}[\![n]\!] &= \lambda s.\mathcal{N}[\![n]\!] \\
\mathcal{A}[\![x]\!] &= \lambda s.sx \\
\mathcal{A}[\![a_1+a_2]\!] &= \lambda s.\mathcal{A}[\![a_1]\!]s + \mathcal{A}[\![a_2]\!]s \\
\mathcal{A}[\![a_1*a_2]\!] &= \lambda s.\mathcal{A}[\![a_1]\!]s \cdot \mathcal{A}[\![a_2]\!]s \\
\mathcal{A}[\![a_1-a_2]\!] &= \lambda s.\mathcal{A}[\![a_1]\!]s - \mathcal{A}[\![a_2]\!]s \\
\mathcal{A}[\![(a)]\!] &= \lambda s.\mathcal{A}[\![a]\!]s.
\end{aligned}
$$

Example 14.7 Let $s_1 \in$ **States** be given by $[\mathsf{x} \mapsto 3, \mathsf{y} \mapsto 14]$. Then

$$
\begin{aligned}
\mathcal{A}[\![\mathsf{x} + 2]\!]s_1 &= (\lambda s.(\mathcal{A}[\![\mathsf{x}]\!]s) + (\mathcal{A}[\![2]\!]s))s_1 \\
&= (\lambda s.((\lambda s.s\mathsf{x})s) + ((\lambda s.\mathcal{N}[\![2]\!])s))s_1 \\
&= (s_1\mathsf{x}) + 2 \\
&= 3 + 2 = 5.
\end{aligned}
$$

Problem 14.8 Let $s \in$ **States** be given by $[\mathsf{x} \mapsto 3, \mathsf{y} \mapsto 14]$. Find, by applying the definition, $\mathcal{A}[\![((\mathsf{x}+\mathsf{x})-2)*(\mathsf{y}-3*\mathsf{x})]\!]s$ and $\mathcal{A}[\![(3+42)+\mathsf{x}*\mathsf{y}]\!]$.

14.3.2 Denotational semantics of Bexp

Bexp is given by the formation rules

$$b ::= a_1 = a_2 \mid a_1 < a_2 \mid \neg b_1 \mid b_1 \wedge b_2 \mid (b_1).$$

The denotational semantics of **Bexp** should depend on that of **Aexp**. Since arithmetic expressions may occur as part of Boolean expressions, the denotation of a Boolean expression also has to depend on the program state.

Consequently, our semantic category is the set **States** $\to \{tt, ff\}$, and our semantic function $\mathcal{B}$ has type

$$\mathcal{B} : \textbf{Bexp} \to (\textbf{States} \to \{tt, ff\}$$

and is defined by

$$\mathcal{B}[\![a_1 = a_2]\!] = \lambda s. if\,(\mathcal{A}[\![a_1]\!]s = \mathcal{A}[\![a_2]\!]s)\ then\ tt\ else\ ff$$
$$\mathcal{B}[\![a_1 < a_2]\!] = \lambda s. if\,(\mathcal{A}[\![a_1]\!]s < \mathcal{A}[\![a_2]\!]s)\ then\ tt\ else\ ff$$
$$\mathcal{B}[\![\neg b]\!] = \lambda s. if\,(\mathcal{B}[\![b]\!]s = tt)\ then\ ff\ else\ tt$$
$$\mathcal{B}[\![b_1 \wedge b_2]\!] = \lambda s. if\,(\mathcal{B}[\![b_1]\!]s = tt)\ and\,(\mathcal{B}[\![b_2]\!]s = tt)\ then\ tt\ else\ ff$$
$$\mathcal{B}[\![(b_1)]\!] = \lambda s. \mathcal{B}[\![b_1]\!]s.$$

A moment's thought 14.9   Let the state $s_1 \in$ **States** be given by

$$s = [\mathbf{x} \mapsto 14, \mathbf{y} \mapsto 3, \mathbf{z} \mapsto 11].$$

Find, using the definition, the value of $\mathcal{B}[\![\mathbf{x} = \mathbf{y+z} \wedge \neg\,(\mathbf{y} < 5)]\!]s_1$.

14.4 Denotational semantics of statements

We are now finally ready for the definition of the denotational semantics of statements in **Bims**.

14.4.1 The denotation of a statement

What should the denotation of a statement be? A statement can change the values of variables, and the values of variables are given by the program state.

Therefore, a statement will, given an initial state, produce a final state. So the denotation of a statement should be a function over the set of states. Sometimes a statement will not produce a final state. This is the case when the statement fails to terminate. This then means that the denotation of a statement should be a *partial function over the set of states*, i.e. a function of type **States** $\rightharpoonup$ **States**. The semantic function $\mathcal{S}$ therefore has type

$$\mathcal{S} : \mathbf{Stm} \to (\mathbf{States} \rightharpoonup \mathbf{States}).$$

A function whose type is **States** $\rightharpoonup$ **States** is often called a *state transformation.*

A moment's thought 14.10 Explain why we do not want the type of $\mathcal{S}$ to be

$$\mathcal{S} : \mathbf{Stm} \to \mathbf{States}.$$

Also explain why we do not want the type of $\mathcal{S}$ to be

$$\mathcal{S} : \mathbf{Stm} \rightharpoonup (\mathbf{States} \rightharpoonup \mathbf{States}).$$

Let us now consider each of the language constructs of **Bims** to get an idea of what its denotation should be.

First, let us find the state transformation that corresponds to `skip`. The statement `skip` does not alter the state, so its denotation should simply be the identity function $\lambda s.s$.

An assignment statement $x := a$ will, given a state s, return a state which is s except that x now has the value of a, where a is evaluated in state s. The denotation of $x := a$ should therefore be the function $\lambda s.s[x \mapsto (\mathcal{A}[\![a]\!]s)]$.

A sequential composition $S_1; S_2$ will first change the state according to the state transformation of S_1 and then change the state according to the state transformation of S_2. So, if our initial state is s, the final state will be $\mathcal{S}[\![S_2]\!](\mathcal{S}[\![S_1]\!]s)$. This then means that the denotation of $S_1; S_2$ should be $\lambda s.\mathcal{S}[\![S_2]\!](\mathcal{S}[\![S_1]\!]s)$. This is simply the *function composition* $\mathcal{S}[\![S_2]\!] \circ \mathcal{S}[\![S1]\!]$.

A conditional statement `if` b `then` S_1 `else` S_2 gives rise to either a state change corresponding to the state transformation of S_1 or the state transformation of S_2, depending on the value of b. The denotation of a conditional statement is therefore $\lambda s.if\,(\mathcal{B}[\![b]\!]s = t\!t)\ then\ \mathcal{S}[\![S_1]\!]s\ else\ \mathcal{S}[\![S_2]\!]s$.

We execute a loop `while` b `do` S in state s by first checking the condition b in state s. If b evaluates to true, then we must execute S in initial state s and then re-enter the loop. Otherwise, nothing happens, and the final state is simply s.

All in all, this leads to the following definition of $\mathcal{S}$:

$$\mathcal{S}[\![\text{skip}]\!] = \lambda s.s$$
$$\mathcal{S}[\![x := a]\!] = \lambda s.s[x \mapsto (\mathcal{A}[\![a]\!]s)]$$
$$\mathcal{S}[\![S_1; S_2]\!] = \mathcal{S}[\![S_2]\!] \circ \mathcal{S}[\![S_1]\!]$$
$$\mathcal{S}[\![\text{if } b \text{ then } S_1 \text{ else } S_2]\!] = \lambda s. \textit{if } (\mathcal{B}[\![b]\!]s = t\!t) \textit{ then } \mathcal{S}[\![S_1]\!]s \textit{ else } \mathcal{S}[\![S_2]\!]s$$
$$\mathcal{S}[\![\text{while } b \text{ do } S]\!] = \lambda s. \textit{if } (\mathcal{B}[\![b]\!]s = t\!t) \textit{ then}$$
$$(\mathcal{S}[\![\text{while } b \text{ do } S]\!] \circ \mathcal{S}[\![S]\!])s$$
$$\textit{else } s.$$

Example 14.11   Let us find

$$\mathcal{S}[\![\text{if } x > 3 \text{ then } (x := \ 3{+}x; y := 4) \text{ else } \ \text{skip}]\!].$$

We have

$$\mathcal{S}[\![\text{if } x > 3 \text{ then } (x := 3{+}x; y := 4) \text{ else skip}]\!] =$$
$$\lambda s. \textit{if} (\mathcal{B}[\![x > 3]\!]s = t\!t) \textit{ then } \mathcal{S}[\![x := 3{+}x; y := 4]\!]s \textit{ else } \mathcal{S}[\![\text{skip}]\!]s =$$
$$\lambda s. \textit{if } (sx > 3) \textit{ then } (\mathcal{S}[\![y := 4]\!] \circ \mathcal{S}[\![x := 3{+}x]\!])s \textit{ else } s =$$
$$\lambda s. \textit{if } (sx > 3) \textit{ then } s[x \mapsto 3 + sx][y \mapsto 4] \textit{ else } s.$$

A moment's thought 14.12   Why is there a section on λ-notation in this chapter?

Problem 14.13   Let S be the statement

x := 3; y:= 0; if (y > x) then y:= 3-y else x:= 42

and let s be given by $sx = 4$. Find $\mathcal{S}[\![S]\!]s$.

Problem 14.14   Let S be the statement

i:= 1; while (x > 0) do (i:= i * x; x:= x-1)

Try finding $\mathcal{S}[\![S]\!]$. Let s be given by $sx = 3$. Find $\mathcal{S}[\![S]\!]s$.

14.4.2 Subtleties in the definition of $\mathcal{S}$

The definition of $\mathcal{S}$ is *not compositional*: On the right-hand side of the definition of the denotation of while b do S we have an occurrence of while b do S. The consequence is that it becomes difficult for us to use the definition for finding the denotation of any statement that involves while-loops.

In fact, one may ask whether the denotation of a while-loop is well defined at all. A slightly different way of phrasing this question is the following. Given a while-loop while b do S, does there exist a state transformation $f :$ **States** $\rightharpoonup$ **States** which satisfies the condition below?

$$f = \lambda s. if\,(\mathcal{B}[\![b]\!]s = t\!t)\; then\;(f \circ \mathcal{S}[\![S]\!])s\; else\; s. \tag{14.3}$$

Fortunately, the answer is *yes*. In general there may be more than one f satisfying (14.3). As a matter of fact, there may be infinitely many. So which one do we choose?

Consider the statement

$$\texttt{while } \neg(\texttt{x=0}) \texttt{ do x:= x-1.}$$

What is $\mathcal{S}[\![\texttt{while } \neg(\texttt{x=0}) \texttt{ do x:= x-1}]\!]$? Consider the two state transformations

- $f_1 = \lambda s. if\,(s\,\mathbf{x} \geq 0)\; then\; s[\mathbf{x} \mapsto 0]\; else\; \underline{undef}$
- $f_2 = \lambda s. s[\mathbf{x} \mapsto 0]$

We can show that f_1 and f_2 both satisfy (14.3). Here we consider the case of f_1. This gives rise to the equation

$$\lambda s. if\,(s\,\mathbf{x} \geq 0)\; then\; s[\mathbf{x} \mapsto 0]\; else\; \underline{undef} = \lambda s. if\,(s\,\mathbf{x} \neq 0)\; then$$
$$((\lambda s. if\,(s\,\mathbf{x} \geq 0)\; then\; s[\mathbf{x} \mapsto 0]$$
$$else\; \underline{undef}) \circ (\lambda s. s[\mathbf{x} \mapsto (s\,\mathbf{x}) - 1])s)$$
$$else\; s.$$

Call the function on the left-hand side f_1' and the function on the right-hand side f_1''. We must now show that $f_1' = f_1''$. Two functions are equal if they return the same value for any choice of argument. Here, this means that for all $s \in$ **States** we have that $f_1's = f_1''s$. There are three cases to consider – states s where $s\mathbf{x} > 0$, states s where $s\mathbf{x} = 0$ and states s where $s\mathbf{x} < 0$. First consider the case where $s\mathbf{x} = 0$. Here we see that

$$f_1's = s[\mathbf{x} \mapsto 0]$$

and that

$$f_1''s = s.$$

But since $s\mathbf{x} = 0$, we have that $s = s[\mathbf{x} \mapsto 0]$. Next consider the case where $s\mathbf{x} > 0$. Here we have that

$$f_1's = s[\mathbf{x} \mapsto 0]$$

and that

$$f_1''s = (\lambda s. s[\mathbf{x} \mapsto 0])s[\mathbf{x} \mapsto (s\,\mathbf{x}) - 1] = s[\mathbf{x} \mapsto 0].$$

The third case, where $sx < 0$, is similar.

Problem 14.15   Prove the case where $sx < 0$.

Problem 14.16 (Important)   Show that f_2 also satisfies (14.3).

So which state transformation should we choose? f_1 or f_2? Intuitively while $\neg(x=0)$ do x:= x-1 corresponds to the following: if we start out in a state where x has a non-negative value, we end up in a state where x has the value 0, whereas if we start in a state where x has a negative value, then the final state is undefined, since the execution of the loop never terminates.

So f_1 is the best choice for the denotation of while $\neg(x=0)$ do x:= x-1. The other state transformations 'say too much'.

Therefore, while there may in general be more than one transformation that satisfies (14.3), we should always choose the one which is minimal in the sense that it does not provide unnecessary information.

The equation (14.3) can be viewed differently. Let us define a function $F : (\textbf{States} \rightharpoonup \textbf{States}) \rightarrow (\textbf{States} \rightharpoonup \textbf{States})$ defined by

$$F = \lambda f.\lambda s.if\,(\mathcal{B}[\![b]\!]s = t\!t)\ then\ f \circ \mathcal{S}[\![S]\!])s\ else\ s.$$

Asking for a solution to (14.3) is tantamount to asking for an f such that $f = F(f)$.

In mathematics, when given a function $g : D \rightarrow D$, we call an x such that $x = g(x)$ a *fixed point* of g. So our denotation of while b do S should be a fixed point of F and it should be a minimal function, where we need a good definition of 'minimal'.

If we can set up reasonable definitions and conditions that will guarantee that F does indeed have such a fixed point, then we can define the semantics of while-loops as such a fixed point.

Setting up the necessary mathematical apparatus for this is the topic of the following chapter.

14.5 Further reading

There are some older books whose main focus is denotational semantics. Stoy, who worked with Christopher Strachey at Oxford University, was the first to write a book about the subject (Stoy, 1977). A few years laters, Gordon wrote a fairly short text (Gordon, 1979), whose emphasis is on applications and does not describe the mathematical underpinnings. Two more technically oriented accounts were given by Schmidt (1986) and Allison (1987).

Many more recent books with a broader focus have chapters devoted to denotational semantics. These include the books by Winskel (1993) and Nielson and Nielson (2007). The latter also describes applications of denotational semantics to static program analysis.

15

Recursive definitions

Recursive definitions appear in many different contexts throughout theoretical computer science and mathematics and are central to the study of programming language semantics and program verification.

In this, the last chapter of the book, we present a general result which will allow us to

- establish sufficient criteria for the existence and uniqueness of a minimal solution to a recursive definition
- find a way to compute the minimal solution to any recursive definition that satisfies these criteria.

As an important application we can now prove that the big-step semantics of **Bims** presented in Chapter 4 and the denotational semantics of **Bims** found in Chapter 14 are equivalent. We do this in Section 15.8.

15.1 A first example

In this section we present an example of a recursive definition and analyze its properties. We shall see that

- We can think of a recursive definition as an equation
- An object which satisfies a recursive definition is a solution to this underlying equation.

15.1.1 A recursively defined language

We define a language L_S by the following recursive definition:

$$L_S = \{a\}L_S\{b\} \cup \{c\} \cup L_S. \tag{15.1}$$

This definition is not as arcane as it might appear at first sight. For we could have defined L_S using a context-free grammar (V, Σ, R, S), where $V = \{S\}$, $\Sigma = \{a, b, c\}$ and the production rules of R are given by

$$S \rightarrow aSb \mid c \mid S. \qquad (15.2)$$

Notice how the grammar of (15.2) corresponds to the definition in (15.1).

15.1.2 Computing a solution

We are now going to present a systematic approach to finding a language U that satisfies (15.1). It is this approach that will be central to the rest of the chapter.

The underlying idea is to use the following procedure.

1. Start out by instantiating the right-hand side of the definition with the minimal candidate for a solution U_0.
2. This gives us a new candidate for a solution U_1. Now instantiate the right-hand side of the definition with U_1. This gives yet another solution candidate, U_2.
3. Continue in this way: obtain a new solution candidate U_{i+1} by instantiating the right-hand side of the definition with U_i.

This procedure gives us a sequence of solution candidates:

$$U_0, U_1, U_2, U_3 \ldots$$

The limit of the sequence is the minimal solution U. It is important to note that *the sequence may be infinite.*

In our example, the minimal solution candidate is the empty language $\emptyset$. We now have

$$
\begin{aligned}
U_1 &= \{a\}U_0\{b\} \cup \{c\} \cup U_0 = \{c\}, \\
U_2 &= \{a\}U_1\{b\} \cup \{c\} \cup U_1 = \{c, acb\}, \\
U_3 &= \{a\}U_2\{b\} \cup \{c\} \cup U_2 = \{c, acb, aacbb\},
\end{aligned}
$$

$$\ldots$$

and we see that the languages form a sequence which is increasing w.r.t. subset inclusion:

$$U_0 \subseteq U_1 \subseteq U_2 \subseteq U_3 \ldots$$

In other words, this is an *increasing sequence*. What is the limit of the sequence $\{U_0, U_1, U_2, \ldots\}$? It must be a language which is a superset of any language found in the sequence. A good candidate for a limit is the language

$$U = \{a^i cb^i \mid i \geq 0\}.$$

If we instantiate (15.1) with U, we get

$$\{c\} \cup \{a\}U\{b\} \cup U = \{c\} \cup \{aa^i cbb^i \mid i \geq 0\} = \{a^i cb^i \mid i \geq 0\} = U,$$

so U is a solution of the equation (15.1).

15.1.3 Existence and uniqueness

We have just seen a way of computing a solution to the equation associated with a recursive definition. However, there may be many solutions to such an equation. In our example, another solution is

$$L_S'' = \{w \in \Sigma^* \mid \exists n \geq 0.w = a^n cccb^n\} \cup \{w \in \Sigma^* \mid \exists n \geq 0.w = a^n cb^n\}.$$

Problem 15.1   Show that L_S'' really is a solution of (15.1). Show that there are in fact *infinitely many* solutions to (15.1). *Hint:* Try some variations of L_S''.

However, L_S'' is not a sensible solution – it contains strings of the form $a^i cccb^i$ that are not mentioned in the definition. In a sense, L_S'' 'tells us more than we want'.

Rather, we are interested in a minimal solution.

15.2 A recursive definition specifies a fixed-point

Every recursive definition is of the form

$$X = F(X), \tag{15.3}$$

where X is the object to be defined (the *definiendum*) and the right-hand side $F(X)$ is the defining property (the *definiens*).

If we know that X is a member of some set D, we can think of the right-hand side $F(X)$ as a function over D, so $F : D \to D$. We call D the *solution domain*.

Definition 15.2 (Fixed-point)   Let D be any set and let $f : D \to D$ be any function over D. We say that $x \in D$ is a *fixed-point* of f if we have $f(x) = x$.

In other words, a fixed point of a function f is a point which is left unchanged by f.

Saying that X satisfies (15.3) is therefore equivalent to saying that X is a fixed point of the right-hand-side function F, and our quest becomes that of computing a fixed point of a function.

15.3 The fixed-point theorem

In this section we shall formulate and prove a very important theorem, Theorem 15.3.

This theorem uses a lot of new concepts that we need to define. The goal of the sections that follow is to define these concepts.

Theorem 15.3 (Fixed-point theorem) *If $(D, \sqsubseteq)$ is a cpo and $f : D \to D$ is a continuous function, then f has a least fixed-point w.r.t. the ordering $\sqsubseteq$. This fixed point, called x^*, is given by*

$$x^* = \lim\{f^i \perp \mid i \geq 0\}, \qquad (15.4)$$

where $\perp$ is the bottom element of D.

15.3.1 Cpos

In this book a cpo stands for a *complete partial order*.

Partially ordered sets

A *partially ordered set* is a set equipped with a relation $\sqsubseteq$ which has properties in common with the relation $\leq$ (less than or equal) on numbers.

We speak of *partially* ordered sets, since we do not require all elements in our set to be comparable under $\sqsubseteq$.

Definition 15.4 (Partially ordered set) Let D be a set, called the set of *points*, and let $\sqsubseteq$ be a binary relation over D. The pair $(D, \sqsubseteq)$ is called a *partially ordered set* if the following conditions are satisfied:

1. $d \sqsubseteq d$ for all $d \in D$ ($\sqsubseteq$ is *reflexive*)
2. For all $d_1, d_2 \in D$: if $d_1 \sqsubseteq d_2$ and $d_2 \sqsubseteq d_1$ then $d_1 = d_2$ ($\sqsubseteq$ is *antisymmetric*)
3. For all $d_1, d_2, d_3 \in D$: if $d_1 \sqsubseteq d_2$ and $d_2 \sqsubseteq d_3$ then $d_1 \sqsubseteq d_3$ ($\sqsubseteq$ is *transitive*).

A partially ordered set $(D, \sqsubseteq)$ is a *totally ordered set* if for all $d_1, d_2 \in D$ we have $d_1 \sqsubseteq d_2$ or $d_2 \sqsubseteq d_1$.

3

2

1

0

Figure 15.1 Part of the Hasse diagram for $(\mathbb{N}, \leq)$

Examples of partially ordered sets

Partially ordered sets occur in many different settings in mathematics.

Example 15.5   Let $\mathbb{R}$ be the set of real numbers and let $\leq$ be defined in the usual way. Then it is easy to show that $(\mathbb{R}, \leq)$ is a partially ordered set: we check the three properties of the definition. It clearly holds for all $x \in \mathbb{R}$ that $x \leq x$. It is also immediately obvious that for any $x, y \in \mathbb{R}$ we have that if $x \leq y$ and $y \leq x$ then $x = y$. Also, if $x \leq y$ and $y \leq z$ we have that $x \leq z$. $(\mathbb{R}, \leq)$ is also a totally ordered set (any two numbers can be compared).

Example 15.6   Let $\mathbb{N}$ be the set of natural numbers and let $\leq$ be defined in the usual way. Then $(N, \leq)$ is a partially ordered set. The proof of this proceeds exactly as in the previous example.

A partially ordered set is often given in the form of a *Hasse diagram*. A Hasse diagram is a directed acyclic graph (a *dag*) whose vertices correspond to the points and whose edges correspond to the ordering relation. The smaller a point is, the closer it is to the bottom of the diagram. An example is shown in Figure 15.1.

Example 15.7   Let Σ be an alphabet and let u and v be strings over Σ. We say that $u \sqsubseteq v$ if there exists a $w \in \Sigma^*$ such that $uw = v$. Then we have that $(\Sigma^*, \sqsubseteq)$ is a partially ordered set. The ordering relation given here is often called the *prefix ordering*, since $u \sqsubseteq v$ if and only if u is a prefix of v.

Problem 15.8   Prove that $(\Sigma^*, \sqsubseteq)$ as defined in Example 15.7 is a partially ordered set. Is it also a totally ordered set?

Increasing sequences and limits

In our setting, a limit is a *least upper bound* of an increasing sequence.

Definition 15.9   Let $(D, \sqsubseteq)$ be a partially ordered set. An *increasing sequence* in D is a subset of points $Y \subseteq D$, where $Y = \{y_1, y_2, y_3 \ldots\}$ and where we have for all $i \geq 1$ that $y_i \sqsubseteq y_{i+1}$.

In the literature on partially ordered sets, an increasing sequence is often called a *chain*.

Definition 15.10   Let $(D, \sqsubseteq)$ be a partially ordered set and let $Y \subseteq D$ be any set of points. The point x is called an *upper bound* of Y if we have for all $y \in Y$ that $y \sqsubseteq x$.

Definition 15.11 (Limit)   Let Y be an increasing sequence in $(D, \sqsubseteq)$. The point $x \in D$ is called a *limit* of Y if the following conditions are satisfied:

1. x is an upper bound of Y
2. For every upper bound z of Y we have $x \sqsubseteq z$.

We denote the limit of Y in D, if it exists, by $\lim Y$ or $\lim_{y \in Y} y$.

Example 15.12   Let $(\mathbb{N}, \leq)$ be the set of natural numbers under the usual ordering. Then 42 is an upper bound of the set $\{9, 17, 23, 38\}$.

Note that the limit of an increasing sequence is unique. Suppose x_1 and x_2 are both limits of Y, then it follows from the second condition of Definition 15.11 that $x_1 \sqsubseteq x_2$, since x_1 is a limit, and that $x_2 \sqsubseteq x_1$, since x_2 is a limit. But then, since a partial order is antisymmetric, we have that $x_1 = x_2$.

A moment's thought 15.13   What is the least upper bound of the set in the above example?

Example 15.14   Consider again $(\mathbb{R}, \leq)$ and let Y be the set of natural numbers, that is, $Y = \{1, 2, 3, 4, \ldots\}$. Then Y has no upper bound, so $\lim Y$ is not defined.

Example 15.15   Let $\mathbb{Q}$ be the set of rational numbers and consider the increasing sequence

$Y = \{x_i | x_i$ is the number whose decimals are the first i decimals of $\pi, i \geq 0\}$.

Then numbers such as 3.1415927, 3.2 and 4 are upper bounds of Y. However, Y has no limit in $\mathbb{Q}$ – the least number greater than or equal to any number in Y is π, which is not a rational number.

If we instead considered Y as an increasing sequence in the set $\mathbb{R}$, we would have $\lim Y = \pi$.

Note that this example also demonstrates that the limit of an increasing sequence need not be an element of the sequence.

Complete partial orders – the definition

A complete partial order $(D, \sqsubseteq)$ is a partially ordered set with a least point and the property that every increasing sequence has its limit within D.

Definition 15.16 (Complete partial order)   A partially ordered set $(D, \sqsubseteq)$ is a complete partial order *(cpo)* if

- For every increasing sequence $Y \subseteq D$ the limit $\lim Y$ exists
- There exists a *least element* $\bot \in D$ (also known as the *bottom element*), that is, a point $\bot$ such that $\bot \sqsubseteq d$ for all $d \in D$

Problem 15.17   Show that a cpo has exactly one bottom element. That is, show that if there are two bottom elements, then they are equal.

Problem 15.18   Prove that $\lim \emptyset = \bot$. That is, show that the second condition of Definition 15.16 is in fact redundant.

Example 15.19 $(\mathbb{R}, \leq)$ is *not* a cpo. For instance the increasing sequence $\{1, 2, 3, 4, 5, \ldots\}$ has no limit. Likewise, $(\mathbb{Q}, \leq)$ is *not* a cpo as evidenced by Example 15.15.

15.3.2 Continuous functions over cpos

When we compute a fixed-point for a function we need to require that the function is *continuous*. In this setting, a function is continuous if it *respects limits*. A consequence is that it makes sense only to speak of continuity of functions whose domain and range are both cpos in the sense of Definition 15.16.

A moment's thought 15.20   Why do we need to assume that both the domain and the range are cpos when we talk of continuity?

We require that a continuous function is *monotone*. A monotone function *respects the ordering relation*.

Definition 15.21 (Monotone function)   Let $(D, \sqsubseteq)$ be a partially ordered set. A function $f : D \rightarrow D$ is *monotone* if it is the case that whenever $d_1 \sqsubseteq d_2$ then also $f(d_1) \sqsubseteq f(d_2)$.

A moment's thought 15.22   What is the difference between this definition of monotonicity and the one that we use in calculus?

Monotone functions satisfy a nice property: they map increasing sequences to increasing sequences.

Lemma 15.23   *Let $(D, \sqsubseteq)$ be a partially ordered set and let $f : D \rightarrow D$ be a monotone function. If $Y = \{d_1, d_2, \ldots\}$ is an increasing sequence, then the sequence $f(Y) = \{f(d_1), f(d_2), \ldots\}$ is also increasing.*

Problem 15.24   Prove Lemma 15.23.

A continuous function is a monotone function that *respect limits of increasing sequences*.

Notation 15.25   If Y is a set of points, we let $f(Y)$ denote the set of resulting function values:

$$f(Y) = \{f(y) \in D \mid y \in Y\}.$$

When we use this notation we can think of continuity as follows: A function f is continuous if we can 'move f underneath a lim':

Definition 15.26 (Continuous function)   Let $(D, \sqsubseteq)$ be a cpo and let $f : D \rightarrow D$ be a monotone function. We say that f is *continuous* if for every increasing sequence Y

$$f(\lim Y) = \lim f(Y) \tag{15.5}$$

Observe that Lemma 15.23 will guarantee that the limit on the right-hand side of (15.5) is well defined.

Our definition of continuity is in fact an extension of the well-known notion of continuity for functions over the reals. A real-valued function is continuous if its graph has no 'holes' and thus preserves limits.

A moment's thought 15.27   Why is preservation of limits the appropriate reformulation of the 'usual' notion of continuity?

15.3.3 Proving the fixed-point theorem

All the necessary definitions are now in place, and we are able to prove Theorem 15.3.

Since we are interested in fixed points, it makes sense only to consider functions whose domain and range coincide. Such functions have type $D \to D$ for some set D and are called *endofunctions*.

A moment's thought 15.28 Why are we interested only in endofunctions?

Let us first recall the definition of fixed points.

Definition 15.29 (Fixed point) Let $f : D \to D$ be an endofunction. A *fixed-point* of f is an $x \in D$ such that $f(x) = x$.

Notation 15.30 $f^i d$ will denote that the function f has been applied i times to the argument d. So $f^0 d = d$ and $f^{i+1} d = f(f^i d)$.

Lemma 15.31 *Let $(D, \sqsubseteq)$ be a partially ordered set and let $f : D \to D$ be monotone. Then the function f^i is monotone for any value of i, that is, if $d_1 \sqsubseteq d_2$ then $f^i d_1 \sqsubseteq f^i d_2$.*

Proof Induction on i. If $d_1 \sqsubseteq d_2$ we immediately see that $d_1 = f^0 d_1 \sqsubseteq f^0 d_2 = d_2$. Now assume that if $d_1 \sqsubseteq d_2$, then $f^i d_1 \sqsubseteq f^i d_2$. We must now prove that the same holds for $i + 1$. Since f is monotone, we get that $f(f^i d_1) \sqsubseteq f(f^i d_2)$, and the proof is complete. □

The following lemma is essential. It tells us that we form an increasing chain by repeatedly applying a monotone function to the bottom element of a cpo.

Lemma 15.32 *Let $(D, \sqsubseteq)$ be a cpo, let $f : D \to D$ be monotone and let $\bot$ be the bottom element of D. Then the set*

$$\{f^i \bot \mid i \geq 0\} = \{\bot, f(\bot), f^2(\bot), \ldots\}$$

is an increasing sequence.

Proof The ith element in our set $\{f^i(\bot) \mid i \geq 0\}$ is $f^i(\bot)$. It is easy to see that $f^i(\bot) \sqsubseteq f^{i+1}(\bot)$. For since $\bot \sqsubseteq f \bot$, Lemma 15.31 tells us that $f^i \bot \sqsubseteq f^{i+1} \bot$. □

Now for the fixed-point theorem and its proof.

Theorem 15.3 (Existence of a least fixed point) *If $(D, \sqsubseteq)$ is a cpo and $f : D \to D$ is continuous, then f will have a least fixed point w.r.t. $\sqsubseteq$, called x^*. The fixed point x^* is found as the limit*

$$x^* = \lim\{f^i \bot \mid i \geq 0\}, \tag{15.6}$$

where $\bot$ is the bottom element of D.

Proof First notice that Lemma 15.32 and the assumption that $(D, \sqsubseteq)$ is a cpo imply that the limit in (15.6) is well defined.

The theorem itself consists of two claims, so there are two claims to prove.

- We must show that x^* actually is a fixed point of f.
- We must show that x^* is the least fixed point of f.

First we must show that x^* is a fixed point. By definition, x^* is a fixed-point if $f(x^*) = x^*$. We use (15.6) to check this:

$$f(x^*) = f(\lim\{f^i \perp \mid i \geq 0\}) \tag{15.7}$$
$$= \lim\{f^{i+1} \perp \mid i \geq 0\} \tag{15.8}$$
$$= \lim\{f^j \perp \mid j \geq 1\} \tag{15.9}$$

To get from (15.7) to (15.8) we made use of the continuity of f to move f underneath the lim. Also, since $\perp$ is the least element of D, we have that $\lim(\{\perp\} \cup Y) = \lim Y$ for any increasing sequence Y. So in particular

$$\lim\{f^j \perp \mid j \geq 1\} = \lim(\{f^j \perp \mid j \geq 1\} \cup \{\perp\}) \tag{15.10}$$
$$= \lim\{f^j \perp \mid j \geq 0\} \tag{15.11}$$
$$= x^* \tag{15.12}$$

which is what we wanted.

Next, we must show that x^* is the least fixed point. So let d be an arbitrary fixed point. To show that x^* is the least fixed point, it suffices to show that $x^* \sqsubseteq d$.

Since $\perp$ is the least element of D, we have that $\perp \sqsubseteq d$. Because f is monotone and d is a fixed point, we have that $f^i(\perp) \sqsubseteq f^i(d) = d$ for all $i \geq 0$ by virtue of Lemma 15.31. d is therefore an upper bound of the set $\{f^i \perp \mid i \geq 0\}$ and thus we get that $\lim\{f^i \perp \mid i \geq 0\} \sqsubseteq d$, so $x^* \sqsubseteq d$ as was to be shown.   □

15.4 How to apply the fixed-point theorem

Theorem 15.3 is extremely useful. If we are given a recursive definition

$$X = F(X)$$

we can use the following strategy when computing a solution to the definition in the form of a fixed point of F.

- First prove that the set of candidate solutions can be described as a cpo $(D, \sqsubseteq)$. To do this, you must first find D and $\sqsubseteq$ and then show that $(D, \sqsubseteq)$ actually satisfies the conditions required of a cpo.

- Next, show that the right-hand-side function F is continuous. To do this, you first show that F is monotone and then that F preserves limits of increasing sequences in $(D, \sqsubseteq)$.
- Finally, compute the least fixed point x^* of F by applying Theorem 15.3.

Theorem 15.3 is only one among a great many fixed-point theorems in mathematics. fixed-point theorems are important not just in theoretical computer science but also in areas such as mathematical economics and theoretical physics. The best known fixed-point theorem in mathematics is probably Brouwer's fixed-point theorem from 1910 (see Shashkin (1991) for an elementary introduction).

If we invert all concepts and instead speak of decreasing sequences, greatest lower bounds, top elements, decreasing sequences and anti-continuous functions (that preserve limits of decreasing sequences) we get a dual result about *greatest* fixed points.

A moment's thought 15.33   What would this dual fixed-point theorem look like?

15.5 Examples of cpos

In this section we shall consider two kinds of cpos that often arise in computer science. We call these *subset cpos* and *function-space cpos*, respectively. In Section 15.6 we will have a look at some examples of functions on these two kinds of cpos.

15.5.1 Subset cpos

Some cpos have *sets* as their points and use set inclusion, $\subseteq$, as the ordering relation. We shall call cpos of this kind *subset cpos*. We now look at some interesting cases.

The power-set cpo

Let S be an arbitrary set. Then if we order the elements of the power set of S w.r.t. set inclusion, we have that $(\mathcal{P}(S), \subseteq)$ is a cpo.

Theorem 15.34   *For any set S, $(\mathcal{P}(S), \subseteq)$ is a partially ordered set.*

Proof   *Reflexivity:* It is obvious that for any $S' \in \mathcal{P}(S)$ we have $S' \subseteq S'$. *Antisymmetry:* If $S_1 \subseteq S_2$ and $S_2 \subseteq S_1$, we immediately get that $S_1 = S_2$. *Transitivity:* Assume that $S_1 \subseteq S_2$ and $S_2 \subseteq S_3$. Let $x \in S_1$. Since $S_1 \subseteq S_2$,

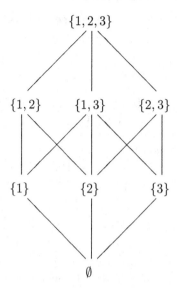

Figure 15.2 A Hasse diagram for $(\mathcal{P}(\{1,2,3\}), \subseteq)$

we have $x \in S_2$. Also, since $S_2 \subseteq S_3$ we have $x \in S_3$. That is, if $x \in S_1$ then $x \in S_3$, and consequently $S_1 \subseteq S_3$. $\qquad\square$

However, $(\mathcal{P}(S), \subseteq)$ fails to be a totally ordered set. A simple counterexample is any set S with two or more elements. Let $x, y \in S$, where $x \neq y$. It is neither the case that $\{x\} \subseteq \{y\}$ nor that $\{y\} \subseteq \{x\}$.

Example 15.35 Let $S = \{1, 2, 3\}$. A Hasse diagram for $(\mathcal{P}(S), \subseteq)$ is shown in Figure 15.2.

Example 15.36 Let $S = \{1, 2, 3\}$ and consider the partially ordered set $(\mathcal{P}(S), \subseteq)$. The set $\{\emptyset, \{1\}, \{1,3\}\}$ is an increasing sequence. On the other hand, $\{\emptyset, \{1\}, \{1,3\}, \{2\}\}$ is not an increasing sequence.

A moment's thought 15.37 Why is $\{\emptyset, \{1\}, \{1,3\}\}$ in the above example an increasing sequence? Why is it *not* the case that $\{\emptyset, \{1\}, \{1,3\}, \{2\}\}$ is an increasing sequence?

Theorem 15.38 *For any set S, $(\mathcal{P}(S), \subseteq)$ is a cpo.*

Proof We must show that $\mathcal{P}(S)$ has a least element and that every increasing sequence has a limit which is a point in $\mathcal{P}(S)$. The first property is easily obtained; the least element is $\emptyset$, since $\emptyset \subseteq S'$ for all $S' \in \mathcal{P}(S)$.

What is the limit of an increasing sequence in $(\mathcal{P}(S), \subseteq)$? Recall that an increasing sequence here is a sequence of sets $Y = \{M_1, M_2 \ldots\}$ such that $M_i \subseteq M_{i+1}$ for all i. Next, recall that the limit of this Y is the least set M such that $M_i \subseteq M$ for all $M_i \in Y$. The union $\bigcup_i M_i$ satisfies this requirement, so we have that $\lim_{M_i \in Y} M_i = \bigcup_i M_i$.   □

A moment's thought 15.39   Again consider the increasing sequence $Y = \{\emptyset, \{1\}, \{1, 3\}\}$ from Example 15.36. What is $\lim Y$?

Problem 15.40   Let S be an arbitrary set and let $\sqsubseteq$ be defined as 'reverse inclusion', so $S_1 \sqsubseteq S_2$ if $S_2 \subseteq S_1$. Show that $(\mathcal{P}(S), \sqsubseteq)$ is a cpo (first check that it is a partially ordered set).

The cpo of languages over Σ

An important example of a subset cpo is the set of languages over some given alphabet. Let Σ be an alphabet. Then Σ^* is the set of all strings over Σ. A language over Σ is a set of strings over Σ, so the set of all languages over Σ is $\mathcal{P}(\Sigma^*)$.

The results in this section tell us that $(\mathcal{P}(\Sigma^*), \subseteq)$ is a cpo.

15.5.2 Function-space cpos

Other cpos have points that are *partial functions*. The set of functions with domain A and range B is often called the *function space from A to B* and cpos of this kind are therefore often referred to as *function-space cpos*.

The cpo of partial functions from A to B

Let A and B be sets. Then $A \rightharpoonup B$ denotes the set of partial functions with domain A and range B. We now show that $A \rightharpoonup B$ can be regarded as a cpo.

Definition 15.41   Let $f : A \rightharpoonup B$ be a partial function. The *graph* of f is the set of pairs defined by

$$\text{graph}(f) = \{(a, b) \mid f(a) = b\}.$$

It is now easy to define an ordering relation for partial functions.

Definition 15.42   Define the ordering $\sqsubseteq$ over $A \rightharpoonup B$ by

$$f_1 \sqsubseteq f_2 \text{ if } \text{graph}(f_1) \subseteq \text{graph}(f_2).$$

The intuition here is that f_1 is 'less than' f_2 if we, by using f_2 instead of f_1, can obtain at least the same results as we could have by using f_1. Notice that if f_1 and f_2 happen to be *total functions*, $f_1 \sqsubseteq f_2$ implies that $f_1 = f_2$.

Example 15.43 Let $A = B = \mathbb{Z}$ and consider

$$f_1(n) = \textit{if } n \textit{ is even then } 0 \textit{ else } \underline{undef}$$

and

$$f_2(n) = 0.$$

We have $f_1 \sqsubseteq f_2$, since

$$\text{graph}(f_1) = \{(n, 0) \mid n \text{ is even}\},$$
$$\text{graph}(f_2) = \{(n, 0) \mid n \in \mathbb{Z}\}.$$

Lemma 15.44 $(A \rightharpoonup B, \sqsubseteq)$ *is a partially ordered set.*

Proof We have defined $\sqsubseteq$ by means of $\subseteq$. Let $\mathcal{G}$ denote the set of graphs of functions in $A \rightharpoonup B$. Since $(\mathcal{G}, \subseteq)$ is a subset cpo, we immediately get that $(A \rightharpoonup B, \sqsubseteq)$ is a partially ordered set. ☐

Lemma 15.45 $(A \rightharpoonup B, \sqsubseteq)$ *is a cpo.*

Proof We must show that for any increasing sequence Y the limit $\lim Y$ is defined. This is the same as saying that if $Y = \{f_0, f_1, \ldots\}$ is a set of functions in $A \rightharpoonup B$, where $f_0 \sqsubseteq f_1 \sqsubseteq f_2 \ldots$, then there exists a function f in $A \rightharpoonup B$ which satisfies that $f_i \sqsubseteq f$ for all $f_i \in Y$ and that for any other upper bound g we have that $f \sqsubseteq g$.

The limit is simply the function f which satisfies that

$$\text{graph}(f) = \bigcup_i \text{graph}(f_i).$$

It is clear that such a function does indeed exist, since all functions in Y agree on their values: if $f_i(a) = b'$ and $f_j(a) = b''$ and $i \leq j$, then we have that $b' = b''$, since $\text{graph}(f_i) \subseteq \text{graph}(f_j)$. It is also not hard to convince oneself that f is in fact an upper bound of Y. If $f(a) = b$ is defined, it must be because $f_i(a) = b$ for some $f_i \in Y$. But since all members of Y agree on their values, we have that $f_j \sqsubseteq f$ for all $f_j \in Y$. Similarly, it is easy to see that f is the least upper bound, since its graph contains exactly those values that are known by the functions in Y. ☐

The least element of the cpo $(A \rightharpoonup B, \sqsubseteq)$ is the fully undefined function $f_\perp$ given by

$$f_\perp(n) = \underline{undef}.$$

The cpo of partial functions over $\mathbb{N}$

The above now tells us that the set of partial functions over $\mathbb{N}$, $\mathbb{N} \rightharpoonup \mathbb{N}$, is a cpo if we use the ordering relation given above.

The cpo of state transformations

A state transformation f is an element of the set **States** $\rightharpoonup$ **States**, and consequently we can regard the set of state transformations as a cpo using the ordering relation defined above.

15.6 Examples of continuous functions

15.6.1 A useful theorem about function composition

Often the most difficult aspect, when examining a recursive definition, is to show that the right-hand-side function is continuous. Here the following result is often extremely useful.

Theorem 15.46 *The composition of two continuous functions yields a continuous function: if the functions $f : D \rightarrow D$ and $g : D \rightarrow D$ are continuous, then the composition $g \circ f : D \rightarrow D$ is also continuous.*

Problem 15.47 Prove Theorem 15.46

15.6.2 Context-free grammars

The grammar (15.2) defines a language over the alphabet $\{a, b, c\}$, so the domain of candidate solutions must be the set of all languages over $\{a, b, c\}$. This set is $\mathcal{P}(\{a, b, c\}^*)$ and can be ordered w.r.t. $\subseteq$. In section 15.5.1 we saw that this solution domain does indeed satisfy the conditions required of a cpo.

The right-hand-side function F must be (15.1) with the recursive call of F 'abstracted out':

$$F(X) = \{a\}X\{b\} \cup \{c\} \cup X$$

F is defined using concatenation and set union, so Theorem 15.46 tells us that if we want to show that F is continuous, it will suffice to show that these two operations are continuous. We omit the proof of this and invite the reader to fill in the details.

Problem 15.48 Show that the concatenation function $\circ$ is a continuous function in each of its arguments over the cpo $(\mathcal{P}(\Sigma^*), \subseteq)$. In other words, show that for any language L the functions

$$f_1(X) = X \circ L$$
$$f_2(X) = L \circ X$$

are both continuous. First show that each of these functions is monotone.

Problem 15.49 Show that the union function $\cup$ is a continuous function in each of its arguments over the cpo $(\mathcal{P}(\Sigma^*), \subseteq)$. Proceed in the same way as in Problem 15.48 by first establishing monotonicity.

15.6.3 Recursive functions over the natural numbers

Here is a recursive function over the natural numbers:

$$g(n) = \textit{if } (n = 0) \textit{ then } 1 \textit{ else } n \cdot g(n - 2)$$

We can rewrite this definition as

$$g(n) = f(n)$$
$$\text{where } f(n) = \textit{if } (n = 0) \textit{ then } 1 \textit{ else } n \cdot f(n - 2).$$

What is the domain D of candidate solutions? We are looking for a recursive function over the natural numbers, and the function need not be defined for all arguments. So D must be the set of partial functions over the natural numbers, $\mathbb{N} \rightharpoonup \mathbb{N}$ ordered w.r.t. the ordering relation $\sqsubseteq$ defined in section 15.5.2

What is the right-hand side function F? It is

$$F(f) = h$$
$$\text{where } h(n) = \textit{if } (n = 0) \textit{ then } 1 \textit{ else } n \cdot f(n - 2).$$

In other words, F is a function over functions over the natural numbers, so F is of type $(\mathbb{N} \rightharpoonup \mathbb{N}) \rightarrow (\mathbb{N} \rightharpoonup \mathbb{N})$.

We now prove that F is continuous. This requires us to first establish the following lemma.

Lemma 15.50 *F is monotone.*

Proof Assume that $f_1 \sqsubseteq f_2$. We must show that $F(f_1) \sqsubseteq F(f_2)$. We have

$$F(f_1) = h_1 \text{ where } h_1(n) = \textit{if } (n = 0) \textit{ then } 1 \textit{ else } n \cdot f_1(n - 2)$$

and

$$F(f_2) = h_1 \text{ where } h_2(n) = \textit{if } (n = 0) \textit{ then } 1 \textit{ else } n \cdot f_2(n - 2).$$

We now show that $h_1 \sqsubseteq h_2$, and we do this by showing that for all $n \in \mathbb{N}$ we have that if $h_1(n) = k$ then also $h_2(n) = k$. If $n = 0$, we have that $h_1(n) = h_2(n) = 1$. If $n \neq 0$, then we have $h_1(n) = nf_1(n - 2)$ and $h_2(n) = nf_2(n - 2)$. If $h_1(n)$ is defined for $n \neq 0$, we have that $f_1(n - 2)$ is defined. Also, since $f_1 \sqsubseteq f_2$, we have that $f_2(n - 2)$ is defined and therefore also that $h_2(n)$ is defined in this case. $\qquad\square$

Lemma 15.51 *F is continuous.*

Proof Let $Y = \{f_0, f_1 \ldots\}$ be an increasing sequence in $(\mathbb{N} \rightharpoonup \mathbb{N}, \sqsubseteq)$. We know from the proof of Lemma 15.45 that $\lim Y$ is the function

$$f(n) = \begin{cases} f_i(n) & \text{if for some } f_i \in Y \text{ the value } f_i(n) \text{ is defined} \\ \text{undef} & \text{otherwise.} \end{cases} \tag{15.13}$$

Now consider the increasing sequence of F-values $FY = \{Ff_i \mid f_i \in Y\}$. We know that $\lim FY$ exists and is the function h defined by

$$h(n) = \begin{cases} (Ff_i)(n) & \text{if for some } (Ff_i) \in FY \text{ the value } (Ff_i)(n) \text{ is defined} \\ \text{undef} & \text{otherwise.} \end{cases}$$

This is again equivalent to

$$h(n) = \begin{cases} (Ff_i)(n) & \text{if for some } f_i \in Y \text{ the value } f_i(n) \text{ is defined} \\ \text{undef} & \text{otherwise.} \end{cases} \tag{15.14}$$

By definition we have that F is continuous if $Ff = h$. We show that this is the case by computing Ff and h and checking that they agree.

For an arbitrary $f_i \in Y$ we have

$$(Ff_i)(n) = \text{if } n = 0 \text{ then } 1 \text{ else } n \cdot f_i(n-2).$$

By substituting this into (15.14) we get

$$h(n) = \begin{cases} 1 & \text{if } n = 0 \\ n \cdot f_i(n-2) & \text{if } n > 0 \text{ and there exists an } f_i \in Y \\ & \text{such that } f_i(n-2) \text{ is defined} \\ \text{undef} & \text{otherwise.} \end{cases} \tag{15.15}$$

When we look at the condition 'if there exists an $f_i \in Y$ such that $f_i(n-2)$ is defined' and recall the definition of f in (15.13), we see that the above is equivalent to

$$(\lim FY)(n) = \begin{cases} 1 & \text{if } n = 0 \\ n \cdot f(n-2) & \text{if } n > 0 \text{ and } f(n-2) \text{ is defined} \\ \text{undef} & \text{otherwise.} \end{cases} \tag{15.16}$$

We have that the function $F(\lim Y)$ is given by

$$(Ff)(n) = \text{if } n = 0 \text{ then } 1 \text{ else } n \cdot f(n-2), \tag{15.17}$$

but this is equivalent to

$$(F(\lim Y))(n) = \begin{cases} 1 & \text{if } n = 0 \\ n \cdot f(n-2) & \text{if } n > 0 \text{ and } f(n-2) \text{ is defined} \\ \text{undef} & \text{otherwise,} \end{cases}$$

$$\tag{15.18}$$

which is precisely (15.16)! □

15.6.4 Denotational semantics

We know from Section 15.5.2 that the set of state transformations $\textbf{States} \rightharpoonup$ $\textbf{States}$ can be seen as a cpo where $\bot$ is the state transformation $\lambda s.\underline{undef}$. We now only need to show that the function $F : \textbf{States} \rightharpoonup \textbf{States}$ given by

$$F = \lambda f.\lambda s.if \ (\mathcal{B}[\![b]\!]s = t\!t) \ then \ (f \circ \mathcal{S}[\![S]\!])s \ else \ s, \qquad (15.19)$$

where we make use of the definition of the semantics of while-loops, is continuous. We omit the proof of this here; the details are straightforward.

Problem 15.52 Prove that the function F in (15.19) is continuous (remember to first show monotonicity).

Given that F is continuous, Theorem 15.3 guarantees the existence of a least fixed-point of F. The final version of the semantics of while-loops is then

$$\mathcal{S}[\![\texttt{while } b \texttt{ do } S]\!] = f^*$$

where f^* is the fixed point of F

where $F = \lambda f.\lambda s.if \ (\mathcal{B}[\![b]\!]s = t\!t) \ then \ (f \circ \mathcal{S}[\![S]\!])s \ else \ s,$

We now take a closer look at the state transformation that f^* corresponds to, and we do so through an example. Let us consider the statement

$$\texttt{while } \neg(\texttt{x=0}) \texttt{ do } \texttt{x:= x-1}.$$

Here we have that

$$F^0 \bot = \bot = \lambda s.\underline{undef}$$
$$F^1 \bot = \lambda s.if \ (sx \neq 0 = t\!t) \ then \ (\lambda s.\underline{undef} \circ \mathcal{S}[\![\texttt{x:= x-1}]\!])s \ else \ s,$$
$$= \lambda s.if \ (sx \neq 0 = t\!t) \ then \ \underline{undef} \ else \ s$$
$$F^2 \bot = \lambda s.if \ (sx \neq 0 = t\!t) \ then$$
$$\qquad ((\lambda s.if \ (sx \neq 0 = t\!t) \ then \ \underline{undef} \ else \ s) \circ \mathcal{S}[\![\texttt{x:= x-1}]\!])s \ else \ s$$
$$\qquad = \lambda s.if \ (sx \neq 0 = t\!t) \ then \ \underline{undef} \ else \ \mathcal{S}[\![\texttt{x:= x-1}]\!]s.$$

The above line of reasoning can be continued, and it turns out that $F^k \bot$ is the state transformation which describes that the while-loop is traversed at most k times.

From Theorem 15.3 we see that the semantics of our while-loop is the limit of all these approximations – and is the state transformation which agrees with all the $F^k \perp$ approximations. This is the state transformation describing an *arbitrary* number of traversals of the loop.

15.7 Examples of computations of fixed-points

In this, the last section, we shall use the cpos and functions from the previous two sections to show how we can compute least fixed points.

15.7.1 Recursive definitions of languages

In Section 15.5.1 we saw that $(\mathcal{P}(\Sigma^*), \subseteq)$ is a cpo and that the least element of this cpo is $\emptyset$. Again consider the function $f_S : \mathcal{P}(\Sigma^*) \to \mathcal{P}(\Sigma^*)$ corresponding to (15.1):

$$f_S(X) = \{a\} \cdot X \cdot \{b\} \cup \{c\} \cup X.$$

If we define the functions $f_1(X) = \{a\} \cdot X$, $f_2(X) = X \cdot \{b\}$, $f_3(X) = X \cup \{c\}$ and $f_4(X) = X \cup X$, we have that $f_S = f_4 \circ f_3 \circ f_2 \circ f_1$.

We can now apply Theorem 15.46, which tells us that it suffices to show that f_1, f_2, f_3 and f_4 are continuous (as one can establish by solving Problems 15.48 and 15.49).

Theorem 15.3 tells us that f_S has a least fixed-point given by $x_S^* = \bigcup \{f_S{}^i \emptyset \mid i \geq 0\}$. We have

$$f_S{}^0 \emptyset = \emptyset$$
$$f_S{}^1 \emptyset = \{c\}$$
$$f_S{}^2 \emptyset = \{acb\} \cup \{c\} = \{a^i cb^i \mid i \leq 1\}$$

and an inductive argument tells us that in general

$$f_S{}^k \emptyset = \{a^i cb^i \mid i < k\}.$$

So $f_S{}^k \emptyset$ describes the set of strings that can be derived by the rules of the grammar using fewer than k derivation steps. This corresponds to the derivation relation $\Rightarrow^k$.

15.7.2 Functions over the natural numbers

Let us now return to the example from Section 15.6.3. We wish to find the limit of the increasing sequence $\{\perp, F^1(\perp), F^2(\perp), \ldots\}$. We can find the elements of the sequence by applying the definition of F:

$$F^0(\bot) = f_0$$
where $f_0(n) = \underline{undef}$,
$$F^1(\bot) = F(F^0(\bot))$$
$$= f_1$$
where $f_1(n) = if\ n = 0\ then\ 1\ else\ \underline{undef}$,
$$F^2(\bot) = F(F^1(\bot))$$
$$= f_2$$
where $f_2(n) = if\ n = 0\ then\ 1\ else$
$if\ n - 2 = 0\ then\ n\ else\ \underline{undef}$,
$$F^3(\bot) = F(F^2(\bot))$$
$$= f_3$$
where $f_3(n) = if\ n = 0\ then\ 1\ else$
$if\ n - 2 = 0\ then\ n\ else$
$if\ n - 2 - 2 = 0\ then\ n \cdot (n - 2)\ else\ \underline{undef}$

$\ldots$

These terms should convince us that in general $F^m(\bot)$ is defined by

$F^m(\bot) = f$ where

$$f(n) = if\ n\ is\ even\ and\ n \leq m\ then\ \prod_{i=1}^{n\ div\ 2} 2i\ else\ \underline{undef}. \qquad (15.20)$$

That this is in fact the case can be shown by induction on m.

Problem 15.53 Prove (15.20) by induction on m. Both the base case and the induction step will require another inductive argument, this time an induction on n.

From (15.20) we see that the limit of the increasing sequence of $F^m(\bot)$-functions is exactly the function g_1 given by

$$g_1(n) = if\ n\ is\ even\ then\ \prod_{i=1}^{n\ div\ 2} 2i\ else\ \underline{undef}.$$

15.8 An equivalence result

In this section we show how the result about least fixed points finally allows us to prove that the operational and denotational semantics of **Bims** are equivalent.

15.8.1 *Equivalence of semantics of expressions*

Our first results express that the big-step semantics of arithmetic and Boolean expressions agree with the corresponding denotational semantics.

Lemma 15.54 $\mathcal{A}[\![a]\!]s = v$ *if and only if* $s \vdash a \to_a v$.

Proof induction on the structure of a. We present only two cases here; the remaining ones are similar or simpler.

$a = x$: We have $\mathcal{A}[\![a]\!]s = sx$ and $s \vdash a \to_a v$ where $sx = v$.

$a = a_1 + a_2$: By virtue of our induction hypothesis, we have that $\mathcal{A}[\![a_1]\!]s = v_1$ if and only if $s \vdash a_1 \to_a v_1$ and $\mathcal{A}[\![a_2]\!]s = v_2$ if and only if $s \vdash a_2 \to_a v_2$. But $\mathcal{A}[\![a_1 + a_2]\!] = \mathcal{A}[\![a_1]\!]s + \mathcal{A}[\![a_2]\!]s = v_1 + v_2$ and $s \vdash a_1 + a_2 \to_a v$ where $v = v_1 + v_2$, and this case now follows. $\square$

Lemma 15.55 $\mathcal{A}[\![b]\!]s = v$ *if and only if* $s \vdash b \to_b v$.

Problem 15.56   Prove the lemma.

15.8.2 *Equivalence of semantics of statements*

The equivalence results were not so hard to prove for expressions. For statements we need to do a little more work.

Definition 15.57   We define the state transformation $\mathcal{S}_{\text{sos}}$ by

$$\mathcal{S}_{\text{sos}}[\![S]\!]s = s' \quad \text{if } \langle S, s \rangle \to s'.$$

The equivalence result now simply says that $\mathcal{S}_{\text{sos}}$ and $\mathcal{S}$ are the same function.

Theorem 15.58   *For every statement S and state s we have* $\mathcal{S}_{\text{sos}}[\![S]\!]s = \mathcal{S}[\![S]\!]s$.

   The proof of this theorem is more involved, because neither the operational nor the denotational semantics is compositional. For this reason we cannot prove the result by structural induction. Instead we have to use the characterization of the denotational semantics as a fixed-point.
   To prove that $\mathcal{S}_{\text{sos}}[\![S]\!] = \mathcal{S}[\![S]\!]$, it suffices to prove that

Lemma 15.59 $\mathcal{S}_{\text{sos}}[\![S]\!] \sqsubseteq \mathcal{S}[\![S]\!]$

and

Lemma 15.60 $\mathcal{S}[\![S]\!] \sqsubseteq \mathcal{S}_{\text{sos}}[\![S]\!]$

where $\sqsubseteq$ is the partial ordering on state transformation functions of Definition 15.42:

$$f_1 \sqsubseteq f_2 \text{ if for all } s, \text{ whenever } f_1 s = s' \text{ then also } f_2 s = s'$$

We first prove Lemma 15.59. To do this, we need the following simple lemma.

Lemma 15.61   *We have*

$$\mathcal{S}[\![\texttt{while } b \texttt{ do } S]\!] = \mathcal{S}[\![\texttt{if } b \texttt{ then } S; \texttt{while } b \texttt{ do } S \texttt{ else skip}]\!].$$

Proof   We have

$$\mathcal{S}[\![\texttt{while } b \texttt{ do } S]\!] = f,$$

where f is the least fixed-point of the function

$$\lambda g.\lambda s. \textit{if } \mathcal{B}[\![S]\!]s \textit{ then } (g \circ \mathcal{S}[\![S]\!])s \textit{ else } s.$$

So

$$\mathcal{S}[\![\texttt{while } b \texttt{ do } S]\!] = \lambda s. \textit{if } \mathcal{B}[\![S]\!]s \textit{ then } ((\mathcal{S}[\![\texttt{while } b \texttt{ do } S]\!]) \circ \mathcal{S}[\![S]\!])s \textit{ else } s.$$

By applying the clauses of the definition of $\mathcal{S}$ we also have

$$\mathcal{S}[\![\texttt{if } b \texttt{ then } S; \texttt{while } b \texttt{ do } S \texttt{ else skip}]\!] =$$
$$\lambda s. \textit{if } \mathcal{B}[\![S]\!]s \textit{ then } ((\mathcal{S}[\![\texttt{while } b \texttt{ do } S]\!]) \circ \mathcal{S}[\![S]\!])s \textit{ else } s$$

$\square$

We can now prove Lemma 15.59.

Proof   The lemma states that whenever $\langle S, s \rangle \to s'$ we have $\mathcal{S}[\![S]\!]s = s'$. So this is a statement about all transitions of the big-step semantics, and the proof is therefore a proof by induction on the transition rules.

[skip$_{\text{bss}}$]: We have $\langle \texttt{skip}, s \rangle \to s$ and $\mathcal{S}[\![\texttt{skip}]\!] = \lambda s.s$, so $\mathcal{S}[\![\texttt{skip}]\!]s = s$.

[ass$_{\text{bss}}$]: Suppose $\langle x := a, s \rangle \to s[x \mapsto v]$, where $s \vdash a \to_a v$. We have
$\mathcal{S}[\![x := a]\!] = \lambda s.s[x \mapsto \mathcal{A}[\![a]\!]s]$. Then by virtue of Lemma 15.54 we
have that $\mathcal{A}[\![a]\!]s = v$, and therefore we get that $\mathcal{S}[\![x := a]\!]s = s[x \mapsto v]$ as desired.

[comp$_{\text{bss}}$]: Suppose $\langle S_1; S_2, s \rangle \to s'$. We must show that $\mathcal{S}[\![S_1; S_2]\!]s = s'$.
The transition was due to

$$\frac{\langle S_1, s \rangle \to s'' \quad \langle S_2, s'' \rangle \to s'}{\langle S_1; S_2, s \rangle \to s'}$$

By virtue of our induction hypothesis, we get that $\mathcal{S}[\![S_1]\!]s = s''$ and $\mathcal{S}[\![S_2]\!]s'' = s'$. But then we have that $\mathcal{S}[\![S_2]\!](\mathcal{S}[\![S_1]\!]s) = s'$, and this completes this case of the proof, since $\mathcal{S}[\![S_1; S_2]\!] = \lambda s.(\mathcal{S}[\![S_2]\!] \circ \mathcal{S}[\![S_1]\!])s$.

[**if-true$_{\text{bss}}$**]: We here consider a state s where $s \vdash b \rightarrow_b tt$. Since Lemma 15.55 holds, we have that $\mathcal{B}[\![b]\!]s = tt$. We have

$$\frac{\langle S_1, s \rangle \rightarrow s'}{\langle \text{if } b \text{ then } S_1 \text{ else } S_2, s \rangle \rightarrow s'}$$

and by virtue of our induction hypothesis $\mathcal{S}[\![S_1]\!]s = s'$. Since we by definition also have

$$\mathcal{S}[\![\text{if } b \text{ then } S_1 \text{ else } S_2]\!] = \lambda s.if \ (\mathcal{B}[\![b]\!]s = tt) \ then \ \mathcal{S}[\![S_1]\!]s \ else \ \mathcal{S}[\![S_2]\!]s$$

we now get $\mathcal{S}[\![\text{if } b \text{ then } S_1 \text{ else } S_2]\!]s = s'$ as desired.

[**if-false$_{\text{bss}}$**]: This case is similar to the previous one and is therefore omitted.

[**while-true$_{\text{bss}}$**]: We here consider a state s where $b \vdash s \rightarrow_b tt$. Since Lemma 15.55 holds and by virtue of Lemma 15.61, we have that $\mathcal{S}[\![\text{while } b \text{ do } S]\!]s = \mathcal{S}[\![S; \text{while } b \text{ do } S]\!]s$.

We have

$$\frac{\langle S, s \rangle \rightarrow s'' \ \langle \text{while } b \text{ do } S, s'' \rangle \rightarrow s'}{\langle \text{while } b \text{ do } S, s \rangle \rightarrow s'}.$$

By virtue of our induction hypothesis, we have $\mathcal{S}[\![S]\!]s = s''$ and $\mathcal{S}[\![\text{while } b \text{ do } S]\!]s'' = s'$. This means that $\mathcal{S}[\![\text{while } b \text{ do } S]\!](\mathcal{S}[\![S]\!]s) = s'$, so we get that $\mathcal{S}[\![S; \text{while } b \text{ do } S]\!]s = s'$, as we were to show.

[**while-false$_{\text{bss}}$**]: We now consider a state s where $s \vdash s \rightarrow_b ff$. Again, since Lemma 15.55 holds and by virtue of Lemma 15.61, we have that $\mathcal{S}[\![\text{while } b \text{ do } S]\!]s = \mathcal{S}[\![\text{skip}]\!]s$. We have

$$\langle \text{while } b \text{ do } S, s \rangle \rightarrow s,$$

completing this case.

$\square$

To prove Lemma 15.60, we need a different strategy. First we need to show the following general result about continuous functions.

Theorem 15.62 *Suppose $(D, \sqsubseteq)$ is a cpo and that $f : D \rightarrow D$ is a continuous function with least fixed point x^*. If a point $d \in D$ satisfies that $fd \sqsubseteq d$, then $x^* \sqsubseteq d$.*

Proof We show that $f^i \perp \sqsubseteq d$ for all $i \geq 0$, for then we have $\lim f^i \perp = x^* \sqsubseteq d$. The proof is by induction on i.

$i = 0$: $f^0 \perp = \perp$, and obviously $\perp \sqsubseteq d$.

Assume for i, prove for $i+1$: We assume that $f^i \perp \sqsubseteq d$. Since f is monotone, we have that $f(f^i \perp) \sqsubseteq fd$. But $f(f^i \perp) = f^{i+1} \perp$ and, since $fd \sqsubseteq d$, the result follows.

$\square$

A point d which satisfies that $fd \sqsubseteq d$ is usually called a *pre-fixed-point*, since fd is 'before' d.

Proof of Lemma 15.60   We now proceed by induction on the structure of S. The difficult case is that of while-loops; we show this and two other cases. The remaining cases are straightforward and are left as an exercise.

$S = \mathtt{skip}$:   We must prove that $\mathcal{S}[\![\mathtt{skip}]\!] \sqsubseteq \mathcal{S}_{\mathrm{sos}}[\![\mathtt{skip}]\!]$. So let s be an arbitrary state. We have that $\mathcal{S}[\![\mathtt{skip}]\!]s = (\lambda s.s)s = s$ and must show that then also $\mathcal{S}_{\mathrm{sos}}[\![\mathtt{skip}]\!]s = s$. But this is immediately apparent from the transition rule [SKIP$_{\mathrm{BSS}}$].

$S = x := a$:   We must show that $\mathcal{S}[\![x := a]\!] \sqsubseteq \mathcal{S}_{\mathrm{sos}}[\![x := a]\!]$. We have that $\mathcal{S}[\![x := a]\!] = \lambda s.s[x \mapsto \mathcal{A}[\![a]\!]s]$; we must show that, if $\mathcal{S}[\![x := a]\!]s = s'$, then $\mathcal{S}_{\mathrm{sos}}[\![x := a]\!]s = s'$. Let s be an arbitrary state. We have $\mathcal{S}[\![x := a]\!]s = s[x \mapsto \mathcal{A}[\![a]\!]s]$. By virtue of Lemma 15.54 we have that $\mathcal{A}[\![a]\!]s = v$ if and only if $s \vdash a \to v$. Since $\mathcal{S}_{\mathrm{sos}}[\![x := a]\!]s = s'$ where $\langle x := a, s \rangle \to s'$ and since $s' = s[x \mapsto v]$ where $s \vdash a \to v$, the result now follows for this case.

$S = \mathtt{while}\ b\ \mathtt{do}\ S$:   We must show that $\mathcal{S}[\![\mathtt{while}\ b\ \mathtt{do}\ S]\!] \sqsubseteq \mathcal{S}_{\mathrm{sos}}[\![\mathtt{while}\ b\ \mathtt{do}\ S]\!]$. We have that

$$\mathcal{S}[\![\mathtt{while}\ b\ \mathtt{do}\ S]\!] = f^*,$$

where f^* is the least fixed point of

$$F = \lambda f.\lambda s.\mathit{if}\,(\mathcal{B}[\![b]\!]s = t\!t)\ \mathit{then}\ (f \circ \mathcal{S}[\![S]\!])s\ \mathit{else}\ s.$$

Let f_{sos} denote the state transformation $\mathcal{S}_{\mathrm{sos}}[\![\mathtt{while}\ b\ \mathtt{do}\ S]\!]$. We must show that $f^* \sqsubseteq f_{\mathrm{sos}}$, and we can do so by showing that $F f_{\mathrm{sos}} \sqsubseteq f_{\mathrm{sos}}$, for then the result follows from Theorem 15.62. We have

$$F f_{\mathrm{sos}} = \lambda s.\mathit{if}\,(\mathcal{B}[\![b]\!]s = t\!t)\ \mathit{then}\ f_{\mathrm{sos}}(\mathcal{S}[\![S]\!]s)\ \mathit{else}\ s.$$

Now suppose $(F f_{\mathrm{sos}})s = s'$. From the definition of $\sqsubseteq$, we see that we need to show that then also $f_{\mathrm{sos}}s = s'$.

Since $(F f_{\mathrm{sos}})s = s'$, and since the definition of F involves $\mathcal{S}[\![S]\!]s$, we must have that $\mathcal{S}[\![S]\!]s = s_1$ for some state s_1 and that $(F f_{\mathrm{sos}})s =$

$f_{\text{sos}} s_1$. There are now two subcases depending on the value of the Boolean expression b.

- If $\mathcal{B}[\![b]\!]s = f\!f$ then $(F f_{\text{sos}})s = s$, so here $s' = s$. By virtue of Lemma 15.55 we have $s \vdash b \rightarrow_b f\!f$, so the transition rule [WHILE-FALSE$_{\text{BSS}}$] applies and we get $\langle \text{while } b \text{ do } S, s \rangle \rightarrow s$. But then we have $f_{\text{sos}} s = s$.

- If $\mathcal{B}[\![b]\!]s = t\!t$ then $(F f_{\text{sos}})s = f_{\text{sos}}(\mathcal{S}[\![S]\!]s) = f_{\text{sos}} s_1$. By virtue of Lemma 15.55 we have $s \vdash b \rightarrow_b t\!t$. We know that $f_{\text{sos}} s_1 = s'$. By virtue of our induction hypothesis we know that $\mathcal{S}_{\text{sos}}[\![S]\!]s = s_1$. Since $f_{\text{sos}} s_1 = s'$, we have the transition $\langle \text{while } b \text{ do } S, s_1 \rangle \rightarrow s'$ and the transition rule [WHILE-TRUE$_{\text{BSS}}$] can be applied. We conclude that there must be a transition $\langle \text{while } b \text{ do } S, s \rangle \rightarrow s'$. But this then implies that $f_{\text{sos}} s = s'$.

$\square$

15.9 Other applications

The mathematical apparatus introduced in this chapter has many other applications. In the following we shall give a short introduction to some of them.

15.9.1 Logical properties of programs

A well-known approach to program verification consists of describing properties of programs as logical formulae, and it is often natural to define such properties recursively.

Let us outline a very simple example. Suppose we want to describe that some property of a **Bims** program will hold eventually (it may even hold now). For instance we might want to describe that our program will terminate eventually, which means that there exists some number of steps after which the program will have terminated.

Here, our definition of a program step will refer to the small-step semantics of **Bims**.

Let Q denote the property that we want to hold eventually and let us write $\bigcirc F$ if the logical formula F can be ensured to hold after the next program step:

$$\langle S, s \rangle \text{ satisfies } \bigcirc F$$

if there exists a γ such that $\langle S, s \rangle \Rightarrow \gamma$ where γ satisfies F

Then we can define the property *eventually Q is true*, written EF_Q, recursively by

$$EF_Q = Q \lor \bigcirc EF_Q.$$

For either it is the case that Q is true now or after the next step it is the case that Q will eventually hold.

We can therefore specify program properties by means of recursively defined formulae. We can then use Theorem 15.3 to compute the set of program configurations which satisfy EF_Q.

The operator $\bigcirc$ is known as a *modality*; logics with operators of this kind are known as *modal logics* and have become very important in computer science. The idea of considering modal logics with recursive declarations dates back to unpublished notes from 1969 by Dana Scott and Jaco de Bakker; after that, the important developments in the area are from the 1980s and onwards. Two particularly important developments of this era are due to Dexter Kozen (1982), who introduced the so-called propositional μ-calculus, and to Emerson and Clarke (1980), who independently of Kozen devised a modal logic with least as well as greatest fixed points.

15.9.2 A recursively defined program equivalence

The 'dual' version of Theorem 15.3, which talks about the existence of a *maximal* fixed-point, has applications in the study of program equivalence. For Definition 8.8 of bisimulation equivalence speaks of the maximal bisimulation relation, and this can be defined recursively. Let us here recall the definition.

Definition 15.63 Let $\mathcal{G} = (\Gamma, A, \xrightarrow{a})$ be a labelled transition system. A *bisimulation* is a relation $R \subseteq \Gamma \times \Gamma$ which satisfies the following conditions.
  If xRy then for all $a \in A$ we have that

1. If $x \xrightarrow{a} x'$ then there exists a y' such that $y \xrightarrow{a} y'$, where $x'Ry'$.
2. If $y \xrightarrow{a} y'$ then there exists an x' such that $x \xrightarrow{a} x'$, where $x'Ry'$.

  If xRy for some bisimulation R over Γ, we say that x and y are *bisimulation equivalent* (or *bisimilar*) and write $x \sim y$.

Another way of putting this is that we have defined a relation $\sim$ by the following recursive definition.

Definition 15.64 Let $\mathcal{G} = (\Gamma, A, \xrightarrow{a})$ be a labelled transition system. Then $\sim$ is the largest relation $\sim \subseteq \Gamma \times \Gamma$ which satisfies the following conditions:
  If xRy then for all $a \in A$ we have that

1. If $x \xrightarrow{a} x'$ then there exists a y' such that $y \xrightarrow{a} y'$, where $x' \sim y'$.
2. If $y \xrightarrow{a} y'$ then there exists an x' such that $x \xrightarrow{a} x'$, where $x' \sim y'$.

When given a labelled transition system, we can then use the dual version of Theorem 15.3 to compute $\sim$; this has been applied to devise efficient algorithms for checking equivalence of processes.

15.9.3 Recursively defined sets

In Chapter 6 we saw a definition of the set

$$\textbf{EnvP} = \textbf{Pnames} \rightharpoonup \textbf{Stm.} \times \textbf{EnvP}$$

In order to be able to solve recursive equations of this kind we need to define an ordering relation $\sqsubseteq$ between cpos, such that we can say that a cpo D_1 is 'less than' another cpo D_2.

If we can do this, we can compute the least solution to the recursive definition.

However, the class of cpos cannot be a cpo in the usual sense. For, if it were, we would have a paradox – the class of cpos would have itself as a member!

We therefore need to generalize the notion of cpo and to generalize Theorem 15.3. This can be done using a branch of mathematics known as category theory; we shall not describe the details of this approach here, but refer to (Gierz *et al.*, 2003).

15.10 Further reading

The results presented in this chapter date back to the work of Tarski and are a very small part of *domain theory*, which is an area that borders on both pure mathematics and theoretical computer science.

There is now a large body of literature on domain theory but two fairly recent books deserve particular mention. That by Gierz *et al.* (2003) gives a clear account of the mathematical theory of domains and the comprehensive text by Amadio and Curien (1998) is a very thorough treatment of how domain theory relates to the λ-calculus.

A good account of modal logics with recursion can be found in a survey chapter by Bradfield and Stirling (2001). Finally, the book by Aceto *et al.* (2007) is recommended for its detailed and clear account of the fixed-point characterization of bisimulation equivalence.

Appendix A
A big-step semantics of **Bip**

In this chapter we present a complete big-step semantics of the language **Bip** assuming static scope rules for variables and procedures. The following description consists of all the elements necessary for a complete semantic definition, namely

- An abstract syntax containing
  - names of all syntactic categories
  - formation rules for each syntactic category
- Definitions of additional sets and auxiliary functions
- Definitions of all transition systems; for each transition system
  - a definition of the set of configurations and the set of terminal configurations
  - a definition of the transition relation by means of a set of transition rules

A.1 Abstract syntax

A.1.1 Syntactic categories

$n \in \mathbf{Num}$ – Numerals
$x \in \mathbf{Var}$ – Variables
$a \in \mathbf{Aexp}$ – Arithmetic expressions
$b \in \mathbf{Bexp}$ – Boolean expressions
$S \in \mathbf{Stm}$ – Statements
$p \in \mathbf{Pnames}$ – Procedure names
$DV \in \mathbf{DecV}$ – Variable declarations
$DP\mathbf{DecP}$ – Procedure declarations

A.1.2 Formation rules

We do not present formation rules for numerals or variables.

$$a ::= n \mid x \mid a_1 + a_2 \mid a_1 * a_2 \mid (a_1)$$
$$b ::= a_1 = a_2 \mid a_1 < a_2 \mid \neg b_1 \mid b_1 \wedge b_2 \mid (b_1)$$
$$S ::= x := a \mid \texttt{skip} \mid S_1; S_2 \mid \texttt{if } b \texttt{ then } S_1 \texttt{ else } S_2$$
$$\mid \texttt{while } b \texttt{ do } S \mid \texttt{begin } D_V \ D_P \ S \texttt{ end} \mid \texttt{call } p$$
$$D_V ::= \texttt{var } x := a; D_V \mid \epsilon$$
$$D_P ::= \texttt{proc } p \quad \texttt{is } S; D_P \mid \epsilon$$

A.2 Additional sets and auxiliary functions

We assume the existence of a function $\mathcal{N} : \mathbf{Num} \rightarrow \mathbb{Z}$ that for each numeral $n \in \mathbf{Num}$ returns the value of n.

The set of *variable environments* is the set of partial functions from variables to locations:

$$\mathbf{EnvV} = \mathbf{Var} \cup \{\text{next}\} \rightharpoonup \mathbf{Loc}.$$

Here, next is a special pointer to the next available location. We let env_V denote an arbitrary member of $\mathbf{EnvV}$.

The function new : $\mathbf{Loc} \rightarrow \mathbf{Loc}$ returns for any location its successor (no matter whether this successor location is available or not).

The set of stores is the set of partial functions from locations to values.

$$\mathbf{Sto} = \mathbf{Loc} \rightharpoonup \mathbb{Z}.$$

We let *sto* denote an arbitrary element of **Sto**.

We again introduce a notation for updating environments and stores. For environments, we write $env_V[x \mapsto l]$ to denote the environment env'_V given by

$$env'_V\, y = \begin{cases} env_V\, y & \text{if } y \neq x \\ l & \text{if } y = x. \end{cases} \tag{A.1}$$

A similar update notation exists for stores, procedure environments etc.

We assume *static scope rules for variables and procedures*, so the set of procedure environments is given by

$$\mathbf{EnvP} = \mathbf{Pnames} \rightharpoonup \mathbf{Stm} \times \mathbf{EnvV} \times \mathbf{EnvP}. \tag{A.2}$$

We let env_P range over **EnvP**.

A.3 Transition systems

Our operational semantics does not define transition systems for **Num** or **Var**.

A.3.1 Transition system for Aexp

$(\Gamma_{\mathbf{Aexp}}, \rightarrow_a, T_{\mathbf{Aexp}})$ is defined below.

Configurations

$$\Gamma_{\mathbf{Aexp}} = \mathbf{Aexp} \cup \mathbb{Z}.$$

Terminal configurations

$$T_{\mathbf{Aexp}} = \mathbb{Z}.$$

The transition relation Transitions in this transition system are relative to an environment–store pair and are therefore of the form

$$env_V, sto \vdash a \rightarrow_a v.$$

$\rightarrow_a$ is defined as the least relation closed under the rules in Table A.1.

A.3.2 Transition system for Bexp

$(\Gamma_{\mathbf{Bexp}}, \rightarrow_b, T_{\mathbf{Bexp}})$ is defined below.

Configurations

$$\Gamma_{\mathbf{Bexp}} = \mathbf{Bexp} \cup \{tt, ff\}.$$

Terminal configurations

$$T_{\mathbf{Bexp}} = \{tt, ff\}.$$

The transition relation Transitions in this transition system are relative to an environment-store pair and are therefore of the form

$$env_V, sto \vdash b \rightarrow_b t.$$

$\rightarrow_b$ is defined as the least relation satisfying the rules in Table A.2.

[PLUS-BIP$_{BSS}$]	$$\frac{env_V, sto \vdash a_1 \rightarrow_a v_1 \quad env_V, sto \vdash a_2 \rightarrow_a v_2}{env_V, sto \vdash a_1 + a_2 \rightarrow_a v}$$

where $v = v_1 + v_2$

[MINUS-BIP$_{BSS}$]	$$\frac{env_V, sto \vdash a_1 \rightarrow_a v_1 \quad env_V, sto \vdash a_2 \rightarrow_a v_2}{env_V, sto \vdash a_1 - a_2 \rightarrow_a v}$$

where $v = v_1 - v_2$

[MULT-BIP$_{BSS}$]	$$\frac{env_V, sto \vdash a_1 \rightarrow_a v_1 \quad env_V, sto \vdash a_2 \rightarrow_a v_2}{env_V, sto \vdash a_1 * a_2 \rightarrow_a v}$$

where $v = v_1 \cdot v_2$

[PARENT-BIP$_{BSS}$]	$$\frac{env_V, sto \vdash a_1 \rightarrow_a v_1}{env_V, sto \vdash (a_1) \rightarrow_a v_1}$$
[NUM-BIP$_{BSS}$]	$env_V, sto \vdash n \rightarrow_a v$ if $\mathcal{N}[\![n]\!] = v$
[VAR-BIP$_{BSS}$]	$env_V, sto \vdash x \rightarrow_a v$ if $env_V\ x = l$ and $sto\ l = v$

Table A.1 *Big-step operational semantics of* **Aexp**

A.3.3 Transition system for Dec V

Our semantics for variable declarations is given by the transition system $(\Gamma_{\textbf{DecV}}, \rightarrow_{DV}, T_{\textbf{DecV}})$.

Configurations

$$\Gamma_{DV} = (\textbf{DecV} \times \textbf{EnvV} \times \textbf{Sto}) \cup (\textbf{EnvV} \times \textbf{Sto}),$$
$$T_{DV} = \textbf{EnvV} \times \textbf{Sto}.$$

Terminal configurations

$$T_{\textbf{DecV}} = \textbf{Env}_V \times \textbf{Sto}.$$

The transition relation Transitions are of the form

$$\langle D_V, env_V, sto \rangle \rightarrow_{DV} (env'_V, sto').$$

and the transition relation $\rightarrow_{DV}$ is defined as the least relation which is closed under the rules in Table A.3.

$[\text{EQUALS-1}_{\text{BSS}}]$
$$\frac{env_V, sto \vdash a_1 \rightarrow_a v_1 \quad env_V, sto \vdash a_2 \rightarrow_a v_2}{env_V, sto \vdash a_1 = a_2 \rightarrow_b t\!t}$$
$$\text{if } v_1 = v_2$$

$[\text{EQUALS-2}_{\text{BSS}}]$
$$\frac{env_V, sto \vdash a_1 \rightarrow_a v_1 \quad env_V, sto \vdash a_2 \rightarrow_a v_2}{env_V, sto \vdash a_1 = a_2 \rightarrow_b f\!\!f}$$
$$\text{if } v_1 \neq v_2$$

$[\text{GREATERTHAN-1}_{\text{BSS}}]$
$$\frac{env_V, sto \vdash a_1 \rightarrow_a v_1 \quad env_V, sto \vdash a_2 \rightarrow_a v_2}{env_V, sto \vdash a_1 < a_2 \rightarrow_b t\!t}$$
$$\text{if } v_1 < v_2$$

$[\text{GREATERTHAN-2}_{\text{BSS}}]$
$$\frac{env_V, sto \vdash a_1 \rightarrow_a v_1 \quad env_V, sto \vdash a_2 \rightarrow_a v_2}{env_V, sto \vdash a_1 < a_2 \rightarrow_b f\!\!f}$$
$$\text{if } v_1 \not< v_2$$

$[\text{NOT-1}_{\text{BSS}}]$
$$\frac{env_V, sto \vdash b \rightarrow_b t\!t}{env_V, sto \vdash \neg b \rightarrow_b f\!\!f}$$

$[\text{NOT-2}_{\text{BSS}}]$
$$\frac{env_V, sto \vdash b \rightarrow_b f\!\!f}{env_V, sto \vdash \neg b \rightarrow_b t\!t}$$

$[\text{PARENT-B}_{\text{BSS}}]$
$$\frac{env_V, sto \vdash b_1 \rightarrow_b v}{env_V, sto \vdash (b_1) \rightarrow_b v}$$

$[\text{AND-1}_{\text{BSS}}]$
$$\frac{env_V, sto \vdash b_1 \rightarrow_b t\!t \quad env_V, sto \vdash b_2 \rightarrow_b t\!t}{env_V, sto \vdash b_1 \wedge b_2 \rightarrow_b t\!t}$$

$[\text{AND-2}_{\text{BSS}}]$
$$\frac{env_V, sto \vdash b_i \rightarrow_b f\!\!f}{env_V, sto \vdash b_1 \wedge b_2 \rightarrow_b f\!\!f}$$
$$(i \in \{1, 2\})$$

Table A.2 *Big-step transition rules for* $\rightarrow_b$

A.3.4 Transition system for DecP

Our semantics is given by the transition system $(\Gamma_{\textbf{DecP}}, \rightarrow_{DP}, T_{\textbf{DecP}})$.

Configurations

$$\Gamma_{DP} = (\textbf{DecP} \times \textbf{EnvP}) \cup \textbf{EnvP},$$
$$T_{DP} = \textbf{EnvP}.$$

$$[\text{VAR-DECL}_{\text{BSS}}] \qquad \frac{\langle D_V, envv'', sto[l \mapsto v]\rangle \rightarrow_{DV} (env'_V, sto')}{\langle \textbf{var } x := a; D_V, env_V, sto\rangle \rightarrow_{DV} (env'_V, sto')}$$

where $env_V, sto \vdash a \rightarrow_a v$
and $l = env_V$ next
and $envv'' = env_V [x \mapsto l][\text{next} \mapsto \text{new } l]$

$[\text{EMPTY-VAR}_{\text{BSS}}] \qquad \langle \epsilon, env_V, sto\rangle \rightarrow_{DV} (env_V, sto)$

Table A.3 *Big-step semantics of variable declarations*

Terminal configurations

$$T_{\textbf{DecP}} = \textbf{EnvP}.$$

The transition relation Transitions are of the form

$$env_V \vdash \langle D_P, env_P\rangle \rightarrow_{DP} env'_P$$

and the transition relation $\rightarrow_{DP}$ is defined as the least relation satisfying the transition rules in Table A.4.

$$[\text{PROC-BIP}_{\text{BSS}}] \qquad \frac{env_V \vdash \langle D_P, env_P[p \mapsto (S, env_V, env_P)]\rangle \rightarrow_{DP} env'_P}{env_V \vdash \langle \textbf{proc } p \textbf{ is } S\,; D_P, env_P\rangle \rightarrow_{DP} env'_P}$$

$[\text{PROC-EMPTY-BIP}_{\text{BSS}}] \qquad env_V \vdash \langle \epsilon, env_P\rangle \rightarrow_{DP} env_P$

Table A.4 *Transition rules for procedure declarations assuming fully static scope rules*

A.3.5 Transition system for Stm

We here have the transition system $(\Gamma_{\textbf{Stm}}, \rightarrow, T_{\textbf{Stm}})$.

Configurations

$$\Gamma_{\textbf{Stm}} = \textbf{Stm} \times \textbf{Sto} \cup \textbf{Sto}.$$

Terminal configurations

$$T_{\mathbf{Stm}} = \mathbf{Sto}.$$

The transition relation Transitions are relative to a variable environment and a procedure environment and are therefore of the form

$$env_V, env_P \vdash \langle S, sto \rangle \rightarrow sto'.$$

The transition relation $\rightarrow$ is the least relation which is closed under the rules in Table A.5.

[ASS-BIP$_{\text{BSS}}$] $env_V, env_P \vdash \langle x := a, sto \rangle \to sto[l \mapsto v]$

where $env_V, sto \vdash a \to_a v$ and $env_V\, x = l$

[SKIP-BIP$_{\text{BSS}}$] $env_V, env_P \vdash \langle \textbf{skip}, sto \rangle \to sto$

[COMP-BIP$_{\text{BSS}}$]
$$\frac{env_V, env_P \vdash \langle S_1, sto \rangle \to sto'' \qquad env_V, env_P \vdash \langle S_2, sto'' \rangle \to sto'}{env_V, env_P \vdash \langle S_1; S_2, sto \rangle \to sto'}$$

[IF-TRUE-BIP$_{\text{BSS}}$]
$$\frac{env_V, env_P \vdash \langle S_1, sto \rangle \to sto'}{env_V, env_P \vdash \langle \textbf{if } b \textbf{ then } S_1 \textbf{ else } S_2, sto \rangle \to sto'}$$

if $env_V, sto \vdash b \to_b tt$

[IF-FALSE-BIP$_{\text{BSS}}$]
$$\frac{env_V, env_P \vdash \langle S_2, sto \rangle \to sto'}{env_V, env_P \vdash \langle \textbf{if } b \textbf{ then } S_1 \textbf{ else } S_2, sto \rangle \to sto'}$$

if $env_V, sto \vdash b \to_b ff$

[WHILE-TRUE-BIP$_{\text{BSS}}$]
$$\frac{env_V, env_P \vdash \langle S, sto \rangle \to sto'' \qquad env_V, env_P \vdash \langle \textbf{while } b \textbf{ do } S, sto'' \rangle \to sto'}{env_V, env_P \vdash \langle \textbf{while } b \textbf{ do } S, sto \rangle \to sto'}$$

if $env_V, sto \vdash b \to_b tt$

[WHILE-FALSE-BIP$_{\text{BSS}}$] $env_V, env_P \vdash \langle \textbf{while } b \textbf{ do } S, sto \rangle \to sto$

if $env_V, sto \vdash b \to_b ff$

[BLOCK-BIP$_{\text{BSS}}$]
$$\frac{\langle D_V, env_V, sto \rangle \to_{DV} (env_V', sto'') \quad env_V' \vdash \langle D_P, env_P \rangle \to_{DP} env_P' \quad env_V', env_P' \vdash \langle S, sto'' \rangle \to sto'}{env_V, env_P \vdash \langle \textbf{begin } D_V\; D_P\; S \textbf{ end}, sto \rangle \to sto'}$$

[CALL-STAT-STAT$_{\text{BSS}}$]
$$\frac{env_V'[\text{next} \mapsto l], env_P' \vdash \langle S, sto \rangle \to sto'}{env_V, env_P \vdash \langle \textbf{call } p, sto \rangle \to sto'}$$

where $env_P\, p = (S, env_V', env_P')$
and $l = env_V\, \text{next}$

Table A.5 *Big-step transition rules for **Bip** statements*

Appendix B

Implementing semantic definitions in SML

This chapter describes how one can implement a structural operational semantics in SML and thereby build a prototype interpreter. We shall look at the operational semantics of **Bims** and the extensions of it with repeat-until loops, nondeterminism and parallelism.

The following presentation uses Standard ML as its starting point (NJ-SML, 2002; Moscow ML, 2002), but the setting is easily adapted to other functional languages such as Ocaml (Hickey, 2007) or Haskell (Peyton Jones, 2003).

B.1 Abstract syntax

The abstract syntax of a language can easily be captured in SML using datatype declarations. For each syntactic category we introduce a datatype, and its formation rules are captured by a datatype constructor for each rule. We also need to agree on the representation of elements of basic syntactic categories **Num** and **Var**.

Compare the following version of the abstract syntax of **Bims** extended with repeat-until loops,

$n \in$ **Num** – Numerals

$x \in$ **Var** – Variables

$a \in$ **Aexp** – Arithmetic expressions

$b \in$ **Bexp** – Boolean expressions

$S \in$ **Stm** – Statements

Formation rules

$$S ::= x{:=}a \mid \text{skip} \mid S_1; S_2 \mid \text{if } b \text{ then } S_1 \text{ else } S_2 \mid$$
$$\text{while } b \text{ do } S \mid \text{repeat } S \text{ until } b$$
$$b ::= a_1 = a_2 \mid a_1 < a_2 \mid \neg b_1 \mid b_1 \wedge b_2 \mid (b_1)$$
$$a ::= n \mid x \mid a_1{+}a_2 \mid a_1{*}a_2 \mid a_1{-}a_2 \mid (a_1)$$

with the SML datatype declaration

```
type Var   = string;

datatype aexp = N of int | V of var |
                Add of aexp * aexp |
                Mult of aexp * aexp |
                Sub of aexp * aexp |
                Parent of aexp;

datatype bexp = TRUE | FALSE |
                Eq of aexp * aexp |
                Le of aexp * aexp |
                Neg of bexp |
                And of bexp * bexp;

datatype stm  = Ass of var * aexp | Skip |
                Comp of stm * stm |
                If of bexp*stm*stm |
                While of bexp * stm |
                Repeat of stm * bexp
```

The program

```
x  := 4;
y  := 2;
repeat
   x := x+y
until x = y
```

can be represented as the datatype value

```
Comp ( (Ass ("x", (N 4))),(Comp (Ass ("y", (N 2))),
       (Repeat  ((Ass
                ( "x" ,(Add ((V "x"),(V "y")))))),
       (Eq (Add (V "x") (V "y")))))))))
```

An obvious addition is to build a *parser* that takes **Bims** source code as input and returns the corresponding datatype value.

B.2 Transition systems

We represent transition systems in a slightly indirect fashion. Let us first consider the big-step semantics of arithmetic expressions and then the semantics of statements.

B.2.1 Program states

We represent the set of program states as the datatype of functions from variables to integers. This becomes

```
type Z    = int
type T    = bool
type States = Var -> Z
```

The program state $[x \mapsto 3, y \mapsto 0]$ is described as

```
fun s_init "x" = 3
  | s_init "y" = 0
```

B.2.2 Semantics of arithmetic and Boolean expressions

We describe the transition relation $\to_a$ by the function

```
a_val :: aexp -> (States -> Z)
```

defined as

$$a\_val \ a \ s = v \ \text{ if } s \vdash a \to_a v.$$

Each transition rule in the definition of $\to_a$ is represented by a clause in the definition of a_val. For instance the rule

$$[\text{MULT}_{\text{BSS}}] \quad \frac{s \vdash a_1 \to_a v_1 \quad s \vdash a_2 \to_a v_2}{s \vdash a_1 * a_2 \to_a v} \quad \text{where } v = v_1 \cdot v_2$$

becomes

```
...
(* other clauses for a_val *)
a_val (Mult (a1, a2)) s = (a_val a1 s) * (a_val a2 s)
```

If we want to find the value that an arithmetic expression evaluates to, we apply a_val to an arithmetic expression and a state as e.g.

```
(* other clauses for a_val *)
a_val (Add ((N 2), (N 2))) s_init
```

B.3 Big-step semantics of statements

We must first define the set of configurations. We do this by declaring the datatype config as

```
datatype config = Inter of Stm * States |
                  Terminal of States
```

The implementation of the big-step semantics of statements follows the same ideas as those of the implementation of the semantics for arithmetic expressions. We implement the transition relation $\rightarrow$ by defining the function bss_stm given by

$$\texttt{bss\_stm } S\ s = s' \text{ if } \langle S, s\rangle \rightarrow s'.$$

There must be a clause in the definition of bss_stm for each transition rule. For instance, the rule

$$[\text{COMP}_{\text{BSS}}]\quad \frac{\langle S_1, s\rangle \rightarrow s''\ \ \langle S_2, s''\rangle \rightarrow s'}{\langle S_1; S_2, s\rangle \rightarrow s'}$$

becomes

```
. . .
(* other clauses for bss_stm *)
bss_stm (Inter ((Comp (ss1, ss2)), s)) =

let val Terminal s'  = bss_stm (Inter (ss1, s))

    val Terminal s'' = bss_stm (Inter (ss2, s'))

in Terminal s''

end;
```

To simulate the execution of a **Bims** program, we apply bss_stm to a configuration.

Problem B.1 (**Important**) Implement an SML datatype which describes derivation trees in the semantics of **Aexp** and define a function `maketree` that for any given configuration $\langle S, s \rangle$ returns the derivation tree whose root is $\langle S, s \rangle \rightarrow s'$, if such a tree exists.

B.4 Small-step semantics of statements

The ideas behind implementation of the small-step semantics of **Bims** are completely analogous to those used to implement the big-step semantics.

We implement the transition relation $\Rightarrow$ as the function `sss_stm` given by

$$\text{sss\_stm } S \ s = \gamma \text{ if } \langle S, s \rangle \Rightarrow \gamma.$$

As before, the transition rules become clauses in a function definition. The rules

$$[\text{COMP-1}_{\text{SSS}}] \quad \frac{\langle S_1, s \rangle \Rightarrow \langle S_1', s' \rangle}{\langle S_1; S_2, s \rangle \Rightarrow \langle S_1'; S_2, s \rangle}$$

$$[\text{COMP-2}_{\text{SSS}}] \quad \frac{\langle S_1, s \rangle \Rightarrow s'}{\langle S_1; S_2, s \rangle \Rightarrow \langle S_2, s' \rangle}$$

become

```
sss_stm (Inter (Comp (ss1, ss2)) s) =

case sss_stm (Inter (ss1, s)) of
     Inter (ss1',s') => Inter (Comp (ss1', ss2)) s'
   | Terminal s' => Inter (ss2,s');
```

Note how the side conditions of the rules correspond to a **case**-construct.

Problem B.2 Implement the small-step semantics of **Aexp**.

B.5 Parallelism

When we implement the transition rules describing a language with a non-deterministic semantics – such as the extensions of **Bims** with nondeterministic choice or parallel composition – we must proceed in a somewhat different manner.

Consider the semantics of **Bims** extended with parallel composition. Here we implement the function `sss_stm`:

$$\texttt{sss\_stm}\ \langle S, s\rangle = \{\gamma \mid \langle S, s\rangle \Rightarrow \gamma\}.$$

That is, for any given configuration we *compute the set of all possible immediate successor configurations*. There is no type for sets in SML, so we define sss_stm such that it returns the *list* of all immediate successor configurations.

Consider the rules

$$[\text{PAR-1}_{\text{SSS}}]\quad \frac{\langle S_1, s\rangle \Rightarrow \langle S_1', s'\rangle}{\langle S_1 \text{ par } S_2, s\rangle \Rightarrow \langle S_1' \text{ par } S_2, s'\rangle}$$

$$[\text{PAR-2}_{\text{SSS}}]\quad \frac{\langle S_1, s\rangle \Rightarrow s'}{\langle S_1 \text{ par } S_2, s\rangle \Rightarrow \langle S_2, s'\rangle}$$

$$[\text{PAR-3}_{\text{SSS}}]\quad \frac{\langle S_2, s\rangle \Rightarrow \langle S_2', s'\rangle}{\langle S_1 \text{ par } S_2, s\rangle \Rightarrow \langle S_1 \text{ par } S_2', s'\rangle}$$

$$[\text{PAR-4}_{\text{SSS}}]\quad \frac{\langle S_2, s\rangle \Rightarrow s'}{\langle S_1 \text{ par } S_2, s\rangle \Rightarrow \langle S_1, s'\rangle}$$

Together, these give rise to the following clauses in the definition of sss_stm. We define the auxiliary functions leftcombine and rightcombine. These combine a list of successor configurations for the left and right component, respectively, with the list of successors for the other parallel component to a new list of configurations.

```
local
fun leftcombine (Inter (ss1,s1) :: ll) ss2 =

(Inter (Par (ss1,ss2),s1)) :: (leftcombine  ll ss2)

   | leftcombine ( (Terminal s1) :: ll) ss2 =

(Inter (ss2,s1)) :: (leftcombine  ll ss2)

   | leftcombine [] ss2 = []
```

```
fun rightcombine ss1 (Inter (ss2,s2) :: 12) =

(Inter (Par (ss1,ss2),s2)) :: (rightcombine   ss1 12)

    | rightcombine ss1 ( (Terminal s2) :: 12) =

(Inter (ss1,s2)) :: (rightcombine   ss1 12)

    | rightcombine ss1 [] = []

in
...
(* other clauses for sss_stm *)

sss_stm (Inter ((Par (ss1, ss2)), s)) =
    let val ss1parts = (sss_stm (Inter (ss1, s)))
        val ss2parts = (sss_stm (Inter (ss1, s)))
        val ss1results = leftcombine ss1parts ss2
        val ss2results = rightcombine ss1 ss2parts
    in
        ss1results @ ss2results
    end;

end;
```

References

Abadi, M., and Gordon, A. D. 1999. A calculus for cryptographic protocols: the spi calculus. *Information and Computation*, **148**(1), 1–70.

Aceto, L., Ingólfsdóttir, A., Larsen, K.G., and Srba, J. 2007. *Reactive Systems: Modelling, Specification and Verification*. Cambridge: Cambridge University Press.

Aczel, P. 1988. *Non-Well-founded Sets*. CSLI Lecture Notes, vol. 14. Stanford: Center for the Study of Language and Information.

Allison, L. 1987. *A Practical Introduction to Denotational Semantics*. Cambridge: Cambridge University Press.

Alves-Foss, J. (ed). 1999. *Formal Syntax and Semantics of Java*. Lecture Notes in Computer Science, vol. 1523. Berlin: Springer-Verlag.

Amadio, R. M., and Curien, P.-L. 1998. *Domains and Lambda-calculi*. Cambridge: Cambridge University Press.

Apt, K. R. 1981. Ten years of Hoare's logic: A survey – Part 1. *ACM Transactions on Programming Languages and Systems*, **3**(4).

Backus, J. 1978. Can programming be liberated from the von Neumann style? *Communications of the ACM*, **21**(8), 613–641.

Backus, J., and Naur, P. 1960. Report on the algorithmic language ALGOL 60. *Communications of the ACM*, **3**, 299–314.

Backus, J., and Naur, P. 1963. Revised report on the algorithmic language ALGOL 60. *Communications of the ACM*, **6**(1), 1–20.

Bengtsson, J., Larsen, K. G., Larsson, F., Pettersson, P., and Yi, W. 1995. UPPAAL - a tool suite for automatic verification of real-time systems. pp. 232–243 in Alur, R., Henzinger, T. A., and Sontag, E. D. (eds), *Hybrid Systems*. Lecture Notes in Computer Science, vol. 1066. Berlin: Springer-Verlag.

Berry, G., and Boudol, G. 1992. The chemical abstract machine. *Theoretical Computer Science*, **96**(1), 217–248.

Board, Ariane 501 Inquiry. 1996. *Report*. http://esamultimedia.esa.int/docs/esa-x-1819eng.pdf.

Börger, E., Fruja, N. G., Gervasi, V., and Stärk, R. F. 2005. A high-level modular definition of the semantics of C#. *Theoretical Computer Science*, **336**(2–3), 235–284.

Bradfield, J. C., and Stirling, C. 2001. Modal logics and mu-calculi: an introduction. Chapter 1.4 in Bergstra, J. A., Ponse, A., and Smolka, S. A. (eds), *Handbook of Process Algebra*. Amsterdam: Elsevier Science.

Chalub, F., and Braga, C. 2007. Maude MSOS Tool. *Electronic Notes in Theoretical Computer Science*, **176**(4), 133–146.

Church, A. 1932. A set of postulates for the foundation of logic. *Annals of Mathematics*, **33**, 346–366.

Church, A. 1936. An unsolvable problem of elementary number theory. *American Journal of Mathematics*, **58**(2), 345–363.

Church, A. 1940. A formulation of the simple theory of types. *Journal of Symbolic Logic*, **5**(2), 56–68.

Church, A. 1941. *The Calculi of Lambda Conversion. (AM-6) (Annals of Mathematics Studies)*. Princeton, NJ: Princeton University Press.

Diehl, S. 2000. Natural semantics-directed generation of compilers and abstract machines. *Formal Aspects of Computing*, **12**(2), 71–99.

Emerson, E. A., and Clarke, E. M. 1980. Characterizing correctness properties of parallel programs using fixpoints. pp. 169–181 in *Proceedings of the 7th Colloquium on Automata, Languages and Programming*. London: Springer-Verlag.

ESA. 2001. *Ariane 5*. http://esapub.esrin.esa.it/br/br200/Ariane-5.pdf.

Giacalone, A., Mishra, P., and Prasad, S. 1989. Facile: A symmetric integration of concurrent and functional programming. *International Journal of Parallel Programming*, **18**(2), 121–160.

Gierz, G., Hofmann, K. H., Keimel, K., Lawson, J. D., Mislove, M., and Scott, D. S. 2003. *Continuous Lattices and Domains*. Encyclopedia of Mathematics and its Applications, vol. 93. Cambridge: Cambridge University Press.

Goguen, J., and Malcolm, G. 1996. *Algebraic Semantics of Imperative Programs*. Cambridge, MA: MIT Press.

Gordon, M. J. C. 1979. *The Denotational Description of Programming Languages: An Introduction*. Berlin: Springer-Verlag.

Gordon, M. J. C., Milner, R., Morris, L., Newey, M. C., and Wadsworth, C. P. 1978. A metalanguage for interactive proof in LCF. pp. 119–130 in *Principles Of Programming Languages*.

Guessarian, I. 1981. *Algebraic Semantics*. Lecture Notes in Computer Science, vol. 99. Berlin: Springer-Verlag.

Hansen, M. R., and Rischel, H. 1999. *Introduction to Programming Using Standard ML*. New York, NY: Addison-Wesley.

Hickey, J. 2007. *Introduction to Objective Caml*. Cambridge University Press.

Hoare, C. A. R. 1969. An axiomatic basis for computer programming. *Communications of the ACM*, **12**(10), 576–580.

Hoare, C.A.R. 1988. *Communicating Sequential Processes*. New York, NY: Prentice–Hall.

Holzmann, G. J. 1990. *Design and Validation of Computer Protocols*. Prentice-Hall.

Hudak, P., Hughes, J., Peyton-Jones, S., and Wadler, P. 2007. A history of Haskell: being lazy with class. In *HOPL III: Proceedings of the Third ACM SIGPLAN Conference on History of Programming Languages*. New York, NY: ACM.

Hutchinson, N. C., Raj, R. K., Black, A. P., Levy, H. M., and Jul, E. 1987 (October). *The Emerald Programming Language Report*. Technical report 87/22. Datalogisk Institut, Københavns Universitet.

INRIA. 1995–2005. *The Caml language*.

Jacopini, G., and Böhm, C. 1966. Flow diagrams, Turing machines and languages with only two formation rules. *Communications of the ACM*, **9**, 366–371.

Jensen, K., and Wirth, N. 1975. *PASCAL, User Manual and Report*. Second edn. Lecture Notes in Computer Science, vol. 18. Berlin: Springer-Verlag.

Knuth, D. E. 1967. The remaining trouble spots in ALGOL 60. *Communications of the ACM*, **10**, 611–18.

Kozen, D. 1982. Results on the propositional μ-calculus. pp. 348–359 in Nielsen, M., and Schmidt, E. M. (eds), *ICALP*. Lecture Notes in Computer Science, vol. 140. Springer-Verlag.

Landin, P. J. 1964. The mechanical evaluation of expressions. *Computer Journal*, **6**(4), 308–320.

Landin, P. J. 1966. The next 700 programming languages. *Communications of the ACM*, **9**(3), 157–166.

Jet Propulsion Laboratories. 1999 (September). *NASA's Mars Climate Orbiter believed to be lost*.

Microsoft. 2009. *F#*. `http://msdn.microsoft.com/fsharp`.

Milner, R. 1978. A theory of type polymorphism in programming. *Journal of Computer and System Sciences*, **17**, 348–375.

Milner, R. 1980. *A Calculus of Communicating Systems*. Lecture Notes in Computer Science. Berlin: Springer-Verlag.

Milner, R. 1989. *Communication and Concurrency*. Prentice-Hall International.

Milner, R. 1992. Functions as processes. *Mathematical Structures in Computer Science*, **2**(2), 119–141.

Milner, R. 1999. *Communicating and Mobile Systems: the π-Calculus*. Cambridge: Cambridge University Press.

Milner, R., Parrow, J., and Walker, D. 1992a. A calculus of mobile processes, I. *Information and Computation*, **100**(1), 1–40.

Milner, R., Parrow, J., and Walker, D. 1992b. A calculus of mobile processes, II. *Information and Computation*, **100**(1), 41–77.

Milner, R., Tofte, M., Harper, R., and MacQueen, D. 1997. *The Definition of Standard ML (Revised)*. Cambridge, MA: MIT Press.

Moscow ML. 2002. *Moscow ML home page*. `http://www.dina.kvl.dk/~sestoft/mosml.html`.

Mosses, P. D. 1975. *Mathematical semantics and compiler generation*. Ph.D. thesis, Oxford University.

Mosses, P. D. 1976. Compiler generation using denotational semantics. pp. 436–441 in Mazurkiewicz, A. W. (ed), *MFCS*. Lecture Notes in Computer Science, vol. 45. Berlin: Springer-Verlag.

NASA. 1999. *Mishap Investigation Board Phase I Report*. `ftp://ftp.hq.nasa.gov/pub/pao/reports/1999/MCO\_report.pdf`.

Nielson, F., and Nielson, H. R. 2007. *Semantics with Applications: An Appetizer*. Berlin: Springer-Verlag.

NJ-SML. 2002. *Standard ML*. `http://cm.bell-labs.com/cm/cs/what/smlnj/index.html`.

Owre, S., Rushby, J. M., and Shankar, N. 1992. PVS: A prototype verification system. pp. 748–752 in Kapur, D. (ed), *CADE*. Lecture Notes in Computer Science, vol. 607. Berlin: Springer-Verlag.

Park, D.M.R. 1981. Concurrency and automata on infinite sequences. pp. 167–183 in Deussen, P. (ed), *Proceedings of 5th GI Conference*. Lecture Notes in Computer Science, vol. 104. Berlin: Springer-Verlag.

Paulson, L. 1982. A semantics-directed compiler generator. pp. 224–233 in *POPL '82: Proceedings of the 9th ACM SIGPLAN-SIGACT symposium on Principles of programming languages*. New York, NY: ACM.

Paulson, L. C. 1996. *ML for the Working Programmer*. Cambridge: Cambridge University Press.

Pettersson, M. 1999. *Compiling natural semantics*. Lecture Notes in Computer Science, vol. 1549. Berlin: Springer-Verlag.

Peyton Jones, S. 2003. *Haskell 98 Language and Libraries: the Revised Report*. Cambridge: Cambridge University Press.

Pierce, B. C. 2002. *Types and Programming Languages*. Cambridge, MA: MIT Press.

Plotkin, G. 1981. *A Structural Approach to Operational Semantics*. Technical report FN-19. Computer Science Department, Aarhus University. Reprinted in *Journal of Logic and Algebraic Programming*, **60–61**, 17–139 (2004).

Plotkin, G. 2004. The origins of structural operational semantics. *Journal of Logic and Algebraic Programming*, **60-61**, 3–15.

Puhlmann, F., and Weske, M. 2005. Using the π-calculus for formalizing workflow patterns. pp. 153–168 in van der Aalst, W. M. P., Benatallah, B., Casati, F., and Curbera, F. (eds), *Business Process Management*. Lecture Notes in Computer Science, vol. 3649. Berlin: Springer-Verlag.

Regev, A., Silverman, W., and Shapiro, E. Y. 2001. Representation and simulation of biochemical processes using the π-calculus process algebra. pp. 459–470 in *Pacific Symposium on Biocomputing*.

Reppy, J.H. 1992. *Higher-Order Concurrency*. Ph.D. thesis, Department of Computer Science, Cornell University.

Reynolds, J. C. 1999. *Theories of Programming Languages*. Cambridge: Cambridge University Press.

Roscoe, A. W. 1995. Modelling and verifying key-exchange protocols using CSP and FDR. pp. 98–107 in *CSFW*. New York, NY: IEEE Computer Society.

Russell, B., and Whitehead, A. N. 1910. *Principia Mathematica*. Cambridge: Cambridge University Press.

Sangiorgi, D. 1998. An interpretation of typed objects into typed pi-calculus. *Information and Computation*, **143**(1), 34–73.

Sangiorgi, D., and Walker, D. 2001. *π-Calculus: A Theory of Mobile Processes*. Cambridge: Cambridge University Press.

Schmidt, D. A. 1986. *Denotational Semantics: A Methodology For Language Development*. Boston, MA: Allyn & Bacon, Inc.

Scott, D., and Strachey, C. 1971. *Toward a Mathematical Semantics for Computer Languages*. Programming Research Group Technical Monograph PRG-6. Oxford University Computing Lab.

Scott, D. S. 2000. Some reflections on Strachey and his work. *Higher-Order and Symbolic Computation*, **13**(1/2), 103–114.

Scott, Dana. 1976. Data types as lattices. *SIAM Journal on Computing*, **5**(3), 522–587.

Shashkin, Y. 1991. *Fixed Points*. New York, NY: American Mathematical Society.

Sipser, M. 2005. *Introduction to the Theory of Computation*. Second edn. Florence, KY: Course Technology.

Stoy, J. E. 1977. *Denotational Semantics: The Scott–Strachey Approach to Programming Language Theory*. Cambridge, MA: MIT Press.

Strachey, C. 1966. Towards a formal semantics. pp. 198–220 in *Formal Language Description Languages for Computer Programming*. Amsterdam: North Holland.

Strachey, C. 1967. *Fundamental Concepts in Programming Languages*. Lecture Notes, International Summer School in Computer Programming, Copenhagen. Reprinted in *Higher-Order and Symbolic Computation*, **13**(1/2), 1–49 (2000).

Tait, W. 1967. Intensional interpretations of functionals of finite type I. *Journal of Symbolic Logic*, **32**(2), 198–212.

Tait, W. 1975. A realizability interpretation of the theory of species. pp. 240–251 in Parikh, R. (ed), *Logic Colloquium*. Lectures Notes in Mathematics, vol. 453. Berlin: Springer-Verlag.

Tarski, A. 1935. Die Wahrheitsbegriff in den formalisierten Sprachen. *Studia Philosophica*, **1**, 261–405.

Velleman, D. J. 2006. *How to Prove It: A Structured Approach*. Second edn. Cambridge: Cambridge University Press.

Walker, D. 1991. Pi-calculus semantics of object-oriented programming languages. pp. 532–547 in Ito, T., and Meyer, A. R. (eds), *TACS*. Lecture Notes in Computer Science, vol. 526. Berlin: Springer-Verlag.

Winskel, G. 1993. *The Formal Semantics Of Programming Languages*. Cambridge, MA: MIT Press.

Index

λ-calculus, 174, 248
  abstraction, 174
  application, 174
  applied, 176
  bound variables, 175
  free variables, 175
  operational semantics, 175
  substitution, 176
  variables, 174
λ-notation, 212
  abstraction, 212
  application of expression, 213
  conditional expression, 213
  higher-order function, 213
  partial function, 213
  type of expression, 212
π-calculus
  alpha-conversion, 127
  bound names, 125, 126, 131
  free names, 125, 131
  scope extrusion, 125
  scope intrusion, 127
  semantics, 129
    labelled semantics, 130
    reduction semantics, 129
  structural congruence, 127
  substitution, 129

abstract syntax, 27
actual parameter, 95, 104
algebraic semantics, 8
ALGOL 60, 5, 100, 211
  call-by-name, 102
  problems in, 5
alpha-conversion, 109, 127, 176
antisymmetric, 225
Ariane 5, 12
axiomatic semantics, 8

Backus, John, 5, 100, 173
base type, 188, 192

behaviour
  global, 115
  local, 114, 115
Berry, Gerard, 114
big-step semantics, 31, 32, 41
Bims, 28
  big-step semantics of **Stm**, 45
    example, 48
  small-step semantics of **Stm**, 53
binding construct, 110
binding construct, 125
Bip, 79
  semantics of **Aexp**, 83
  semantics of **Bexp**, 83
  semantics of **Stm**, 85
  semantics of declarations, 84
bisimulation, 247
bisimulation equivalence, 70, 247
block, 80
Boudol, Gerard, 114
Bump, 94

Cab, 113
call-by-name, 100
call-by-reference, 96
call-by-value, 99
cardinality, 91
CCS, 7, 113
chain, 227
channel, 113
Chemical Abstract Machine, 114
Chemical Abstract Machine, 127
Church, Alonzo, 174
class, 142
  declaration, 142, 143
Coat, 134, 142
Cola, 161
communication
  asynchronous, 119
  synchronous, 115

complete partial order, 225
composite type, 189
composite element, 28
compositional, 35, 215, 218
  example of a non-compositional rule, 36, 48
concurrency, 76
  attempt at big-step semantics, 77
  small-step semantics, 77
configuration, 30, 33
  terminal, 30, 33
confusion-free, 202
connective, 18
  and, 18
  not, 18
  or, 18
constant, 176
constant-folding problem, 211
continuous function, 228, 229
  composition of, 236
  examples of, 236
cpo, 225, 228
  examples, 232
  function space, 234
  powerset, 232, 233
  subset, 232
CSP, 113

de Bakker, Jaco, 247
de Bruijn index, 108
declaration of
  classes, 143, 146
  methods, 147, 161
  objects, 147, 161
  procedures, 85
    with parameters, 96
  records, 139
  variables, 84, 161
denotation, 214
  of a statement, 216
denotational semantics, 7, 211, 239
  of **Aexp**, 214
  of **Bexp**, 216
  of **Stm**, 216
  x **Stm**, 218
  equivalence with structural operational semantics, 10, 241
derivation tree, 34
  construction of, 48–52
deterministic, 38, 61
domain theory, 91, 248

Emerald, 161
endofunction, 230
environment
  method environment, 163
  object environment, 145
  procedure environment, 82
  record environment, 136
  type environment, 199

variable environment, 80
  variable environment, 81, 144, 154
environment–store model, 80
  update notation, 81
environment-store model
  for objects, 144
equivalence
  of big-step and small-step semantics, 55
equivalence relation, 22, 70
evaluation context, 156

fixed-point, 224, 230
  theorem, 225, 229, 230
    applications, 231
Flan, 177
  big-step semantics, 178, 179
  bound variables, 202
  closure, 178
  free variables, 201
  recursive closure, 178
  small-step semantics, 180, 199, 201
for-loop, 71
formal parameter, 95
formal parameter, 104
formation rule, 28
function, 22
  partial, 23
  total, 23
function space, 23
functional programming language, 171
functional programming language
  impure, 172
functional programming language
  pure, 171

generalized procedure name, 139
generalized variable, 137

Haskell, 174
Hasse diagram, 226, 233

immediate constituents, 28
imperative language, 171
implicit parallelism, 121
increasing sequence, 227
induction, 16
  on the length of transition sequences, 55
interleaving, 163

Jensen, Jørn, 103

Knuth, D. E., 5
Kozen, Dexter, 247

labelled transition system, 247
least upper bound, 227
least element, 228
least upper bound, 227
limit, 227
Lisp, 172, 173, 211
locations, 81
logic of programs, 246
logical relation, 206

loops forever
  in the big-step semantics, 52
  in the small-step semantics, 54

Mars Climate Orbiter, 13
McCarthy, John, 5
metavariable, 28
method
  declaration, 146
  environment, 146
method environment, 163
Milner, Robin, 123, 209
ML, 173, 177
  OCaml, 172, 174
  Standard ML, 172, 174
modal logic, 247
  recursive, 247
monotone function, 228, 229

name clash, 107–109, 127, 129, 131, 176
Naur, Peter, 5, 100
new, 81
next, 81, 145
nondeterminism, 73
  angelic, 65, 75
  big-step semantics, 74
  bounded, 74
  demonic, 65, 75
  small-step semantics, 75
not compositional, 218

object
  declaration, 147
  dynamically created, 143, 144
  path expression, 143
  sequence, 148

parameter
  actual, 95, 104
  formal, 95, 104
  mechanism, 95
parameters, 94
  name, 100
  reference, 96
  value, 99
Parrow, Joachim, 123
partial function
  cpo, 234, 235
partial order, 225
  example, 226
  Hasse diagram, 226
Pascal, 5, 6, 100, 172, 211
Pif, 121
polymorphic type, 205, 209
power set
  cpo, 232, 233
pre-fixed-point, 245
prefix ordering, 227
premise, 32
procedure call, 80
  dynamic scope rules

  big-step semantics, 89
  mixed scope rules
    big-step semantics, 91
  recursive, 90, 97, 98, 158
  remote, 161, 162
  static scope rules
    big-step semantics, 93
    small-step semantics, 159
procedure declaration
  dynamic scope rules, 89
  mixed scope rules, 90
  static scope rules, 92, 254
procedure environment, 85, 95, 104
  for dynamic scope rules, 89
  for mixed scope rules, 90
  for static scope rules, 92
process calculus, 113, 123
proof by
  induction on the length of transition se-
    quences, 61
proof by
  induction on the length of transition se-
    quences, 58
  mathematical induction, 16
  transition induction, 39, 56, 60

quantifier
  existential, 18
  universal, 18

record, 134, 135
recursive definition, 222, 224
  definiendum, 224
  definiens, 224
  of **EnvP**, 91, 248
  of function over $\mathbb{N}$, 237, 240
  of language, 222, 224, 236, 240
  of set, 248
  solution, 223
  solution to, 223
recursively defined set, 91
referentially transparent, 172
reflexive, 22, 225
relation, 21
  binary, 21
rendezvous, 114, 162
repeat-loop, 66
run-time stack, 154, 155, 163
Russell, Bertrand, 186

safe, 192
scope rules
  according to the ALGOL 60 report, 103
  dynamic, 86, 89, 159
    big-step semantics, 89
  example, 88
  mixed, 90
  static, 86, 92, 158
Scott, Dana, 7, 80, 211, 247
SECD machine, 173

semantic category, 214
semantic equivalence, 70
semantic function, 214
set, 19
   cardinality, 91
   Cartesian product, 21
   equality, 19
   intersection, 20
   power set, 20, 167
   subset, 19
   union, 20
set abstraction, 19
side condition, 32
slack, 197
small-step semantics, 31, 36, 41
Standard ML, 172
state, 44
   update, 44
state transformation, 217, 220
   cpo, 236
store, 80, 81, 154
Strachey, Christopher, 7, 80, 211
structural operational semantics, 8
   equivalence with denotational semantics, 10, 241
structured declaration, 134
   object, 134
   record, 134
   struct, 134
substitution, 129
   for **Aexp**, 105
   for **Bexp**, 106
   for call-by-name in **Bump**, 104
      in **DecP**, 109
      in **DecV**, 109
      in **Stm**, 110
Sweden, 19
symmetric, 22
syntactic category, 27, 28

Tarski, A., 4
terminal configuration, 30, 33
terminates
   in the small-step semantics, 54
   in the big-step semantics, 52

totally ordered set, 225
transition, 30
transition induction, 56
transition rule, 27, 32, 33
   conclusion, 32
   premises, 32
   side condition, 32
transition sequence, 37
transition system, 27, 30
   configuration, 30
   definition of, 30
   global, 164, 166
   labelled, 115, 164
   local, 164
   terminal configuration, 30
transitive, 22, 225
type, 186
   checking, 186, 187
   derivation, 193, 194, 203
   environment, 190
      update, 190
   inference, 187, 209
   judgment, 186, 190, 199, 203
   rule, 186
   safety, 192
      in **Bump**, 193, 195
type environment, 199
type system, 185
   for **Bump**, 188
   for **Flan**, 198
   slack, 197

upper bound, 227

verification, 11
   tools, 14

Walker, David, 123
well-typed, 187, 188
while-loop
   big-step semantics, 47
   denotational semantics, 217, 218
   denotational semantics of, 239
   semantics as a fixed-point, 239
   small-step semantics, 53
Whitehead, A. N., 186
Wirth, Niklaus, 6

Printed in the United States
By Bookmasters